HER LITTLE MAJESTY

The Life of Queen Victoria

——◦∞◦——

CAROLLY ERICKSON

SIMON & SCHUSTER

SIMON & SCHUSTER
Rockefeller Center
1230 Avenue of the Americas
New York, NY 10020

Simon & Schuster and colophon are registered trademarks
of Simon & Schuster Inc.

Designed by Chris Welch
Manufactured in the United States of America

1 3 5 7 9 10 8 6 4 2

Library of Congress Cataloging-in-Publication Data
Erickson, Carolly, date.
Her little majesty : the life of Queen Victoria / Carolly Erickson.
p.   cm.
Includes bibliographical references (p.   ) and index.
1. Victoria, Queen of Great Britain, 1819–1901. 2. Great Britain—History—
Victoria, 1837–1901. 3. Queens—Great Britain—Biography.
I. Title.
DA554.E75   1997
941.081'092—dc20   96–35041 CIP
[B]
ISBN 0–684–80765–3

All photographs courtesy of Hulton Deutsch

TO MY READERS, WITH THANKS

Chapter 1

THE KING, SEATED IN his elegant painted phaeton, the reins of his fine team of matched horses held in his pudgy, beringed hands, looked out over the gardens of Windsor Great Park and was content. The sun was sparkling on the blue waters of the lake, the mingled scents of roses and honeysuckle and wisteria filled the air and in the distance, the royal band was playing a lilting operatic air. All was in readiness for the afternoon's entertainment: a royal fishing party, with many of the king's relatives, his courtiers, his circle of friends and admirers in attendance.

The year was 1826, and George IV, in his sixty-fourth year, was rapidly aging. He was weak in the knees, his eyesight was going, he had to take laudanum—which made him bilious—to ease the severe pain of a bladder complaint, and a lifetime of gorging himself on rich French food and potent liqueurs had made him so hugely fat that it took his dressers hours to stuff him into his corsets and sew him into his plum-colored silk jackets and enormously wide white pantaloons. His sallow, bulging cheeks had to be smeared with rouge, his full lips artificially reddened and his sparse gray hair covered with a dark wig to disguise his senescence, and even then court gossips whispered to one another about his obvious decline. Before long, they said, he would suffer the fate of his father, George III, who had taken complete leave of his senses and died a feeble lunatic, his mind ravaged by delusions.

That he might indeed go mad was a thought never far from King George's mind, even on the sunniest of days devoted, as most of his days were, to pleasure, and any reminder of his increasing incapacity, either mental or physical, filled him with dread. For he would one day die, and then his throne, his wealth, all that he had spent a lifetime accumulating would pass, not to a child of his own body, but to his greedy, ungrateful, unworthy brothers. To Frederick, his oldest brother, handsome but stupid, and quite possibly, since Frederick had no children, to his second brother William, farcical and grotesque, the family joke and disgrace, and then, as William was elderly and childless, to the king's little niece Alexandrina Victoria.

King George had had his eye on his young niece for some time. She was the only child of his late brother Edward, Duke of Kent—an odious man, the king thought, debt-ridden, brutish, a boor in society, a bully in the family. Edward was no loss, but his child, now seven years old and living with her mother in a set of shabby apartments in Kensington Palace, was worthy of her royal uncle's attention. For one thing, she was unique: the only living legitimate grandchild of George III. (There had been others, most notably King George IV's daughter Charlotte, but they had all died young.) If the king and his siblings continued to be childless, Alexandrina Victoria would one day be queen. For another thing, George's advisers and spies assured him that she was a sturdy, healthy child, with good strong Hanoverian blood, and that the vicious rumors about her, rumors that spoke of ill health, weak limbs and diseased feet, were unfounded. Then there was the possibility that the king might outlive both Frederick and William and that the crown might pass directly to the young princess on George's death. In that event, the king thought, he would like to have the chance to mold his successor himself.

He had been thinking of bringing Alexandrina Victoria to live with him, so that he could begin to shape her tastes and design her education. His Prime Minister, the Duke of Wellington, had advised against it, and this was causing the king to think twice about his plan. But he had decided to invite the princess, along with her mother and half sister, to visit Windsor so that he could see her for himself. She would attend the fishing party this afternoon, in fact. Entertaining her would be one of the many pleasures he anticipated, to distract him from the gathering pains in his body and the annoying paperwork that had been accumulating on his desk for many months. The nuisance of governing, he decided, he would leave to Wellington; he had enough to worry about without letting the everyday work of ruling burden him too.

As the king drove his phaeton along the path by the lake, passing the Chinese Pagoda and the tents erected on the grass for the buffet, a pony cart was approaching from the opposite direction, a small vehicle with rock-hard seats and no springs, its cramped passengers jostling uncomfortably against each other with every bump and dip in the uneven surface of the road. In the cart were the princess, a plump, ringleted, rather plain child who looked to be no more than five or six years old, her blooming, pink-cheeked half sister Feodore, who was eighteen and bewitchingly pretty, the princess's middle-aged governess Louise Lehzen, and the Duchess of Kent, mother of both girls and by far the most prepossessing figure of the four.

The Kent party had been invited to stay at Cumberland Lodge by the king himself, and this mark of his favor was as welcome to the duchess as it was unexpected. Until very recently, George IV had been no friend to the duchess or her children; indeed he had gone out of his way to demonstrate not only coldness but outright hostility to the family of his late brother Edward. When the young princess was born the king, who was not on speaking terms with her father, behaved ungraciously at her christening and refused to allow her to be named "Georgiana" after him, or Charlotte, after his daughter. And when, eight months later, Edward of Kent was on his deathbed, his royal brother did not come to see him but only sent a curt message of "anxious solicitude." King George had never shown the slightest concern for the financial well-being of his widowed sister-in-law, even though she had been in a near-desperate state and only the timely generosity of her brother Leopold had saved her from ruin and her children from want. In fact, until very recently King George had let it be known that he wanted the Kents to leave England and go to live in obscurity among the duchess's German relatives.

But in the last few months there had been signs that he was having a change of heart. He had written to the duchess about her older daughter Feodore—her child by her first husband, Prince Emich Charles of Leiningen—and had made frequent private inquiries about Alexandrina Victoria. Now he was entertaining the family at Windsor, inviting them to dine with him and his many other guests at the royal lodge, where the food was ambrosial and the plate solid gold. Clearly things were changing, and the change was making the duchess nervous.

As she reached her fortieth year Victoire, Duchess of Kent was still an uncommonly handsome woman, with chestnut hair, wide brown eyes and a fine high forehead. She carried her head proudly on a long graceful neck, and she dressed to emphasize her importance as mother to the child third in line for the throne, in deep dark velvets, ropes of pearls and very large, wide-brimmed hats with sweeping ostrich plumes. No one who saw the duchess ever forgot her, though cruel observers said behind her back that her conversation was insipid and her intellect mediocre. She knew that nearly all her royal in-laws were contemptuous of her, with the exception of her sister-in-law Adelaide, William's wife, who was a font of genuine kindness and Christian forbearance, and her sister-in-law Sophia, King George's youngest sister, who was unstable but friendly and who occupied apartments adjoining those of the Kents in Kensington Palace.

The duchess was in no doubt that the king's invitation to join his pleasure party was only incidentally extended to her. No, it was Feodore and Alexandrina Victoria he wanted to see. But why, exactly? Could he possibly have his eye on Feodore as a prospective bride? A fresh young girl who could give him an heir? And could he be planning to take the little Alexandrina Victoria away from her, in order to counteract the duchess's influence over her and ensure that, if the young princess should come to the throne while still a child, someone other than her mother would be appointed as regent for her until she reached her majority?

The child herself, caught up in admiring the beauty of the gardens and the splendor of her surroundings, took scant heed of her mother's misgivings. There was so much to marvel at: the gazelles and goats kept in their special enclosure, the gorgeous rooms at Cumberland Lodge, each with its own character, decorated with carved, polished furniture and sofas upholstered in rich brocade and deep-piled carpets, the cream cakes served on fragile painted china, so thin it was almost translucent, the king's grooms in their scarlet and blue liveries, the king himself, like a huge, waddling doll, painted and gilded, fragrant with scent and oily with unguents, who talked to her in a friendly way and gave her a diamond pin with his own portrait in miniature.

Alexandrina Victoria decided that she liked her "Uncle King," as her mother said she must call him. Not as well as she liked her Uncle Leopold, who was like a father to her, or her Uncle Frederick, the tall, shy old soldier who had always been kind to her and gave her lovely presents, including the donkey she loved to ride with Feodore walking along on one side and her nurse on the other. But far better than her Uncle Sussex, the towering giant of whom she was terrified, or Uncle Cumberland, whose horribly scarred face and malevolent expression sent her running to Lehzen.

The little girl did not yet understand why this visit to Windsor to see Uncle King was so important, why her mother was more than usually ill at ease, or why Lehzen, ever anxious, was tight-faced with strain. She did not know her own significance in the succession. She only knew that, for a few days at least, she was being allowed a glimpse of a wider, more comfortable, and happier life than the one she led at Kensington Palace, where all seemed cramped, dingy, and miserable, and where she was often very lonely and sad.

The king in his phaeton came up to the pony cart and both vehicles stopped. The king leaned down and addressed the Kents.

"Pop her in," he said, meaning Alexandrina Victoria. The duchess hesitated, evidently fearful, then allowed her daughter to be handed across into the phaeton. The king's sister Mary, who was sitting beside him, grabbed the child around the waist and put her on the seat. The king flicked his whip, and the phaeton moved on.

Many years later, Alexandrina Victoria recalled that afternoon as one of the happiest of her childhood. The ride with His Majesty, the music floating out over the lake, the crowd of beautifully dressed people gathered at the Fishing Temple to indulge in the idle sport of fishing for carp, the king's constant attention to herself and her pretty sister, all were to stand out in her memory as part of an enchanted idyll. She was to remember in particular King George's grave and regal charm, the way he won her over by bending down and addressing her as if she were quite grown up, asking her what tune she would like the band to play. For weeks afterward she enjoyed the happy afterglow of her time with her Uncle King, never suspecting that he, soon bored with the elaborate fishing party, and more than a little disappointed with his homely young niece (who reminded him disturbingly of her hated father), had soon stopped thinking of her at all and let his thoughts drift to his indigestion, his annoyance with his valets, and a mare he had running at Newmarket.

IT MUST HAVE seemed to Drina that she had always lived in the sprawling old brick mansion known as Kensington Palace. She had no memory of any other house, having been far too young to remember the seaside cottage at Sidmouth where the family had been living in 1820 when her father died. Kensington was her home, its overgrown formal gardens, long straight paths and clipped hedges her playground, its tall old trees and time-blackened statues, cracked and chipped, as familiar to her as the face of her governess Lehzen.

With Mrs. Brock, her nurse, or one of the palace footmen trailing behind her, she wandered along the endless dim corridors and huge, echoing rooms of the dilapidated house, rooms largely bare of furnishings as the palace had not been lived in by a reigning monarch for well over a century and had fallen into neglect. Everywhere the princess looked she saw evidence of decay—in the stagnant, silent fountains that no longer ran, the frayed, faded hangings that clung to the walls, the broken locks on doors hanging crooked on their hinges. The floors creaked, there were water stains on the once pristine plasterwork ceilings, and even the portraits on the walls, portraits of men and women in the quaint stiff gowns, ruffs and square hats of another era, were indistinct and dark with age.

No one told Drina that she was a poor relation of the royal family, living on sufferance in a tumbledown house, but as she grew older she must have come to understand that this was so. Years later she recalled how, as a child, she never had a room to herself, nor a sofa nor an easy chair, how all the carpets in the rooms she and her mother lived in were threadbare, and how her mother was forever preoccupied with expenses and bankers and debt. Having seen Windsor Castle when she was seven, and having spent time at her Uncle Leopold's comfortable house Claremont, she had had a taste of luxury, and knew that Kensington represented its opposite.

And she must have realized too, as she grew older, that the constant tension and conflict in the household went along with the want of money and comfort, that her mother's highly variable moods, her irascible temper, resulted in part from her financial uncertainties, and the expedients she was forced to employ to relieve them.

The duchess was deeply in debt, and each year her debts mounted higher. Her husband's estate was insolvent, and although, by 1826, she had a parliamentary grant of £6,000 a year to live on, plus an additional £3,000 from her brother Leopold, these sums were barely sufficient to pay the interest on her debts, much less provide the furnishings of an aristocratic household and pay for its upkeep. The duchess felt deprived—and aggrieved. Other members of the royal family received much larger parliamentary grants than she did; her brother Leopold, for example, a widower who had at one time been married to King George IV's daughter Charlotte, was grandly recompensed at £50,000 a year.

Economy was essential, but the duchess could not cut back on her expenses. She had to keep up appearances, to pay servants and tutors for the princess and dressmakers and milliners and purveyors of food and drink. Meanwhile the bankers kept demanding more, and the duchess had no means of raising more cash to pay them. She possessed only one thing of real value: young Drina's birthright. One day, before long, Drina would be queen, with riches unimaginable, and she, the duchess, would be regent. Then all debts could be paid and there would be such an abundance of wealth left over that she could not possibly spend it, not if she tried for a lifetime. On the strength of these hopeful expectations, the duchess applied for more loans.

But the bankers insisted that she supply more substantive collateral than her daughter's expectations. There had to be land, houses, concrete valuables to back the debts. Because of this the duchess was drawn into an unholy bargain, one she lived to regret in time.

In charge of her finances, as controller of her household, was an ambitious, good-looking, extremely hardworking Anglo-Irishman named John Conroy. Conroy had entered the military as a young man in the early years of the century, and had soon shown outstanding ability with horses and money—able to judge the one and attract, juggle and manipulate the other. These talents brought him to the attention of the Duke of Kent, who was perpetually short of money and who needed a steady supply of horses for his large stable. The duke made

Conroy his equerry and came to rely on him as a friend. On his deathbed the duke entrusted the well-being of his wife and baby daughter to his equerry—a fact of which Conroy reminded the duchess again and again.

Captain Conroy offered to put up his own property and possessions to guarantee the duchess's loans, and was more than willing to help her secure them. For Conroy intended to share in the wealth that would one day be showered on Princess Drina and her mother, and the duchess acquiesced in his ambitions. A bargain was sealed between them, that if Conroy would continue to pledge his collateral, and to handle the duchess's finances in such a way as to keep her creditors at bay, she would repay him once her daughter ascended the throne.

Their bargain may or may not have had an erotic dimension—Wellington thought it had—but it locked the duchess and her financial partner in a stormy intimacy marked by frequent quarrels. Both sought power and wealth through influence over the princess; each sought to gain the upper hand over the other. Factions formed, with Conroy winning to his side, among others, the duchess's son and oldest child, Charles, who had inherited the Principality of Leiningen but came to live in England in 1824. The disputes and disagreements swirled around Drina, clouding her childhood and making her hate Conroy more and more as it became apparent that he was winning the battle for control. The duchess, whether ultimately convinced of the superior wisdom of her financial partner or simply beaten down by his alternate bullying and cajoling, gave way. By the time Drina was eight or nine years old Conroy was firmly in command, making all decisions, both financial and personal, for the household.

Conroy ruled with an iron hand. Though his orders were delivered by the duchess, who was nominally in charge, in actuality he dictated all—or so Charles of Leiningen told a confidant much later, looking back over the dark years at Kensington Palace. Conroy had a talent beyond those of judging horseflesh and handling money: he knew how to handle and manipulate women, and attain a degree of control over susceptible ones, a control that had something sordid about it. Indeed Conroy was a shady character, not merely an opportunist but a fraud, an exploiter, a weaver of fictions. The Duchess of Kent believed his fictions, as did the eccentric, mentally wayward Princess Sophia, who was also drawn in by him and supplied him with information about her brother the king and the other royals. Sophia turned her ample resources over to Conroy to manage, and even put him in her will. In the year that the Kents visited Windsor, 1826, Conroy came into possession of an estate worth £18,000—a gift from Princess Sophia.

Drina, Feodore, the duchess, all the servants—everyone was governed by Conroy's rules, which were intended to keep the princess in a safe, stifling cocoon until her accession. She was never to be left alone, without supervision. She was to be kept in isolation from other children, except Conroy's children. She was to be kept away, as much as possible, from her disreputable royal relatives, those uncles around whom scandal gathered, and she was not to leave the palace grounds except on carefully chaperoned excursions to the theater. If she showed affection or partiality to a servant, the servant must be dismissed. And if the princess misbehaved, as she very often did, she was to be put out on the landing with her hands tied behind her back, until she became contrite.

Misery descended on the Duchess of Kent's apartments. Drina was watched, hovered over, protected, all but smothered. From the time she arose in the morning until she got into her small French bed at night in her mother's room, the princess was kept under the strictest control, and everything she said and did was reported to Conroy. No word she spoke, no sneeze, no choice of hair ribbon, no detail of her instruction escaped his scrutiny. When she went up and down stairs, someone was nearby to hold her hand lest she trip and fall. When she walked through a room or along a garden path, a footman in gold and green followed close behind her. When she sat down to eat, the food set before her was tasted by someone else to be sure it contained no poison—a precaution taken to satisfy the duchess, who feared that Drina's Uncle Ernest would stop at nothing, not even murder, to remove her from the succession.

Treated like a fragile, precious piece of carved glass or china, instead of like the sturdy, feisty child she was, Drina suffered, and smoldered with pent-up fury.

"I had led a very unhappy life as a child," she told her own daughter as she reached middle age. "I had no scope for my very violent feelings of affection—had no brothers and sisters to live with—never had a father—from my unfortunate circumstances was not on a comfortable or at all intimate or confidential footing with my mother . . . and did not know what a happy domestic life was!"[1] "I was extremely crushed," she remembered on another occasion, "and kept under and hardly dared say a word."[2]

Drina's half sister Feodore too was hobbled and suppressed by the restricting rules. Because she was so much older than her sister, the closeness between the two was not like that of siblings, it had more the character of parent and child. Drina adored Feodore, but was often kept away from her. Feodore loved Drina, but was jealous of her, and believed that the duchess loved her younger daughter more; she did not accept her mother's wan assurances that she loved both of her daughters equally. When as a mature woman Feodore looked back on her years at Kensington Palace she wrote of them as "years of trial," and thanked God that they were over. In a letter to Drina she remembered with some bitterness how she had been deprived of the pleasures of youth, immured like a nun and prevented from forming friendships or meeting anyone. Even the innocent satisfactions of conversation were denied her. "Not one cheerful thought in that dismal existence of ours was very hard," she wrote. "My only happy time was going or driving out with you and Lehzen; then I could speak or look as I liked."[3]

Feodore's life, though curtailed, was not in fact devoid of adventure or romance. The other royal occupant of Kensington Palace, besides Drina and Princess Sophia, was Augustus, Duke of Sussex, and he had a son and namesake, a cavalry officer, who glimpsed Feodore and fell in love with her when he was in his early thirties and she seventeen.[4] The young officer soon discovered that he could not gain access to Feodore; Conroy permitted no visitors. But one of the duchess's attendants, Baroness Späth, an old woman who had been in service with the family for decades and was utterly devoted to both Feodore and Drina, agreed to take young Augustus's messages to Feodore and deliver them in secret.[5]

A clandestine correspondence began, no doubt as exciting to Feodore as it was encouraging to the eager officer. When he became more serious, however, and sent Feodore two gold rings via the baroness, Feodore could not bring herself to accept them, or to give Augustus a promise of marriage. Even though she was desperate to escape, and confided to Drina when both were adults that she would have married almost anyone if it meant release from Kensington Palace, she panicked, and confessed her secret to her mother.

As she might have expected, the duchess was furious, not only because she had no intention of letting her pretty daughter marry a nonentity with no social standing and no money, but because Feodore had proven that the security of the household could be breached. Also, the duchess had to tell Conroy what had happened, and face his wrath.

In the end, Feodore was given a harsh lecture, the Duke of Sussex was put in his place and told to keep his son in check, and the lovelorn cavalry officer felt the full brunt of his father's anger. Conroy was resentful toward Baroness Späth, and determined to marry Feodore off to the first presentable candidate for her hand, to prevent her from causing any more disruption.

If Feodore's reaction to her repressive environment was to welcome clandestine adventure, Drina's was, in her earliest years, to rebel.

As a very young child she had screamed with fury, pounding her fists and shouting herself hoarse whenever Mrs. Brock or Lehzen tried to correct her or discipline her. Once she angrily threw a pair of scissors at Lehzen, who often remarked that she had never known a child as passionate and naughty as Drina.[6] She refused to learn her alphabet, threw fits when made to wash, or have her hair brushed, or dress in the stiff, uncomfortable layers of linen, lace and velvet her mother insisted on. Storms of tears broke over the nursery every day, many times a day, and when the storms subsided, Drina was left comfortless.

Amid the tensions, conflicts and festering resentments of Kensington Palace, an emotional forcing house if ever there was one, Drina's young character took form. Shy, nervous, ill at ease beneath her passionate surface, the little girl struggled to find her place.

"I was always taught to consider myself a soldier's child," she later remarked, and indeed she became, inwardly, a little soldier, toughening herself against the hard knocks of fate, standing her ground firmly and stubbornly in the face of enemy attack, loyal to her allies and implacably opposed to her enemies—and given to categorize anyone she encountered as either friend or foe. She adopted a soldier's simple, straightforward code of honor: she never lied (though she often concealed the truth of her feelings), she never abandoned her friends, she never retreated, she sought victory through stolid endurance and respected those who did the same. She stood at her post, uncomplaining, for as long as she possibly could. She hated deceit and intrigue; these constituted betrayal, and invited defeat. She distrusted subtlety, flights of intellect, obfuscation. Dilemmas, crises of conscience she would always minimize, believing firmly that rightmindedness would dissolve all apparent contradictions in human affairs.

Thus embattled, the round, stout fair child who was third in line for the British throne girded herself to face the challenges that lay ahead for her, her blue eyes often sad but always observant, her small mouth often agape, her mind determined, at whatever cost, to meet and overcome disaster.

Chapter 2

———— ✧ ————

IN THE FALL OF 1829, when the princess was ten years old, Conroy ordered sweeping changes in the Duchess of Kent's household. Old Baroness Späth, who had served the duchess for twenty-five years, was told to leave and Louise Lehzen too was made to understand that her services were no longer wanted. Späth and Lehzen belonged to the duchess's German past (Späth spoke English very badly), but the duchess was becoming an Englishwoman now, and needed to surround herself and the princess with English servants. She was rising in the world, her status had advanced, for the princess's Uncle Frederick had died and Drina was now heir presumptive, second in line for the throne.

To mark her newfound importance the duchess began to give grand dinners in her run-down rooms, inviting not only Princess Sophia and the Duke of Sussex but other members of the extensive royal family, along with nobles and ambassadors. The expense of feeding twenty to twenty-five guests, plus the hiring of chefs, waiters and extra servants, strained the duchess's already overstrained credit, and there were additional dressmakers' and milliners' bills as well, but as always Conroy

made all possible. Indeed he encouraged the giving of more such entertainments, at which the duchess, dowdy but animated, presided
with a happily self-important air.

The princess appeared before the guests, scrubbed and polished
until she shone, her darkening blond hair curled charmingly around
her face, dressed in the stiff organdy gowns, wide satin sashes and lace-
trimmed pantalets then in fashion for girls. The guests could not help
noticing how short she was for a child of ten, but she held herself
well—her mother trained her to hold up her head by pinning holly
under her chin, so that if her head drooped, the sharp thorns pricked
her neck. Her good manners were noted and approved, and she was
able, if called upon, to recite French and German poetry and to sit
down at the pianoforte and play "There's No Place Like Home" or
"The Battle of Prague" to polite applause. She sang duets with her
mother, who had a good ear for music and composed songs; the
princess's voice, high, clear and true, lacked richness and warmth of
tone but was pleasingly sweet.

The princess, who was no longer called Drina but Victoria—the
more dignified name thought to be more appropriate to her higher
status—was indirectly responsible for the upheaval in the household.
She saw something she shouldn't have seen—a touch, an embrace, a
conspiratorial whisper with an erotic promise hinted at—between her
mother and Conroy, and she confided it to Späth.[1] The latter, who had
been in Conroy's bad graces for several years, chastised her mistress
the duchess, and was ordered out of the palace.

Victoria was very fond of the elderly, ugly Baroness Späth, and her
departure must have been a hard blow to the princess—and a cause of
increased resentment against the all-powerful Conroy. Späth had
spoiled Victoria to the point of idolatry, kneeling before her, looking
fondly on while she covered cardboard boxes with tinsel or rode her
pony or learned her lessons. Späth was one of a group of grandmotherly figures who had been in the background of Victoria's life since her
birth: they included her baby nurse, Mrs. Brock ("not a pleasant person," Victoria recalled as an adult); Mrs. Louis, whom Victoria called
"good Louis" and who lived at Claremont, Uncle Leopold's estate, and
Princess Amelia Carolath, a relative of Aunt Adelaide's whom Victoria
knew well as a young child.[2] Mrs. Louis, Amelia Carolath and Späth
adored, petted and caressed the young princess, Späth most of all.
Their smiles and nods of approval may have helped to counteract the

unpredictable, irritable Duchess of Kent, whose moods were "so variable" and who was touchy and jealous.

Späth's departure followed closely on another major turning point in Victoria's emotional life. In 1828 her sister Feodore had married Prince Ernest of Hohenlohe-Langenburg, a handsome if impecunious German nobleman, and had left England for faraway Schloss Langenburg. Although Feodore continued to write regularly, her little sister missed her terribly.

Without Feodore or Baroness Späth, Victoria turned more and more to Lehzen as not only a governess but a surrogate mother. But Lehzen was a complex character, who as Victoria realized later "had not much softness" and whose marked intelligence was devoted at times to mischief and intrigue. Lehzen was much more circumspect than Späth had been; she knew how to hold her tongue and keep her position, and in fact she did not follow Späth into exile on the Continent. Though she must have been fully aware of all the machinations in the palace she did not complain about them, or draw Conroy's wrath or injure the duchess's pride. She did, however, contrive to win the princess's loyalty and confided in her, making her keep secrets from her mother. Lehzen was also at times quite stern with Victoria, who feared as well as loved her. If Conroy governed the household, Lehzen meant to govern at least her own small part of it, and that the most important part, the heart of the princess.

By the age of ten Victoria was spending four hours a day at her lessons, though she was not a particularly apt student and disliked learning. The urge to rebel that had made her resist memorizing the alphabet until she was five now made her a difficult student to manage. She was not trained to become a ruler; apart from learning to speak French and German, and absorbing a smattering of history and geography, there was nothing in her education to set her apart from any other highborn girl. Accomplishments, not intellectual training, or a wide breadth of knowledge, were the goal. The duchess and Conroy wanted Victoria to become an ornament to the drawing room, able to recite, sing and play, to dance a quadrille, and to draw for her own amusement.

A variety of tutors provided instruction, besides Lehzen: a French dancing mistress, a German pastor, an Anglican clergyman who tried, often unsuccessfully, to teach his pupil ancient history and the rudiments of Latin, and made her read what she later recalled as "many dull books." Victoria liked arithmetic, and thought she had a talent for it. She loved dancing, enjoyed her piano and singing lessons, and always looked forward to the arrival of her drawing master, the academician Richard Westall.

Drawing was the princess's only conspicuous talent, and under Westall's indulgent and patient tutelage her talent began to expand. She copied the sketches he made for her, she sketched from memory stage performers she had seen, her pets, and the people in her household. At the age of eleven, she undertook, all on her own, to copy a Thomas Lawrence portrait—though how true a copy it was can only be conjectured.

Victoria's Uncle Leopold, the sanest and most disinterested of her relations, might have guided her education quite differently had he been in charge of it, for he had foresight and considerable political sophistication; he believed that his niece would one day rule England, and even if, like everyone else, he expected her to rule through trusted male advisers, and not to make her own decisions, still he recognized how important it was that she be well informed and able to think clearly and with discrimination. But as Victoria reached her tenth year, Leopold was distracted by other concerns.

An able man, mature and worldly, popular with the English (though not with King George, who called him "Monsieur peu-à-peu" and thought him ridiculously cautious and deliberate), Leopold was respected abroad. When in 1829 the Greeks won independence from the Turkish Empire, Leopold was invited to become King of Greece. He wanted to accept, but declined with regret, after months of negotiations, at the insistence of King George and his ministers. Soon afterward, however, a better situation presented itself. The Belgians rebelled against the King of Holland and eventually, with the blessing of the British government, asked Leopold to become their ruler. He accepted gladly and prepared to move to Brussels, where his new responsibilities absorbed him and left him little time to spare for Victoria. He wrote to her, and kept himself informed of events in England, but his new preoccupations allowed the conniving Conroy to work against him, and advance his own interests still further.

The glittering prize of a regency continued to draw Conroy and the duchess like a magnet, and all Conroy had to do to alarm the latter was to suggest that she might never achieve the prize she sought. Now he told her that her brother Leopold, having won the crown of Belgium, was scheming in secret to become regent for the princess. So bold was the new king's plan that he had actually drawn up legal papers establishing his authority in the event the princess became queen before she reached the age of eighteen, Conroy said—and the duchess believed him. Leopold's influence with his sister, already in decline, reached a new low.

Between struggling through her lessons and displaying her accomplishments, Victoria enjoyed a closely supervised leisure. She played with her favorite dog Fanny, collected seashells, wrote letters to Feodore and Uncle Leopold, and read illustrated annuals bound in watered silk that showed her an idealized, sentimentalized world filled with simpering, retiring women, bold, dashing men and antique houses dwarfed by towering mountains and vast expanses of heath. She admired her mother's copies of *La Belle Assemblée*, a woman's periodical combining pictures of dainty Paris gowns with stories of tempestuous love, bloodcurdling crime and daring adventure. Her slightly protuberant blue eyes widened at the pictures of menacing phantoms and howling savages, her strong little heart pounded when she read of maidens rescued from fates unspeakable and unnatural beings stalking human prey. She lay at night in her chintz-curtained bed, knowing that her mother was asleep in her own bed just across the room, and listened to the constant ticking of her father's old tortoiseshell watch kept in the watch pocket on her mother's bedstead, its ticking the gauge that marked the passing hours of her childhood.

Day by day, she enfolded herself in a special fantasy world. She made dolls. Taking small ceramic figures five or six inches high, Victoria and Lehzen dressed them in tiny silk and velvet gowns with minute lace aprons and feathered hats and linen pantalets. These miniature ladies all had names and characters, invented by the princess, and lived imaginary lives; their husbands, their children, their aristocratic titles and country houses were all spelled out in detail. Many of the dolls were dressed as ballet dancers, for Victoria was enchanted with the ballet, and others were dressed like actors and opera singers in favorite roles.

The making of the dolls reinforced the growing bond between Victoria and Lehzen. The German governess, who was so conscientious and loyal that she never took time for herself, not one day or even one afternoon off, sat with Victoria by the hour and cut and stitched and glued the bits of braid and satin ribbon that adorned her dolls. She entered Victoria's fantasies and shared them, earning the child's undying trust and affection.

Had Victoria not been a royal child she would have had playmates with whom to make and enjoy her dozens of dolls. But she was not allowed playmates, other than Conroy's daughter Victoire—named for the Duchess of Kent—who was a companion forced upon her and deeply resented.[3]

Little is known about Victoire Conroy, and as she was the closest thing the princess had to a sibling her own age, the void in the historical record is to be regretted. Of the two, Victoire was the elder, though not by much; she was almost certainly bigger and taller; and she was much prettier, with dark hair and hazel eyes, and small regular features.[4]

Victoria was by nature affectionate, and she was certainly lonely. Had Conroy's daughter been warm and friendly, the princess would probably have become fond of her. But no fondness developed—only dislike and distrust. Perhaps no daughter of the man Victoria hated as her jailer and persecutor could have surmounted her inherent wariness and resentment. Or perhaps Victoire was not a likable child. Certainly the princess came to believe that Conroy used Victoire against her, instructing Victoire to tell tales about her royal playmate's babyish ways and fragile health and difficulties in learning her lessons. It must have been a particularly unpleasant form of torment for Victoria, being thrown together constantly with another child for whom she felt only detestation, never being allowed to refuse the detested one's company, having to coexist on strained terms, always watched, her doings and sayings always repeated.

The unwelcome presence of the Conroy children must have been especially galling to Victoria at Christmastime, when following the German custom pine trees in pots were set out on long tables, the trees decorated with colored wax candles in blue, green, red and white, the tables heaped with gifts—toys for the children, gloves, pocket handkerchiefs, books, work boxes, jewelry and other mementos for the adults. Having to share her holiday with Conroy and his brood, especially Victoire, can only have been a bitter reminder to Victoria of her awkward, painful situation, with no father, a distant and often irascible mother and a haughty, self-important martinet at the head of everything.

Conroy was more insufferable than ever, having been made a knight, and thus "Sir John Conroy." His knighthood was not very distinguished—he was a mere Knight Commander of the Hanoverian Order, a title Princess Sophia procured for him from her ailing brother King George—but his hauteur was as great as if he had been made a royal duke. In the spring of 1830, as Victoria approached her eleventh birthday and the aged, fatally ill king struggled to hold on to life, Conroy and the Duchess of Kent both "held themselves very high," according to the mordantly observant Princess Lieven, wife of the Russian ambassador, "as if the throne were to be theirs tomorrow." Bursting with self-importance, Conroy strode about in his dress uniform, reacting irritably to any perceived slight, exploding into wrath at any thwarting of his designs. He and the duchess were both waiting eagerly for word from the palace that the king was dead, and when the long-expected news finally arrived, at the end of June, 1830, they sprang into action.

A letter was carried to the Prime Minister, signed by the Duchess of Kent but composed by Conroy, asserting Victoria's rights as heir apparent. She needed a larger staff, more suitable quarters, a more generous allowance, the letter said. The duchess herself needed a larger income, in keeping with her role as Dowager Princess of Wales (the late Duke of Kent being posthumously promoted to Prince of Wales). And she insisted, in language that was bound to cause friction by its arrogance, that she be made regent for her daughter.

It was a needlessly combative beginning to the new reign, one that put Victoria in an awkward position. The new monarch and his wife, King William IV and Queen Adelaide, had always shown kindness and benevolence toward Victoria, and now when Adelaide came to visit her at Kensington Palace she discovered that she had to wait for admittance; the duchess had given orders that all visitors, even the queen, had to be formally announced before being allowed into Victoria's presence. Such absurd posturing (Princess Lieven referred to it as "that German *morgue* and little-mindedness") gained nothing and cost Victoria some of the respect she actually deserved. Adelaide gently chided the duchess, and suggested, none too subtly, that Conroy was overreaching himself and ought to be kept in his place. King William, nervous and ill at ease in his role as ruler, took the demands and arch attitudes issuing from Kensington Palace badly and became suspicious of Victoria as a result. When she attended her first chapter of the Order of the Garter, wearing a black gown with a hugely long train, walking behind Adelaide, William squinted at her through her long black veil to see whether she looked any different. And when, early in 1831, the princess was present for the first time at a royal Drawing Room—no doubt filled with amazement at the grandeur around her and at the same time shy and painfully self-conscious—William again scrutinized her, and did not like what he saw. Her gaze was "stony," he said, when she turned it on him. He saw, or thought he saw, in that basilisk stare the hardening influence of the strong-willed, self-regarding Duchess of Kent; in actuality, Victoria was seeking to hide her nervousness behind an expression of regal reserve, and her feelings toward her uncle the king were warm if slightly wary.

For King William, an odd, red-faced, blustering old fool, was a far different creature from his brother George. Where George had been unctuous and punctilious about etiquette, with perfect manners and a particularly gracious bow, William was brusque to the point of rudeness, informal to the point of vulgarity, coarse in manner and careless of his person and habits. Visitors to William's court noticed with horrified amusement that the king had a way of wiping his bulbous red nose with his forefinger instead of using a scented silk handkerchief as his predecessor would have done. This was but one of his many "grotesque ways"; he was inclined to be suspicious, he meddled ceaselessly with the trivia of palace affairs, he refused to surround himself with an appropriate barrier of social distance, and insisted upon walking at large in the streets of London's West End, or inviting acquaintances to ride in his royal coach, or even opening the palace gardens to any and all of his subjects.

King William was an anomaly, in every sense. So unkingly a sovereign had not occupied the throne for centuries—not since the time of James I, in fact, whose bawdy jokes and lewd merrymaking (he liked to drop his trousers to scandalize the well behaved) had caused the prestige of the monarchy to plummet.

Worst of all, and most unsettling to his niece Princess Victoria, King William tended to talk wildly and constantly, throwing his arms about in great agitation. Often irritated, he would suddenly become empurpled with rage, his wildness frightening the servants and court officials and leading them to speculate that he would soon sink into the madness that had afflicted his father. But the king's eruptions of garrulity always subsided eventually, and he was restored to his brash, thoughtless self—a self that, at its best, had an appealing side.

To those who knew William's story, he was a sympathetic figure.

The third son of King George and Queen Charlotte, he was never expected to reign and was sent into the navy at a young age and left to his own devices. Believing himself unloved by his parents, who much preferred their two older sons, William developed into a rakehell who fought and drank and fornicated his way up through the ranks, leaving a trail of broken heads and wrecked brothels and inconvenient bastards wherever he went. ("Oh, for England and the pretty girls of Westminster," was his inebriated *cri de coeur,* "at least to such as would not clap or pox me every time I fucked."[5]) William was not mean-spirited, merely uncontrolled; his careless hell-raising was thoughtless and childish, but he was never dissolute, and lacked the overrefined tastes of a voluptuary. Plain William liked plain food, and had no use for culture or elegance; fine art he referred to as "nick-nackery," and he hated gilded walls and marbled furnishings.

It was just as well that William preferred simple living, for he never had much money, and what little he had went to support his numerous children, all of them illegitimate and most of them greedy and demanding. His ten children by the comic actress Dorothy Jordan, known to London hostesses as "Les Bâtards," were the most conspicuous of his progeny. They lived with him and off him, and when his funds failed, Mrs. Jordan's stage profits made up the difference.[6]

William's second illegitimate family was more obscure, in fact its existence did not become public knowledge until after the king's death, but a bastard son born while the young William was living in Hanover had been raised in his father's home and destined for a naval career. He died young, drowning off the African coast during the Napoleonic Wars.[7]

For forty years and more William lived his singular life, a king's son yet disregarded by most of his relatives and considered an embarrassment by society. "Nobody ever invited him into their house, or thought it necessary to honor him with any mark of attention or respect," wrote the diarist Greville, who was in a position to know.[8] Even after he became heir apparent on the death of his brother Frederick, William was not brought forward into the limelight. He was too strange, too loquacious, too liable to burst into apoplectic wrath to be lionized as Britain's future king. The only notoriety he received came not from his position in the succession but from an unfortunate physical trait: he had a head that came nearly to a point, and was ridiculed as "Coconut."

By his side the Coconut had what a visitor from abroad called "undoubtedly the plainest woman in her dominions." This was Queen Adelaide, who was thirty-seven in 1830 (King William was sixty-five). Only the most sympathetic of her courtiers could bear to look for long at her poor afflicted face, crusty with sores and blazing with red blotches, but those who did saw there a look of sorrow, and an almost poetic melancholy. Adelaide was easily moved to tears, so tender was her nature, and though some saw only weakness and insecurity in her watering eyes—her doctor called her "a poor, wishy-washy thing"—others thought she was merely acutely sensitive, and that she possessed an exceptionally able mind.[9]

Adelaide was an excellent wife to William, tolerant and benevolent, willing to overlook his obstreperous outbursts and happy to share her home with his ten children by Mrs. Jordan, children who were now well grown with children of their own. To her sorrow, she had no living children, her one baby daughter having died at the age of four months.[10]

The great event of 1831 was to be King William's coronation, and the London season that spring and early summer was unusually festive. Balls and fetes were held every night, grand military reviews went on in Hyde Park and the late-rising fashionable world attended elaborate "breakfasts" served in the open air at six o'clock in the evening. Paganini played at the Opera House, the theater season sparkled, and everyone who was anyone crowded into the salons and dining rooms of the London mansions, eager to see and to be seen, gratified that King George and his stale grandeur had been swept away and that a fresh new spirit prevailed.

The new spirit was much in evidence in the planning of the coronation. King William, impatient with formality, had at first proposed eliminating the costly coronation ceremony entirely, substituting a brief oath-taking in the presence of Parliament. This was going too far; the conservatives in William's government insisted that there be a traditional crowning ceremony, but with a minimum of fuss and expense. Preparations went forward with an intent to save cost. Participants in the festivities were told that they had to provide their own liveries, robes and gowns. The customary banquet in Westminster Hall would not be held. Even the queen economized by not ordering a new crown made for herself; instead she had some of her own jewels made into a crown, paying for the new setting out of her private income.

King William seemed uneasy amid the excitement of the gala season, his gawky figure lost in the crowd of gaudy notables that so often surrounded him. He sat at a plain table and gazed out of the window at the Windsor flower garden, clearly worried about his responsibilities and unhappy to be burdened with them. He could not trust his ministers. Adelaide vexed him. His children hounded him with requests for money, titles, marks of distinction. And his annoying sister-in-law, the Duchess of Kent, was a constant, and increasingly galling, irritant.

"She is the most restless persevering troublesome devil possible," wrote the MP Thomas Creevey, an observant if bilious diarist. She made frequent demands for alterations to her apartments at Kensington Palace, insisting that new furniture be provided, new rooms added, the entire suite enlarged. She wrote to the king himself, to his new Prime Minister Lord Grey, Wellington's successor, and to the harassed officers of the Board of Works, whose nemesis she had quickly become, in a tone of injured dignity. When her requests were ignored, she sent Conroy (who was no doubt the instigator of many of the duchess's demands) to the Board of Works in person to express her extreme dissatisfaction with the king and his Prime Minister.

Like sandpaper the duchess's shrill requests, repeated almost daily, abraded what goodwill the king felt toward his heir and her self-important mother. William began to resent the sight of the dowdy duchess, who was now present at all important court functions, dressed, observers thought, with "a certain German homeliness," her face set in a rictus of determination.

That the king and his ministers were Tories and the duchess a staunch Whig only made the situation worse, as did the rising tide of political dissent, the demand for democratic reform that seemed to advance as the new king's reign went along. To William, his sister-in-law was one more member of the opposition, albeit a particularly obstreperous one, nagging at him to take action he preferred not to take.

"The squabbles that have been going on at Kensington Palace do not surprise me," Princess Lieven wrote. In her view it was inevitable that the confused, beleaguered king and the pushy Duchess—pushed by Conroy—would clash resoundingly. "Those people are wrong-headed to the utmost possible degree," she added, meaning the duchess and Conroy, "which, however, is a great pity, for, after all, the future of England is placed in their hands."

Victoria was England's future. It was Victoria, Lady Wharncliffe thought when she saw her, who would "save us from Democracy, for it is impossible she should not be popular when she is older and more seen." Lady Wharncliffe saw the princess from time to time at the duchess's soirées, and was delighted with her. "She is very much grown though short for her age," she recorded, "has a nice countenance and distingué figure, though not very good, and her manner is the most perfect mixture of childishness and civility I ever saw."[11] The princess was polite, natural and unaffected; she spoke with charming grace of manner about her liking for music and her drawing lessons and her dolls, and when the evening was over, Lady Wharncliffe noted, she took leave of the company—who stood up out of respect for her—by kissing her Aunt Sophia, "curtseying first to one side, and then the other, to all the Ladies," and then walking off with Lehzen.

Victoria was still Victoria—but only just. Ministers of the king, contemplating the future, thought seriously about changing her name to Charlotte. Charlotte had been the popular name of George IV's mourned daughter, dead for fifteen years but still remembered fondly and a bit tearfully by the English. Charlotte had been the name of Victoria's grandmother, George III's queen. (Of unhappy memory. William IV said of his mother, "I only wish the accursed bitch would have spewed her soul up, and then we should have had some peace in the house."[12]) Charlotte was a good German name, while Victoria was neither English nor German, but French, and France was England's hereditary enemy. Victoria was also the name of the Duchess of Kent, and William was coming to despise it, and her, more every day.

When it was announced to the duchess that her daughter's name was to be changed she was amenable, but before long she altered her view, and became recalcitrant. Victoria herself, though "grieved beyond measure at the thought of any change," said nothing; she was no longer rebellious, but indrawn, keeping her feelings, however strong, to herself.[13] Time passed, another name was suggested, the name Elizabeth, and finally, six months after the original suggestion had been made, the plan was dropped, ostensibly because the English were accustomed to hearing the princess called Victoria and liked the name.[14] The princess was greatly delighted, though the king was furious.

As the day of the royal coronation approached, more imperious pronouncements issued from Kensington Palace. Victoria would assume the place of honor in the king's procession, the duchess insisted;

she would walk immediately behind His Majesty. The response from the king was negative. His brothers, Ernest and Augustus and Adolphus, would follow him. The princess would follow them.

Vexed beyond measure, not only by King William's insult to his heir but by his government's insultingly small increase in the duchess's allowance, she decided to express her indignation in the strongest way she knew. She would remove Victoria from the coronation ceremony entirely. She wrote a letter to the king saying that the princess had fallen and injured her knee, and could not attend. Then she took Victoria and the servants off to Norris Castle on the Isle of Wight, far from the noise and excitement of London, to wait until the festivities were over.

The great day came, September 8, 1831. Trumpets blared, horses clopped down freshly swept streets, crowds gathered to cheer King Billy, and to catch a glimpse of his peculiar head. Inside Westminster Abbey, its dim recesses brightened with the most economical velvets and laces and embroidered liveries that a stringent budget would allow, a hushed congregation watched the old king make his slow way down the aisle toward the throne. They took note of his "very infirm" walk, the way he wore his robes as though they were made of iron, the defeated slope of his shoulders and his lowered head and furrowed brow.[15] They looked in vain for the little twelve-year-old princess, and were dismayed by her absence.

She too was dismayed, though she did her best to hide her feelings from her mother. She went down to the beach and walked in the sand, wading out into the icy water, looking down into the tide pools, watching the sunlight gleam across the choppy waters of the Solent. No one had consulted her about whether or not she wanted to attend her uncle's coronation. No one cared that she was so very disappointed not to be able to go. Her mother was angry at the king, he was very angry back—and would now be angry with Victoria too. Everything would be worse than before.

In her depressed state, Victoria got out her dolls and laid them out one by one, hoping that their familiar presence would comfort her. Instead of comfort, they deepened her distress. She wept inconsolably, for her situation, for her sorrow, for the fate that awaited her when, on some future day, she would herself become queen.

Chapter 3

———— ❦ ————

THE LONDON CROWDS THAT had cheered lustily for the king on his coronation day turned angry and rebellious when, a month later, the bill to reform Parliament was defeated in the House of Lords.

Agitation for reform had become a national obsession. The old political order, in place for hundreds of years, vested political power in the hands of a tiny minority of wealthy and privileged families who controlled the government, the military and the church. Advocates of change demanded a broadening of the franchise, to include the more affluent middle classes, and more equitable representation, so that the swiftly growing industrial cities would have a voice in the Commons.

As reasonable as these demands might seem, they were opposed, vehemently and strenuously, by the Tories who controlled Parliament and by many in the country who saw the reformers as dangerous radicals bent on destroying the constitution and unleashing chaos.

And chaos there was, both before and after the fateful vote that defeated the bill. Financial stability was undermined as people rushed to buy gold. Mobs attacked politicians' town houses, episcopal palaces (the bishops were against political reform), jails and municipal offices. Mass meetings of protest, many thousands strong, degenerated into riots.

In the countryside, crops were burned and laborers formed themselves into armed bands demanding "bread or blood." In the towns, associations of working people came into existence whose object was to force employers to raise wages—by violence if need be. Some of these groups armed themselves, spreading panic throughout the industrial areas of the north, and convincing terrified citizens that revolution was all but inevitable. The forces of order offered little reassurance; only London had a police force, and it was new and small, while the army, never large, had shrunk since the days of the Napoleonic Wars and regiments of local yeomanry were inexperienced and often inept.

Britain was still, in 1831, stronger and more stable than any of the European countries, and far richer. Yet it was precisely because of her stability and wealth that the groups in power felt so fearful. They had a great deal to lose, and they tended to see all around them an advancing horde of marauders, political and economic, who were determined to wrest it from them.

It was not only fear of reform that clutched at the vitals of the wealthy and powerful: it was a deeper fear, a dread that the urbane, cultivated secularism that had marked the early decades of the century was rapidly giving way to greed, brute force and religious excess—in short, a fear that all that had come to represent civilized life was unraveling at a dizzying pace.

Underlying all the upheaval was the mechanization of labor, that sweeping change that made it possible for a machine to do the work of hundreds of men and women. For two generations machines, brought together into factories, had been producing manufactured goods in rapidly expanding quantities, while at the same time hugely increasing Britain's coal output. The resulting wealth was staggering, and was growing each year, but this growth came at a high price in social dislocation, human suffering and periodic anxiety. An exploding population swarmed into England's burgeoning manufacturing cities from rural areas and from Ireland, finding work in factories but discovering too late that factory wages were too low and too erratic to provide healthful food and decent shelter. Tens of thousands of workers, men, women and especially children—died from the combined effects of long working hours, malnutrition and cold, and living conditions that bred disease and despair. And even though there were always more willing hands to take their place, the seemingly endless supply of laborers could not prevent the sudden bursts of expansion and equally sudden contractions that sent waves of alarm through the entire industrial community. Both owners and workers were constantly on a knife edge of insecurity, whether in boom times or when work dried up and machines were idle. The only certainty seemed to be that prosperity never lasted, and want was sure to descend in time.

Mechanical inventions engendered the tremendous social and economic upheaval, a greatly expanded population perpetuated it, but it was greed that drove it forward, greed and acquisitiveness—or so many contemporaries believed. And the greedier those with money and power became, the more they drew to themselves the wrath of those who were not allowed to share in the incoming tide of prosperity when it was at its full. Their anger curdled into hatred, and then into violence.

Many of those who witnessed the destructive rioting, rick-burnings and violent protests of 1830 and 1831 remembered all too vividly the horrors of the French Revolution, when in a fearful upwelling of savagery thousands of French aristocrats were slaughtered, the ground under the guillotines saturated with their blood. Many more remembered the Luddites, machine-breakers armed with pickaxes and huge menacing hammers who rose up in the north of England and spread mayhem and destruction. Now a force stronger and more widespread than either the sansculottes or the Luddites threatened to burst free of all civilizing restraint, with a brutishness that seemed, to those with so much to lose, to have something transmogrifying about it. The protesters, the crop-burners were men (and not a few women), yet they were less than human; their frenzied malice seemed to herald the bestialization of humanity. Reason, refinement, moderation were swept aside as irrational desires, crude lusts and uncontrolled passions took the lead.

And as the debasing of humanity proceeded, another distinctive phenomenon was occurring, equally threatening to the old order of things. Serious-mindedness was on the rise, that earnest, impassioned determination on the part of a revivified Christian community to rescue fallen humanity from godless, joyless vice and guide it upward into the light of piety, decency and the hope of betterment. As marked a change, as thoroughgoing a revolution in worldview as any political program, serious-mindedness gave moral legitimacy to the clamor for reform and lent its vision to the turbulent era. For if change was all but inevitable, the evangelists said with fervor, then let it be not only change, but improvement. The onrushing transformation of society need not be dreaded, the evangelicals insisted, not if it brought a higher standard of humanity, a higher calling for brother to help brother (and sister) in its wake.

The moral rigor of the evangelicals was, at its best, a fresh and purifying force, yet it spelled the end of the tolerant, detached worldliness that had been the hallmark of the Georgian era. And just as the whirlwind of industrialization and the fear of violence created a febrile excitement and a dread of irremediable displacement, so serious-mindedness created a boundless and pervasive anxiety wherever it took hold. For it imposed new imperatives: no more latitude, no more ease, was the battle cry of the serious. Life must be lived with a fierce urgency, in view of the mission at hand, which was to save the world from itself. Tense with purpose, the evangelicals went about their work, handing out tracts, building churches, entering slums and offering a way out to prostitutes and thieves, teaching poor children, verbally assaulting those who profaned the Sabbath. Their perfervid tension was a touchstone for the age.

When the cold weather set in, late in the autumn of 1831, acts of violent protest diminished but suspicion and resentment directed toward the government did not. A cholera epidemic had been moving westward across Europe from St. Petersburg for over a year, and when it reached England there were rumors that the fever was being spread deliberately among the laboring classes to thin their ranks and dilute their demands for reform.[1] In midwinter the first London cases appeared, and soon thousands were dying amid ghastly suffering.

When the London season arrived it was subdued, its usual gaiety blighted by political dissension and the ongoing debate over the Reform Bill, whose proponents were determined to see it pass despite embattled opposition. Families were divided, party guests almost came to blows. The king, worried and worn down by responsibilities he was incapable of meeting, unable to offer leadership yet equally unable to trust his ministers to lead wisely, seemed to age rapidly; his idiot grin seemed fixed, his bursts of talkative animation wilder and less coherent than ever.

Finally, in May of 1832, the Reform Bill became law, with King William playing a key role in its passage by threatening to create, should this become necessary, enough reform-minded new peers to insure passage of the Bill in the reactionary House of Lords. Centuries of political tradition gave way to a new system that awarded seats in Parliament to the previously unrepresented cities and widened the franchise to include the wealthiest men of the middle classes. The Tories, arch conservatives, could no longer dominate the country politically, although their influence could not be discounted.

Moderate though the actual changes were, in comparison with those envisioned by the radicals, the privileged classes continued to feel deeply uneasy. The impregnable castle, the safe political bastion behind which the wealthy carried on their lives, was no longer invulnerable to siege. If a modest breach in the walls could be achieved, then much larger breaches were possible. In time the walls themselves would come tumbling down, and the extremists would rush in and take over. Until then, they would continue their disconcerting campaign of rioting, window-breaking and noisy protest.

Through the midst of all the tumult rode the thirteen-year-old heir to the throne, Princess Victoria, in a handsome barouche drawn by matched gray horses. Postboys in pink silk jackets and black hats escorted the carriage, and the horses had pink silk reins decorated with nosegays of flowers. Victoria, her mother, and an entourage of several dozen others set off in August of 1832 to tour Wales.

If the princess was aware of the political ferment in the country she did not record it in the journal she began to keep on that Welsh journey. Her journal entries, she knew, would be read by her mother and Lehzen, and could not be of a very personal nature. But she was by now so practiced in hiding her innermost feelings that circumspection came naturally to her. Even when she made that most momentous of discoveries, the realization that she would one day be queen, Victoria concealed her reaction, at least from her mother.[2]

In actuality, as Victoria became aware, through her history lessons, that she was close to the throne she dreaded the responsibility that overshadowed her and wished that her Aunt Adelaide would have a child so that she could avoid her fate.[3] When, eventually, she had to accept the likelihood of becoming queen, she broke down. "I cried much on learning it," she wrote, "and ever deplored this contingency."[4]

A prospect of misery, not delight, seemed to stretch before the unhappy Victoria, increasingly hemmed in by the inescapable fact of her personal significance. As she grew out of childhood her life was more confined and regimented than ever, while the great battle for control of her swirled around her. Her mother and Conroy fought with one another, while joining forces in combat against the royal court. Skirmishes between the princess's household and the king's were frequent and tense, and when Victoria went to court to take part in minor ceremonies she was always nervous and self-conscious, aware that everything she did was closely watched, and was part of a carefully orchestrated competition with herself as the ultimate prize. Even the journey to Wales was part of this ongoing competition, for it symbolized Victoria's role as Princess of Wales and it was intended to enhance her visibility and popularity.

Off she went in her traveling barouche, with Lehzen, her mother, her beloved pony Rosa and the entire Conroy family in tow. She had just turned thirteen, but looked more like a child of ten, plain of feature, direct of gaze, and with a disconcerting habit of holding her mouth open. A few months earlier Charles Greville had noted that Victoria was "a short vulgar-looking child," lacking distinction; even though dressed up to attend a royal Drawing Room, she seemed to him quite ordinary. Nature had not favored her. Like her father, she was round, stout, and fair, with not a bit of the handsome Coburg blood that graced her mother and Uncle Leopold. Her face was appealingly full, her brown hair thick and glossy, but she lacked grace. Clearly she would not grow up to be other than a short, plain, thick-waisted woman. Conroy unkindly told her that she resembled the king's cousin "Silly Billy" Gloucester, a plump-cheeked, hook-nosed nonentity who was a figure of ridicule.

Impressive or not, Victoria drew great crowds everywhere she went, from a populace that accorded her the welcome owed to their future ruler. They were delighted to see her, her very ordinariness was a comfort for it made her seem as familiar as one of themselves. She was dressed simply and sensibly, with a touch of primness to her girlish dresses. Pantalets, flat shoes and a straw hat worn straight across her guileless brow, its only adornment a ribbon, completed her costume.

As she entered each town, troops of soldiers escorted her barouche through specially erected arches, garlanded with flowers. Massed choirs sang and bands played, cannon were fired and speeches were delivered. At Caernarvon, the Conway children were deputed to walk ahead of the princess's carriage and spread flowers on the road; at Anglesey, Victoria and her mother went sailing, and afterward the princess took Rosa for an invigorating gallop.

All the flowers and bunting could not disguise the poverty of some districts the traveling party went through, and Victoria was appalled at the "strange and extraordinary appearance" of the coal towns, where people, buildings, and even plants were coated in a pall of black grit. She wrote in her journal of the "engines flaming, coals, in abundance, everywhere, smoking and burning coal heaps, intermingled with wretched huts and carts and little ragged children."[5] The factory towns too made an impression, the orange fires of the works flaming night and day, their noise deafening, black smoke pouring from their smoke-stacks at an astonishing rate. But Victoria's attention was arrested less by these evidences of industrial upheaval than by the decoration of the aristocratic houses she stayed in, their picture galleries and conservatories and gardens, the gold plate on which she was served, the events of a hunt she attended, where the fox's "beautiful brush" was presented to her.

On throughout the autumn the tour of Wales and the Midlands continued, through town after singing, cheering town, the rigors of travel broken by stays at country houses. In mid-October Victoria and her party arrived at Lord Grosvenor's immense mansion of Eaton Hall, near Chester, at the end of a long day. To prevent her from becoming overtired, Victoria dined upstairs in her room with only Lehzen as company. The duchess, however, dined formally with Lord and Lady Grosvenor and their children, staying up until nearly eleven despite a headache. Lady Grosvenor was impressed with the duchess, finding her to be "good humored and kind and ready and able to talk *sense* when allowed."

On the following day Victoria and her mother went into Chester to receive formal documents of welcome from the Mayor and other dignitaries. Afterward, Victoria went walking in the gardens with three of the Grosvenor daughters and, in the afternoon, drove out in a carriage through the park. After a lavish dinner the company played games and had a musicale, with Victoria and her mother both singing. No doubt their singing was applauded, but most likely it fell far short of excellence, and may have been embarrassingly bad. On another occasion, after listening to the duchess and the princess perform a duet, Lady Holland wrote that "the singing of mother and daughter was exceedingly inharmonious, but of course was highly lauded."[6]

The third day of their stay at Eaton Hall was by far the most taxing. Bright skies and a warm sun favored the princess and her party as they made their way to Chester, along roads lined with hundreds of well-wishers shouting "God save the Princess Victoria." As they approached the magnificent ruins of Chester Castle high on its sandstone crag, guns boomed out a salute, and from the many boats in the river, crowded with passengers, came more cheers and salutes.

The duchess made a short speech and declared the "Victoria Bridge" open, and then the visitors moved on to tour the dungeon and armory of the castle, the cathedral, and the town's well-preserved medieval and Tudor-era buildings. The Bishop of Chester made a speech, and the duchess, though very nervous, delivered a response that struck one on-looker as having just the right touch of modesty and charm. Victoria too played her role "perfectly and with great simplicity and good na-ture," despite the heckling of two obnoxious men, one of whom thrust himself rudely on the princess "as if mad or drunk," and set the crowd to murmuring disapprovingly about his brutish bad manners.[7]

The next day it poured, and Victoria and her entourage were housebound. Another impromptu musicale was arranged at Eaton Hall, and in the afternoon, after the weather cleared, there was a re-ception on the grounds. People thronged in from all over Cheshire. Victoria circulated, making polite acquaintance with so many people that, hour by hour, her head must have begun to ache and her feet to swell painfully. Then the Royal British Bowmen gathered and gave an archery exhibition, after which an immense dinner was held, with nearly three hundred people sitting down to honor Victoria. After din-ner many toasts were offered around the long tables, and then the Chester gleesingers entertained the company until ten, when at last, exhausted yet poised and charming, Victoria took her leave.

So it went from day to day, house to house. Many who met Victoria were struck by her unaffected dignity, her strong sense of herself and her maturity and self-command. Only a few glimpsed the apprehen-sive child hidden behind the carapace of calm reserve. While at Eaton Hall Victoria revealed a bit of what lay beneath her surface control. "She hardly ever sleeps," Lady Grosvenor wrote to her mother when the royal visit ended, "occasioned, I believe, by her constant anxiety as to the future."[8]

Winter brought a respite from the fatigues and pressures of appear-ing in public and maintaining a public role. At Christmas, the house-hold exchanged the gifts they had been working on—for all well-bred young girls and women in the 1830s occupied themselves with knit-ting, embroidery or lace-making. Victoria made her mother a white bag, and the duchess in turn gave her daughter an embroidered pink bag with a small sachet. In addition Victoria received an opal brooch and earrings, prints and books, including a music book from Lehzen, a pink satin dress and a fur-lined cloak. The Conroys too presented gifts, though Victoria must have winced when she accepted them. Conroy gave Victoria a silver brush, and Victoire presented her with another of the ubiquitous embroidered bags.

The best gift, though, from Victoria's point of view, was one that Conroy made to her mother early in 1833. The black King Charles spaniel Dash, who quickly became Victoria's dog, was her most beloved companion, eclipsing the pony Rosa, the parakeet and canary, every other object of affection in the household. "Dear Dashy" was mentioned often in her journal, and she liked dressing him up in a red coat and blue trousers, and perhaps making up stories about him, just as she had once enjoyed dressing up her dolls and inventing lives for them. "Little Dash is perfection," she wrote in her journal. He became the playmate she had always craved, a source of devotion and uncritical affection in Victoria's increasingly fraught world.

The ungentlemanly assaults made on the princess during her recent journey were a reminder that despite the passage of the Reform Bill, there remained a great deal of unrest and political disaffection. In May of 1833, as Victoria reached her fourteenth birthday, the committee of the National Union of the Working Classes called a mass meeting for the purpose of discussing a National Convention (an ominous term, a reminder of the National Convention in France that had abolished the monarchy). Though the proposed meeting was declared to be illegal, a large crowd assembled anyway, with many people carrying banners reading "Death or Liberty." The meeting was barely under way when a large force of police appeared, whipping out their truncheons and flailing away indiscriminately at protesters and bystanders until the frightened crowd was scattered.

The "massacre" at Cold Bath Fields provoked a national outcry, but it was not allowed to disturb the dinner parties the Duchess of Kent was giving that spring. Five or six times a month she assembled an array of notables, prominent among them politicians known to be opposed to the king's views, and presided over long sociable evenings at which Victoria was the centerpiece. After dinner tables were set up for whist, and the guests had no choice but to humor their hostess and play with her, though she played badly.[9]

One guest was conspicuously absent. This was Ernest, Duke of Cumberland, the Duchess of Kent's loathsome brother-in-law and Victoria's most famously wicked uncle. After Princess Victoria, Ernest was next in line for the throne, though his scandalous past, hateful personality and grotesquely scarred face were liabilities so severe that most people hoped passionately that no harm might come to Victoria.

Two scandals dogged Ernest. First, it was widely believed that he had murdered his valet in the sordid aftermath of a homosexual affair. The official account of what happened exonerated Ernest, but popular opinion continued to suspect him of being a murderer, and the site of the valet's death, in St. James's Palace, continued to attract thrill-seeking sightseers. A second, and much more recent, piece of gossip— one that reached the newspapers—claimed that Ernest was the father of his sister Sophia's illegitimate child. True or not, this particularly ugly rumor added to the stigma of depravity that clung to all the children of George III. To an increasingly moralistic, seriousminded age, Ernest seemed merely the most malign of a thoroughly malignant clan.

If possible, Conroy and the Duchess of Kent wanted the British public to forget that Victoria had a wicked uncle, but in this they were thwarted of success. For Ernest, his loud voice and ferocious manner making him stand out in any gathering, however large, would not go away. He was the duchess's archenemy; whenever the two of them were in the same room—as happened at Windsor—Ernest hectored his sister-in-law incessantly, reminding her that her late husband had promised him he would never marry, and that he had broken his promise. Ernest blamed the duchess for cheating him of his opportunity to reign by giving birth to Victoria. When words failed him, he walked up to her and stomped on her toes.[10]

Summer 1833 found the princess making another tour, this time of the south coast. Once again she walked and rode amid cheering crowds, admired displays of flowers and painted banners and choral tributes. But the looming shadow of violent protest left its mark on this journey. While staying at Norris Castle on the Isle of Wight, Victoria and her mother went aboard the royal yacht at Cowes and were towed to Southampton, where only two weeks earlier angry boatmen had demolished a newly built pier, which the duchess had been asked to christen. The damage was severe; piles had been cut away, stone- and ironwork broken, the entire effect spoiled. Still, with the Mayor and corporation eager to go ahead with the ceremony, makeshift repairs had been carried out, and a crowd of twenty-five thousand waited in the pouring rain to see the young princess and her mother.

A military guard from the South Hants Militia stood stiffly on the shaky pier, beside a dais and a marquee, when the royal party landed. Hundreds of small boats were drawn up around the pier as guns boomed a salute. Doing their best to ignore the wreckage that still scarred the coastline, Victoria and her mother took their places on the dais, the duchess observing "that it was a great advantage to the Princess to be taught thus early the importance to be attached to works of utility." She might have added how advantageous it was for Victoria to see at first hand what destructive conflict there was in the realm she would soon inherit, but this observation was not in Conroy's script.[11]

The attention Victoria drew on her journeys was vexing to the aging king, whose own popularity was rapidly waning. Where early in his reign King William and Queen Adelaide had been greeted with affection, they were now objects of ridicule and scorn. "Never was a King less respected," Greville commented; when he walked through the London streets "he was very coolly received," and his opinions provoked nothing but laughter.[12] Queen Adelaide, tarnished by rumors of an affair with her Chancellor, lost her popularity as well, and retreated to her little cottage on the grounds at Windsor, red-eyed and full of mortification.[13]

Petty warfare between the king and the Duchess of Kent continued, with the king forbidding the firing of cannon to acknowledge Princess Victoria and the duchess encouraging it. The king wanted his niece and heir to come to court frequently, and the duchess continually threw up obstacles to her attendance at court functions, though Victoria did go to Windsor sometimes. The atmosphere there was always tense, and the princess herself was "always on pins and needles, with the whole family hardly on speaking terms." She felt herself to be "between two fires," doing her best to be civil to her royal uncle yet scolded by her mother and Conroy for her civility.[14] She saw no menace in the doddering, foolish old king, only harmless bluster; she had long since ceased to be alarmed by his stream of outraged chatter, and saw beneath it a well-meaning but ineffectual man struggling with an impossible task.

If Windsor was tense and uncomfortable, Kensington Palace was becoming all but unbearable. "Painful and disagreeable scenes" were all too frequent, making the princess's adolescence "a time of great misery and oppression." Everyone knew that the elderly king could not live much longer, and Conroy, who felt that his moment of glory was coming closer every day, was working overtime to ensure that when Victoria became queen, his own status and influence would rise with hers.

This invariably led to debates and conflict with the duchess, who was never entirely under Conroy's control, and to more skirmishes with the king and his agents, who were alarmed at the debts Conroy was taking on in expectation of paying them off with Victoria's future fortune.

Conroy confidently expected to become Victoria's personal secretary, the primary manager of her personal affairs—the role he had played for her mother for so many years and before that, for her father. He saw clearly that the princess disliked him, and most likely he disliked her. He referred to her slightingly as "the little woman" and wrote that she was "arch, sly, and artless."[15] But whatever their personal relationship, practicality had to be addressed. Victoria was after all a young woman, in need of a man to handle her business, and he believed that he could, if necessary, bully her into accepting his help.

He was not subtle. Victoria complained to her half brother Charles about Conroy's "personal affronts."[16] Probably he ordered her to do this and that, as he might have ordered a child or a superior servant. Undoubtedly he took charge of making her daily schedule, particularly when traveling, without consulting her. Haughty and self-important, he probably swept in and out of her room in his assumed role of master of the house, barking out commands, taking charge, ignoring Victoria's protests and disregarding her wishes. In doing so he did more injury than he knew, for he not only made Victoria hate him, and estranged her from her mother, whom she saw as his ally, but he drove Victoria more deeply into herself, helping to bring out those facets of her diamond-hard character that made her feel embattled—and abandoned.

Conroy's bullying stiffened Victoria's resistance, yet at the same time it may have led her to dwell on the father she never knew. When she sketched, again and again she drew a scene that haunted her. It was a scene from Rossini's opera *Otello*, a popular work in the 1830s, in which Desdemona laments "If even my father abandons me, from whom can I hope for pity?"[17] Victoria had lost her father; therefore she had no one. Her mother had been co-opted by Conroy. Her beloved sister Feodore, who made an all too brief, bittersweet visit to

England in 1834 with her children, was for the most part far away. She felt alone—except for "dear good Lehzen," of whom she wrote in her journal that "she is the most affectionate, devoted, attached and disinterested friend I have." Yet however devoted, Lehzen was a servant, an inferior. Her devotion could not take the place of parental love.

Beleaguered and abandoned, not knowing where to turn for solace, Victoria took refuge in her dolls, in riding Rosa and playing with Dash and her other dogs and her pet waxbills, and above all in the theater.

In spring 1834, the operatic soprano Giulia Grisi made her first London appearances. Her voice was dazzling, her acting affecting. To Victoria, who was much moved by music, Grisi was perfection, not only because of her singing but because, to the fifteen-year-old princess, she was so beautiful and ladylike. Like Victoria, Grisi was below average in height, with thick black hair and a pale, sweet face. In her journal Victoria noted in detail the soprano's dress and coiffure at each performance, even recording minor costume changes she missed, whether she had lost or gained weight, whether she looked refreshed or tired.

At fifteen, Victoria sought escape in the world of the theater, and Grisi, along with the dancer Marie Taglioni, were her models and her inspiration. She heard Grisi sing *I Puritani* so many times that she almost knew it by heart, costume changes and all. She saw Taglioni dance the same ballets many times, and when she went home afterward, she dressed herself like her idol had been dressed, and pretended that she too was leaping and pirouetting across the stage, lost to all mundane concerns.

There were no Conroys in her balletic or operatic fantasies, no irascible mothers, no crowds to encounter or ungentlemanly subjects to give offense. In the world of her imagination, she sang beautifully, she danced divinely, and her future was no more troubling than a wisp of cloud on the sunniest of summer afternoons.

Chapter 4

THE FIRST SIGNS THAT all was not well with Victoria came in early October, just when the weather was turning cold and a chill wind was whipping the water to froth in Ramsgate harbor. The year was 1835, she was nearly sixteen and a half and for the past several months she had been overly tired and suffering from insomnia. The incessant touring her mother and Conroy insisted on had become a fatiguing chore, made worse by King William's loud complaints and clumsy attempts to intervene.

She began to feel unwell, ill at ease, with pains in her joints and a general lethargy. The mood of depression that accompanied these discomforts she attributed to circumstances, for she was about to lose the treasured company of Uncle Leopold and his new young wife Louise, daughter of the French king Louis Philippe.[1]

Leopold had once again become an influential presence in Victoria's life, corresponding with her frequently, sending her books and autographs, giving her much-needed tutelage in an effort to prepare her for the infinitely nuanced, labyrinthine arena of politics over which she would soon preside. Victoria was no stranger to politics; for years she had been both participant in and witness to a political struggle within her own household. But Conroy's high-handedness and manipulative intrigues had given her a jaundiced view of power, and an exaggerated fear of her own powerlessness. Leopold saw clearly that her education had been incomplete, and damaging.

By the time Leopold and Louise said their good-byes Victoria was quite ill, and over the next several days she became feverish and then delirious. She had come down with typhoid, which was often fatal, and as her symptoms worsened it became apparent that she might die.[2]

Lehzen never left Victoria's side, as her fever continued to rise and periods of mental confusion and delirium became more prolonged. Her hair began to fall out, she lost weight and became hollow-eyed and emaciated. She was far too ill to write in her journal, even if she had had the mental acuity to form sentences.

The duchess and Conroy were beside themselves. What if, after all their years of effort, the princess died before she could reign? Or what if she became permanently incapacitated, as her grandfather George III had been? It did not bear thinking about. Yet Conroy, at least, thought long and hard about a number of horrifying possibilities, and realized that he had to secure his position in case disaster struck.

The succession was after all particularly shaky in the fall of 1835. The king had announced that he did not expect to live much longer, and his halting walk, asthmatic cough and vacant expression underscored his words. His doctors were treating him for heart disease and severe bronchitis, and while earlier in the year there had been rumors that Adelaide was pregnant—rumors that had died down by the time Victoria fell ill—no one seriously believed that William was capable of fathering a child.

The king's fragile sanity seemed at times to snap. His ministers, who regarded him as "a silly bustling old fellow" and considered him a nuisance, were alarmed when he insisted that Great Britain should go to war with China, and annoyed when he pestered them about buying the island of St. Bartholomew from Denmark in order to keep it out of the hands of the Russians.[3] "There is a very strong impression abroad that the King is cracked," Greville wrote, "and I dare say there is some truth in it. He gets so very choleric, and is so indecent in his wrath."[4] Victoria's Uncle Ernest, ever eager to hasten the progress of the succession, tried to gather support to persuade the ministers to declare the king insane and institute a regency. No doubt Ernest imagined that he would be declared regent.

It was clear to Conroy that he had to act quickly, given Victoria's worsening crisis and the king's evident decline. Heedless of the princess's condition, Conroy approached her sickbed, over Lehzen's protests. Most likely he told Victoria, in his usual hectoring way, that it was very important that she assent to his becoming her personal secretary, and that she give some legally binding proof that this was her intent. When she resisted, he pressed his case more strongly, ignoring the distress his insistence was causing her. Yet again she refused to do as he asked, and given his choleric temper, he must have been highly exasperated.

Never doubting that he would win her compliance eventually, Conroy brought the duchess in to help persuade the princess to do the sensible thing and grant him the authority he required. But weak though she was, Victoria continued to withstand their combined pressure, until Conroy began lecturing her severely and giving Lehzen a tongue-lashing.

How painful this must have been to the suffering and enfeebled Victoria, in her exhaustion and intermittent feverish delirium, can only be imagined. She couldn't sleep, she could hardly eat anything, her eyes were sunken and dark-rimmed and her once thick, lustrous hair hung lank and sparse. Her mirror showed her a greatly altered self. Instead of the plumply blooming girl she had been, she now saw a dull-eyed, wasted creature, alternately pale and flushed with fever. Her weeks of anguish marked her expression. In the third or fourth week of her illness, Lehzen cut short her greatly thinned hair; shorn of her one beauty, she must have mourned the loss of an important part of herself.

How she must have wished for a strong protector, someone who could banish the hateful Conroy from her presence forever. Her mother, who ought to have protected her, instead betrayed her by aligning herself with the enemy. On Victoria's side there was only Lehzen, and though, to her credit, Lehzen did not flinch under Conroy's withering vituperation, she could hardly go on the offensive and order him out of the sickroom.

The days of her ordeal at Ramsgate were the worst of Victoria's young life—and during those bitter days, the lamp of life itself burned dim. Struggling against succumbing to the symptoms that tormented her, wounded by her mother's betrayal, battered by Conroy's repeated onslaughts—which, at their worst, amounted to outright physical co-ercion—Victoria somehow found the strength to turn her head and murmur a faint but distinct "No."

She would not sign the document her enemy demanded that she sign. She would be a good soldier, standing her ground, never retreat-ing, undaunted to the last. She would not give in. Not one inch. No matter what effort it cost her.

And in that flinty resolve, she may have found the strength to re-cover. After nearly four weeks, she was able to note in her journal that she had begun to eat a bit of soup and meat. She was still an invalid, so weak that walking was a great effort, but she had begun to come back among the living. The worst was over. And as she grew stronger day by day, the crisis that had impelled Conroy to act receded. He stopped hounding her, for the time being.

But something had changed. An older, sadly wiser Victoria now viewed her situation in a different light.

For she was learning, at last, and in her own way. Her formal educa-tion had never gone very deep, her teachers had not succeeded in forming her mind, merely in feeding her information. Now, however, under Leopold's growing influence, she was reading more, on her own, and relating what she read to her own experience. "Reading history is one of my greatest delights," she told her uncle. On his recommenda-tion she had made her way through the memoirs of the Duc de Sully, Henry IV's remarkable minister, and through Sully's eyes had wit-nessed the treacheries and cunning subtleties of the sixteenth-century French court.[5] The memoirs were an education in ruthlessness, devi-ousness, political and religious cynicism—in short, they taught Victo-ria much about human nature in high places.

While she was reading Sully, Victoria was at the same time listen-ing to Lehzen read to her from the letters of Madame de Sévigné ("How truly elegant and natural her style is," Victoria wrote), and ab-sorbing from them a wider sense of the repertoire of feeling. Opera too widened her experience vicariously, and fed the romantic side of her nature, the side that savored melodrama. Stark emotion reigned in the operas and plays of the 1830s, and Victoria relished every grimace of horror, every pang of remorse, every grief-stricken collapse and every lovesick swoon. Love triumphant, sweet revenge, tragic death

were meat and drink to her, for she was a full-fledged child of the romantic era, believing firmly in the sacredness of love, the nobility of
individual destiny, sublime heights of passion and dismal abysses of
shame. In the romantic canon, extremes were all, and Victoria found
in the extremes of the stage an echo of her own violent, yet rigidly
suppressed, emotions.

Her tastes were forming, and she was learning to express them un-
inhibitedly. She criticized long theological works, found *King Lear*
"horrid," was bored by Handel's *Messiah* and disparaged the novels of
Fanny Kemble as "very pertly and oddly written." On the other hand,
she adored Walter Scott, admired the Bishop of Chester's *Exposition of
the Gospel of St. Matthew* as "full of truth and good feeling" and struggled through Hume and Milton and even Clarendon's *History of the
Rebellion* ("It is drily written, but full of instruction").[6] Racine's
baroque tragedies were stark enough to thrill her, though their magnificent poetry was probably beyond her shallow aesthetic range.

The diligent effort she had always refused to put into her Latin
lessons she now devoted to investigating books on her own. "I love to
be employed," she noted in her journal. "I hate to be idle."[7] Leopold
had cautioned her against wasting her time, urging her to set aside
time for reflection and self-examination. She should clear her mind of
trifles, and seek to understand her own motives and those of others, he
told her, for she would soon, as queen, come under the harsh scrutiny
of the world.

"The position of what is generally called great people has of late
become extremely difficult," Leopold told his niece. "They are more
attacked and calumniated, and judged with less indulgence than private individuals. . . . Ever since the revolution of 1790 they are much
less secure than they used to be."[8] The princess paid close attention to
her uncle, whom she called her "second father," "or rather 'solo padre'
for he is indeed like my real father, as I have none!"[9] She examined her
motives, probed her conscience, and looked with a new and less for-
giving eye on the motives of others.

The last shreds of her tolerance for her mother and Conroy fell
away. She saw clearly that they were using her to grasp for power and
wealth. Both relatively humbly born, both cursed with limited sympathies and extreme narrowness of view, their pettiness ruled them; presented with a boundless opportunity in the guise of Victoria's
prospects, they took the low road. Judged with impartiality, one might

understand their choice, while deploring their behavior. But Victoria was not impartial. She had suffered far too much at their hands.

Where before her illness she had resolved "to try and comfort my dear Mamma in all her griefs, trials and anxieties," now she was pitiless. She barely spoke to her mother, and treated Conroy with icy, close-mouthed contempt. And she noticed that, though they tried harder than ever to control her, they did not succeed in punishing her for her attitude.[10] She knew—everyone now knew—that it was only a matter of months, or at the very most, a year or two, until her long unhappy waiting period ended and the throne passed to her. She began to feel her power.

Soon she would rule. And that inevitably meant that soon she would marry.

In her early teens Victoria had teased those around her by saying solemnly that she would never marry.[11] But it was unthinkable, in the era that was redefining women as helpless, delicate creatures, ethereal and retiring, pillars of goodness in need of male protection from the vileness of the world, that the heir to the throne of England would rule without the guidance and support of a husband.[12]

But which husband? It was all but axiomatic that a female sovereign ought not to choose her consort from among her own nobility; that could lead to envy and disunity. She had to choose a foreigner, albeit one without obligations in his own land—i.e., a younger son of a highborn foreign family. He had to be a Protestant, he had to be amenable to playing the rather difficult role of husband to a queen—self-effacing yet dignified—and, of course, he had to be capable of fathering an heir to the throne, preferably several heirs.

Where better to look for such a person than among the broad ranks of Victoria's cousins? There were so many of them, from Uncle Ernest's blind son George to Uncle Adolphus's very handsome son George (called George Cambridge to distinguish him from the other Georges at court), who was Victoria's age and who lived at court with William and Adelaide. In the early 1830s the king favored a match between Victoria and George Cambridge, and the latter, along with a carefully selected handful of other young men, was brought together with the princess at court events and danced several slow, stately quadrilles with her at a ball celebrating her fourteenth birthday in 1833. Whether or not Victoria may have felt any affection for George

Cambridge is undiscoverable, though by 1836 she had begun to dislike him.

Among the princess's many German cousins were Hugo and Alfonso Mensdorff, sons of her mother's sister Sophie von Mensdorff-Pouilly.[13] They came to visit her at Kensington Palace in 1832, but they made a far weaker impression than Alexander and Ernst Württemberg, sons of her mother's sister Antoinette. The latter pair were tall, good-humored worldlings—the debonair Alexander was already embarked on a career of debauchery—who entertained their sheltered royal cousin with stories of their military campaigns against the Turks.[14] For a few weeks they brought a bracing draft of fresh air into the stale old palace and into Victoria's life—and something more telling as well. She noted in her journal that Alexander "took such care of me in getting out of the boat," which she found gratifying; his attentiveness pleased her. She would demand attentiveness in the man she eventually chose to share her life.

Victoria was nearly seventeen, and much altered in strength of personality in the aftermath of her severe illness and her conflict with Conroy and her mother, when she met her cousins Ferdinand and Augustus of Saxe-Coburg, the sons of her mother's brother Ferdinand. Ferdinand, by far the more prepossessing of the two young men, was blond with "beautiful" dark brown eyes though his attractions were attenuated by his nasal drawl; Victoria liked the way he came and sat near her during a ball, and "talked so dearly and so sensibly." "I do so love him," she added. This was no more than cousinly affection, to be sure, for Ferdinand was already married to another of Victoria's cousins, the Queen of Portugal, Maria da Gloria. Augustus, or "Gusty," was taciturn and a bit backward, "like a good affectionate child," Victoria wrote, but they had fun together, laughing like children over a mishap that occurred when they were sealing some letters. Gusty "never is in the way," she noted approvingly; though he was phlegmatic, and eclipsed by his brother, he made her feel safe.[15] She was sorry to see both young men leave.

Meanwhile another conflict between Kensington Palace and Windsor had arisen over another pair of cousins, the sons of the Duchess of Kent's brother Ernest. The older of these brothers, Ernest of Saxe-Coburg-Gotha, would inherit his father's title and responsibilities and would therefore not be a likely marriage prospect for Victoria. But the younger son, Albert, who was just Victoria's age and who had showed himself to be exceptional in looks, intelligence, disposition and talents—in short, a paragon—was by far the most outstanding candidate to become Victoria's husband.

She had known for some time that all her Coburg relations were in favor of her marrying Albert—including the one relation whose advice and opinion meant most to her, Uncle Leopold. In 1836, Leopold had never enjoyed higher admiration from his niece, and by her own admission, her love for him "approached to a sort of adoration."[16] Feodore had written to Victoria praising both brothers, though she preferred the elder to the younger. "Ernest is my favorite," Feodore wrote to her half sister, "although Albert is much handsomer, and cleverer too, but Ernest is so honest and good-natured."[17] Yet Victoria, her backbone recently stiffened against all attempts to coerce her, was clearly reserving judgment on her cousins from Coburg until she met them, especially in the light of all the dark stories being told about the family.

Scandal hung over the Ernestine branch of the Coburgs. The marriage of Duke Ernest and his beautiful, much younger wife Duchess Louise, Ernest and Albert's mother, had become the object of far-reaching gossip in the 1820s. The duke had had mistresses, the duchess lovers; eventually the duchess had run off with one of her lovers, leaving her two small children bereft. Such situations were hardly rare, but the duke's response was all but unheard-of: he divorced the duchess, and married his niece Marie, daughter of his sister Antoinette.

Everyone gossiped about the disgraceful Coburgs. In particular, society condemned Louise, and went on condemning her, even though she paid for her transgressions with an early death. As her sons grew it was rumored that the younger, fair one, Albert, was not the duke's son at all but the scion of Louise's Jewish lover. As for the duke, while his amours were not in themselves condemned—after all, he was a man, and neither fidelity nor purity were expected of men—still he had broken an unwritten law in taking the appalling step of divorcing his wife.

The scandal had not died down by 1836, and gossip flew when it became known in court circles that Ernest and Albert Coburg were coming to visit. The king, infuriated as usual that his permission had not been sought by the duchess for her nephews' stay in England and determined that no one but himself should choose the princess's future husband, objected strenuously to the impending arrival of the two brothers, though he stopped short of taking official steps to prevent them from landing on British soil.

Persuaded by his ministers that he ought not to intervene, William nonetheless acted aggressively. He had decided that Victoria should marry the younger son of the Prince of Orange, Alexander, and to this end he arranged for Alexander and his brother William to come to court and meet the princess. On May 13, 1836, a ball was held in honor of the two young Princes of Orange at St. James's Palace. But far from being enraptured with Alexander, Victoria rejected him as stolid and sluggish, with none of the spark of gaiety and playfulness she had prized in her favorite male cousins. She danced with him, but she did not enjoy it, and wrote to Leopold scornfully about the plainness of both young men's features, with "a mixture of Kalmuck and Dutch in their faces."[18]

Ernest and Albert of Coburg, however, were another story entirely. When Victoria met them, only days after her encounter with Alexander and William of Orange, she scrutinized their faces and figures minutely and pronounced them superior. The tall, dark Ernest, nearly eighteen, had "fine dark eyes and eyebrows," she wrote in her journal, and a "most kind, honest and intelligent expression," but Albert's large blue eyes, "beautiful nose and very sweet mouth with fine teeth" were even better. Beyond that, Albert's "most delightful" expression, "full of goodness and sweetness, and very clever and intelligent," pleased her beyond words.[19]

Victoria knew that she was expected to be pleased with Albert, and given her contrary streak she must have been prepared to resist his charm, yet her journal entries show that she was clearly entranced. For once, that which was expected of her coincided with her own natural choice—a rare and happy coincidence that must have lifted her spirits mightily.

Young as he was—he had not quite reached his seventeenth birthday—Albert was well aware of the somewhat thorny position in which he found himself. He had always known that his relatives wanted him to marry Victoria, and he must in consequence have felt considerable trepidation on meeting her. He also knew that the king opposed the Coburg marriage plan, and that he himself was the subject of particularly unsavory gossip.[20] To marry the future Queen of England, to share her immense renown and vast wealth was an almost unimaginable distinction for the younger son of an undistinguished family, and Albert knew it. But he was the sort of person who was not swayed by worldly honors; when he contemplated becoming Victoria's husband he thought of duty, sacrifice, and the opportunity to serve. He may even have thought, with regret, of another of his cousins, Uncle Ferdinand's pretty daughter Vecto, whom at one time he had hoped to marry.

Victoria took her amiable cousins to the opera, where Albert appeared to be just as enraptured by the music as she was. On evenings when they did not visit the opera, they sketched together, or the princess sang for her guests (she had recently begun singing lessons with the renowned bass Luigi Lablache). Victoria was delighted to learn that Albert was a talented pianist and organist and that both brothers composed music. They were, she noted in her journal, "very fond of occupation," just as she was; idleness was abhorrent to them.

But where Victoria threw herself eagerly into the balls, receptions, and late-night parties of the Season, Albert faded, wilted and either fell asleep early or became ill. His constitution was not suited for the stresses of prolonged socializing; he tended to feel faint midway through the evening. He wrote to his stepmother that "the climate of this country, the different way of living, and the late hours, do not agree with me," and no doubt he was relieved when after three weeks in England the day of departure came, and he and Ernest went home.[21]

Albert's delicate health did not mar the overall success of the visit. After her cousins left, Victoria announced to Leopold that she was more than content with Albert, and had concluded that "he possessed every quality that could be desired to render me perfectly happy." Indeed "the prospect of great happiness" now stretched before her, for the first time in her oppressed life,[22] though the issue of her eventual marriage would not be settled for some time to come.

The prospect of future happiness, and the approach of her eighteenth birthday, must have heartened Victoria over the course of the next very difficult year. While keeping her more "crushed and kept under" than ever, and stifling her every utterance, the duchess and Conroy aggressively advanced the princess's importance in the eyes of the public and combated the king's equally aggressive opposition.

King William chose the occasion of his birthday banquet in August to make a highly public declaration of his fury. In the presence of a hundred guests, he stood and declared that he hoped to live long enough to be able to leave the "royal authority" to Victoria herself, once she turned eighteen, and not to "a person now near me, who is surrounded by evil advisers and who is herself incompetent to act with propriety in the station in which she would be placed." No one could doubt that he was referring to the Duchess of Kent, who sat in silence throughout his tirade, even when he grew excited and loud and shouted that he had been "grossly and continually insulted" by that same person.[23]

By the time the king finished, Victoria was in tears. Every time they came to Windsor, it seemed, there was a painful scene of some kind; it made the princess dread and hate the drafty old castle.

Throughout the exceptionally severe winter of 1836 and the frigid spring that followed, the battle lines were drawn. The king, shaking with palsy, fighting for breath and so in danger of fainting that he had to be pushed from room to room in a wheeled chair, seemed grimly to focus all his flagging energies on surviving until May 24, Victoria's eighteenth birthday, while the duchess and Conroy were equally bent on circumventing the old king's plans by arranging to extend the regency into Victoria's nineteenth year—and beyond, if they could manage it.

Caught between the two warring camps, with the distant Leopold her only ally in the family and Lehzen her only friend, so "embroiled" with her mother, as she recalled later, "as to be almost at that time at enmity with her" and harassed by the hateful Conroy, Victoria waited for the king to die and for power to descend upon her.[24]

On May 19, five days before her eighteenth birthday, liberation began to dawn. The Lord Chamberlain, Lord Conyngham, arrived at Kensington Palace with an urgent written message from the king that he was empowered to deliver into the princess's hands and no one else's. Conroy attempted in vain to intervene and take the document, and when the Lord Chamberlain handed it to Victoria the duchess also attempted, without success, to take it out of his hand. Victoria read it, then handed it to her mother. It contained nothing less than an offer of a private income of £10,000, to be administered by her own Lord Privy Purse who would not be under the control of anyone but herself—in short, the king was offering his heir full independence from her mother and Conroy.

But Victoria was not yet eighteen, and was still under her mother's guardianship. Much as she wanted to confer privately with the Prime Minister Lord Melbourne, her mother prevented her from doing so. It was still in the duchess's power to lock her daughter up, threaten her physically, even starve her into refusing the king's generous offer. And so, on the following day, Victoria was coerced, no doubt at Conroy's harsh insistence, into signing a letter to the king in which she said that she had no desire to change her circumstances, and wanted to remain with her "dear mother." The money would be welcome, but not the independence.

So matters stood on the morning of May 24, when Victoria attained the significant age of eighteen. Lying in her small bed in her mother's room, she was awakened by the bright harmonies of a chorus, greeting her on this birthday morning. The singers shivered in the brisk air, as did the servants who tidied the palace grounds and put up special birthday decorations. All along the old, winding Kensington High Street the grocers and linen drapers and gentlemen's outfitters displayed banners and signs in their shop windows wishing the princess a happy birthday, and in the great houses in Kensington Square, along Church Street and in Campden Hill people readied themselves for the grand reception to be held at the palace in honor of Victoria.

Carriages began rolling into the palace courtyard early in the morning, while the princess and her mother were still dressing. Some had come from a hundred or even a hundred and fifty miles away, bearing visitors eager to attend the princess's reception and sign their names in her guest book. Deputations from Manchester, Birmingham, and other towns arrived, along with crowds of Londoners, the women in their best bow-trimmed full-skirted dresses and poke bonnets, the men in tight coats and gaudily patterned waistcoats, their necks stiff in high heavy collars and wide neckcloths.

Among the visitors was one Mr. Potter, a strong advocate of reform who wrote down his observations after seeing Victoria and her mother and paying his respects. "The Duchess," he noted, "was, we thought, anxious and harassed, but was finely dressed, and had a fine neck to show, though rather a stout one." A magnificent plumed hat crowned her formal gown. "The Princess stood beside her," wrote Potter, "also in an evening dress and a hat. She was pretty, but her face, somehow, was not quite satisfactory . . . . I was less taken with her than with her mother."[25]

Victoria's "not quite satisfactory" look resulted, no doubt, from her extreme discomfort; outwardly cool, as Potter noted, she was inwardly doing battle with violent feelings of rage toward her mother and frustration at the obstructions she still faced. Longing to break free, to end her years of subjection and compulsion, she nonetheless felt she had no choice but to keep up a pretense of civility and subordination. So nearly flawless was her self-possession that few in the crowd noticed any hint of her unease. When the members of the town deputations read their addresses to her, she did not answer, but deferred to her mother just as she had in the past. The duchess answered each address, and then Victoria spoke briefly, Potter wrote. "I am very thankful for your kindness," she told the speakers, "and my mother has expressed all my feelings."

Not quite all. Not by any means. She was in fact contemplating composing a written protest against the letter the duchess and Conroy had forced her to sign, accepting the money but rejecting the freedom the king had offered her. She had set her mind and heart against submitting to any further coercion. She was determined to find a way out.

The gala day passed in a round of receptions and appearances, ending, at ten-thirty in the evening, in a festive ball at St. James's. King William was too ill to attend, but sent Victoria a piano as his birthday gift. She bore up well under the strain of the long day and longer evening, a charming miniature amid the much taller ladies and gentlemen who gathered to congratulate her. She kept her peace with her mother, though they were barely on speaking terms. She kept out of Conroy's way. And when the ball was over, and she was once again in the room she shared with her mother at Kensington Palace, she took out her journal and described her day.

"Today is my eighteenth birthday!" she wrote. "How old! and yet how far am I from being what I should be. I shall from this day take the firm resolution to study with renewed assiduity, to keep my attention always well fixed on whatever I am about, and to strive to become every day less trifling and more fit for what, if Heaven wills it, I'm some day to be!"[26]

"Some day" was nearly at hand. Victoria felt moved by all those who had come to see her and cheer her, the throngs who had lined up along the parks and streets to wave at her and shout out their enthusi-astic affection as she rode past in her carriage. It was heartening to re-alize that very soon they would be, not merely her well-wishers, but her loyal subjects.

"The courtyard and the streets were crammed when we went to the Ball," she concluded before going to sleep, "and the anxiety of the people to see poor stupid me was very great, and I must say I am quite touched by it, and feel proud which I always have done of my country and of the English Nation."

Chapter 5

———∾———

THE KING WAS DYING. For a month he had been sinking rapidly, like an old battleship, restless and in pain from a dozen ailments, any one of which, his physicians said, could carry him off in a matter of hours. He could not breathe lying down, so his servants sat him up in a leather chair, resting his gaunt old pointed head against a pile of cushions.

Having lived to see Victoria's eighteenth birthday, he wanted to continue to cheat death to savor one more important event—Waterloo Day, June 18. But with each long, warm June day it seemed less and less likely that William would survive to see the anniversary of the battle.

During these critical days his heir, nominally independent but still tightly "kept under" by Conroy and her mother, was nonetheless continuing to assert herself. She composed a statement of protest against the letter she had been forced to sign refusing King William's offer of a separate establishment and an independent income. She continued to resist pressure to appoint Conroy her private secretary, and when her half brother Charles, who had come from Leiningen to add his voice to the chorus of persuasion and reproof, repeatedly tried to intervene she told him curtly to mind his own business. She managed, with much difficulty, to have a private interview with a disinterested peer, Lord Liverpool, who advised her to continue to resist Conroy's campaign of coercion and to rely on the Prime Minister to advise her once she became queen. That she managed to see Liverpool alone was a significant sign that the balance of power in the household was shifting; day by day, as the new reign came closer, Victoria was laying the groundwork for her autonomy.

Most important, for the future, was the counsel offered by Leopold's emissary, Baron Christian Stockmar. Cool, shrewd, alert, cynical, Baron Stockmar had been Leopold's trusted adviser for many years, and was uniquely suited to guide Victoria through the coming months. ("An excellent man," Melbourne said of Stockmar. "He has rather a contempt of human affairs and means; a bad digestion."[1]) Leopold, who was very well informed himself, thought that Stockmar was "a living dictionary of all matters scientific and politic that happened these thirty years," and constantly turned to him for information.[2] Not only did Stockmar have an exceptionally able and well furnished mind, but he was plainspoken and sensible, and he had another rare quality: he wanted nothing for himself—not power, not money, not honors or worldly status. He was content, it seems, to play a behind-the-scenes role, knowing that his suggestions had far-reaching impact.

Victoria found Stockmar's candor and discretion invaluable. She called him "my good and honest friend, Stockmar," or, later, simply "Stocky." "He is one of those few people who tell plain honest truth," she wrote, "don't flatter, give wholesome necessary advice, and strive to do good and smooth all dissensions."[3]

Stockmar saw through Conroy's brittle façade to his sordid, unprincipled core and told him bluntly that his behavior toward the princess had earned him her disrespect; he could not expect to serve her in any capacity once she became queen. Conroy fought back, using every wile he knew. He blamed Lehzen for poisoning Victoria's mind against him, he fumed that Victoria was light-minded at best, at worst, mentally unbalanced. He predicted that, if the management of the princess's affairs were to leave his hands, immediate disaster would be the result.

Nothing availed. Victoria sent Stockmar to Melbourne to tell him not to listen to any messages conveyed by Conroy and to state her own wishes, and the Prime Minister, disturbed that he had been misled, agreed.

On the nineteenth of June a rumor spread in London that the king was dead. People put on black, shop windows were framed in drooping swags of crape and dressmakers in the West End hurried to finish the somber gowns and capes that had been ordered in anticipation of the royal demise. Victoria, whose lessons had been suspended for several days and who was being kept closeted at Kensington Palace with her mother, was not aware of the funereal bustle in town, but waited for medical bulletins and tried to compose herself. It was not easy, for she struggled with her own feelings for the much reviled old king ("Poor old man! I feel sorry for him; he was always personally kind to me, and I should be ungrateful and devoid of feeling if I did not remember this"[4]) while at the same time expecting, at any moment, to be told that her own exciting elevation had occurred. The news from the king's bedside seemed to vary widely from hour to hour; one bulletin announced that the king could not possibly survive another twenty-four hours, and the next announced that he had rallied. Still, the fateful announcement seemed imminent, as Victoria sat down to write to her Uncle Leopold.

"I look forward to the event which it seems is likely to occur soon, with calmness and quietness," she told him. "I am not alarmed at it, and yet I do not suppose myself quite equal to all; I trust, however, that with good-will, honesty, and courage I shall not, at all events, fail."[5] Her composure was still in place early the following morning, June 20, when the Lord Chamberlain and the Archbishop of Canterbury came to Kensington Palace to tell her that the king had died during the night.

She received the long-expected news calmly, as dignified, standing there in her dressing gown and slippers, as if she had been wearing her coronation robes. A few hours later, dressed in mourning for the late king, she breakfasted with Stockmar and sent notes to the two people she loved best, Leopold and her half sister Feodore. Melbourne came, "in full dress," at midmorning and discussed with the new queen the procedures necessary to inaugurate her reign.

"I like him very much and feel confidence in him," Victoria wrote in her journal that afternoon. "He is a very straightforward, honest, clever and good man." In all she met with the Prime Minister three times that day, and each time her trust in him grew. "I had a very important and a very comfortable conversation with him . . . . I find him very kind in his manner too."[6] Comfort, trustworthiness and kindness: a potent combination for the young queen who for the most part had been surrounded by people who made her uncomfortable, who betrayed her and treated her unkindly. Even if he had not been the leader of the Whigs, and she a confirmed hater of Tories, she would have liked him.

Victoria stepped into her new role as queen with grace and capability and assurance, dumbfounding those who had been convinced that "the royal girl" would founder. Though barely eighteen, and surrounded by seasoned politicians and veteran courtiers three and four times her age, she not only held her own but commanded a degree of respect that neither the foolish William IV nor the oily, eccentric George IV had been able to elicit. "I have seen the Queen twice," Princess Lieven wrote to an acquaintance. "She has an aplomb, an air of command and dignity that, with her childlike face, her tiny figure and pretty smile create one of the most extraordinary impressions it is possible to imagine."[7]

The transition from King William's governance to that of Queen Victoria was managed with the utmost tranquillity; the diarist Greville noted with surprise that "everything goes on as if she had been on the throne six years instead of six days." Relying on Melbourne and Lehzen, who remained with Victoria from dawn to dusk except when she was meeting with her ministers, the queen altered her private living arrangements overnight. She moved to her own suite of apartments. She gave orders that all the Conroys were to be kept away from the palace, and that Sir John be allowed entrance only on official business. And the Duchess of Kent, her injured sense of self-importance disregarded, was pushed discreetly into the background as the demands of rulership took center stage.

To Victoria's immense satisfaction, fulfilling those demands was turning out to be more pleasure than burden. "I have so many communications from the Ministers, and from me to them, and I get so many papers to sign every day, that I have always a very great deal to do," she wrote in her journal, "but for want of time and space I do not write these things down. I delight in this work."[8]

Though crowded with meetings and discussions, and though she had to learn a great deal and make decisions on a wide range of matters from the running of her household to the governing of Britain's empire, Victoria's life for the first time seemed spacious and deeply satisfying. The great anxieties under which she had labored for so many years were lifted from her, and her spirits rose. She worked during most of the long days, then in the warm summer evenings, she drove out in the country, full of a sense of accomplishment and happily anticipating the next day's challenges. Occasionally she suffered from bad headaches, and at times others noted in her "slight signs of a peremptory disposition," yet these were small clouds on a vast clear horizon.[9] For the young queen, the summer passed in a blissful trance of contentment. Later, looking back on those early months of her reign, she would call it "the dream," a season in which, bemused by the multiple diversions of her high office, and the unaccustomed joy of being free to do as she liked, with no one to threaten or constrain her, Victoria blossomed.

"Everything is new and delightful to her," Greville wrote. "She is surrounded with the most exciting and interesting enjoyments; her occupations, her pleasures, her business, her court, all present an unceasing round of gratifications. With all her prudence and discretion she has great animal spirits, and enters into the magnificent novelties of her position with the zest and curiosity of a child."[10]

Like a child Victoria savored the treasures that were hers as queen, among them the great imperial crown, originally made for George IV, which was much too large for her and had to be adjusted; the royal jewelers, Rundell and Bridge, made the adjustment, adding a particularly brilliant large sapphire to the dazzling array of existing jewels and fitting the crown with a purple velvet cap with an ermine border.

But the crown was only the beginning. There were roomfuls of jewels, sparkling necklaces and gleaming tiaras and earrings of diamonds and pearls. The Windsor hoard was a warehouse of gilded plate, candelabra, goblets and *objets d'art*. Beyond the magnificent furnishings, glowing tapestries, and fine paintings that adorned the ancient castle's living quarters, there were riches brought from India, booty taken from Tippoo Sahib, including a golden tiger's head and a sparkling sculpted peacock studded with rubies and emeralds.

To pay her official household of 445 servants, Victoria was given a parliamentary grant of nearly £400,000—an immense fortune—most of which went to pay salaries and costs of provisioning, furnishing, remodeling and repairs. Victoria's household was not as large as the im-

mense royal establishments in Tudor and Stuart times, but it was extensive nonetheless, with many dozens of servants attached to the
kitchens, the laundry, the stables and the larders. The royal Rat Killer
was paid slightly more than the Poet Laureate, whose salary was £72;
posts such as Lace Cleaner in Ordinary, Body Linen Laundress, Clock
Winder and Stove and Fire Lighter were much sought after, not only
for the generous fees that went with them but for the prestige that attended even the most menial service at the royal court.

Despite her new and heavy workload, the queen found time to pay
close attention to her servants, not only her ladies- and lords-in-
waiting—one of whom, she discovered, was a cousin of the late and in-
famously wicked Lord Byron—but the maids and chimney sweeps.
The latter, in particular, gave her concern. The queen was not indifferent to the plight of the tiny boys, sometimes as young as five or six,
who were sent up into the scalding, smoke-choked chimney flues to
clean them out, and were frequently injured, sometimes fatally, in the
process. Flue-cleaning machines had been invented that could replace
the boys (and, at Windsor, at least two girls), but about a third of
Windsor's 250 flues were too narrow to accommodate the machinery.
So, to Victoria's dismay, there was no alternative to using the children
to clean them.[11]

When Victoria became queen, she pensioned off a number of servants who had belonged to the households of her uncles William and
George, granting them apartments in the castle where appropriate.
Some of the pages and personal housemaids had served thirty years or
more, and were "very infirm"; one, Sarah Randall, a housemaid who
had sat up with William in his last illness and spent many long nights
at his side, was awarded a pension of £40 with thanks for her faithful
attendance.

Servants could be troublesome, and their complicated lives could
cause the sovereign considerable nuisance. One of Victoria's pages,
George Pocock, owed a considerable sum to an apothecary and because he was in the queen's service and under her protection Pocock's
creditor appealed to the queen for repayment.[12] The matter became
murky when Pocock claimed that the debt was not his but his estranged wife's—and the wife, who claimed that Pocock had mistreated
and discarded her, denied everything he said. Eventually the Lord
Chamberlain, tired of all the fuss, waived Pocock's immunity from arrest and he was taken to jail—only to be bailed out by the queen. Sen-

timent played a role in all this, as Pocock, personally unpleasant though he probably was, had once served Melbourne's mother as a sedan-chair man, and so had a claim on the Prime Minister's nostalgic affection.

At the head of Victoria's wardrobe, overseeing all the practical work of ordering all her clothing, shoes, hats, gloves and undergarments, was Marianne Skerrett, Head Dresser to the queen. She kept the wardrobe accounts, checking all the bills to make certain no one tried to cheat her mistress, and supervised the purveyors, hairdressers, dressmakers and pearl-sewers whose task it was to keep the royal wardrobe in good repair. The queen and her Head Dresser had much in common. Both were very short of stature, though Marianne was quite thin where Victoria was, at eighteen, pleasingly rounded. Both were intelligent, loved animals, spoke several languages and told the truth bluntly, without guile or dissimulation. Also the queen and her dresser shared a great interest in painting and painters. Marianne was well educated, with cultivated tastes, and in time to come Victoria would rely on her to help with the purchase of paintings and in corresponding with artists.

A crowd of older women surrounded the very young queen. Her eight bedchamber ladies and robes mistress were Whig aristocrats whose court appointments involved no real work, only the honor of serving as the queen's official attendants. Some of them, such as the wealthy and beautiful Duchess of Sutherland ("so handsome," the queen commented), were popular celebrities and social leaders. The stout Duchess of Bedford and the even stouter Marchioness of Normanby were middle-aged and rather dowdy; the Marchioness of Lansdowne, fiftyish, cool and stately, disliked court balls and was prone to secret weeping fits.

The eight maids of honor and seven bedchamber women formed an inner circle around the queen, acting as companions and attendants. They were chosen, one suspects, with considerable attention to their appearance, as it would have been important for them not to upstage Victoria. For though her loyal admirers paid chivalrous compliments to her looks, in truth the young queen was more plain than pretty, with her round child's face, perpetually open mouth and slightly deformed lip, and exophthalmic eyes. Even at eighteen, and presumably at her most appealing, her figure lacked distinction, and it was not hard to see that her Hanoverian physique would one day run to fat. It is no surprise, then, that her maids of honor included the "not at all pretty" Mary Davys, and another young woman, Miss Spring Rice, who was more "clever-looking" than attractive.[13]

The maids of honor were seriously underemployed, and they filled the long empty hours following morning prayers with visits to one another's sitting rooms, where they amused themselves playing parlor tricks and embroidering *"Honi soit qui mal y pense"* on chair cushions. Each of them wore, as a badge of office, a heavy gold bracelet that bore the initials *VR* in turquoise and that opened to reveal a lock of the queen's hair. Sometimes they wore Victoria's cast-off gowns as well.

Victoria's newfound lightheartedness came through in her relationships with her waiting maids. Jokes, teasing and banter made the queen laugh—and she liked nothing better than to laugh "until her gums showed," completely letting herself go. With her maids of honor she could talk over anything from the current fad for being "magnetised" ("I said it was very disagreeable to be magnetised, as people got to say such odd things in this magnetic state") to the influenza epidemic to the latest horrific murder reported in the London papers. The queen was not yet a novel reader but she listened to the others describe fashionable novels such as *Eugene Aram*, Lytton Bulwer's story of a sadistic schoolmaster, and entered into discussions of more serious books such as Jeremy Taylor's *Holy Living and Holy Dying*, which most of the waiting maids had read.

As ever, when women gathered, there was talk of clothes, and of the sleek, smooth hair styles of that season, with long corkscrew curls emphasizing the cheeks, worn with the wreaths of artificial or real flowers that Victoria loved, and of the pain of tight corsets. No doubt Victoria turned to her maids of honor for opinions on her gowns, and shared with them her regret over her short stature and her dismay at having unlovely hands, which she tried to disguise by wearing many rings.

The summer of 1837, Victoria wrote, was the happiest summer of her life. In July she moved from Kensington Palace to Buckingham Palace, where thousands of her subjects came to be presented to her and where she eagerly and tirelessly danced until dawn at court balls. The many inconveniences of the soot-filled, smoky, cluttered and disordered palace, with its lack of running water and its broken water closets and its pervasive stench from the "noxious effluvia" of bad drains, could not quench Victoria's newfound enthusiasm, and when in August she moved on to Windsor, which she had always detested, it too seemed to her a brighter, more cheerful place, reflecting back her own high spirits.

For several years, following her serious attack of typhoid, she had not gone riding, but now, on fine afternoons, she led riding parties through the park, galloping recklessly ahead of a large group of her household officers and heads of government departments on one of the horses from the royal mews or on a favorite horse that she christened Leopold, after her uncle. She ordered a riding habit made in the same style as that worn by the Windsor gentlemen, navy blue with red trim, and in this outfit, with her riding whip and Garter sash, she made a smart leader for her little pack.

Greville noticed that the queen liked to gather as large a following as possible on her rides, with Melbourne galloping along beside her on one of his superb horses and a handsome equerry on her other side. Lehzen sometimes trailed behind the group in a pony carriage. During the two hours or more that these mounted excursions lasted Victoria kept a close watch on her troop, scrutinizing everyone with her "quick and observant" eye and taking note of any absentees. By the time the entire throng thundered into the palace courtyard, the horses lathered and the courtiers too tired and winded, the queen's observant eyes were bright and her cheeks glowed pink with health.

By now some of the pain and anxiety of the recent past had begun to recede. Secure with Lehzen and the ever-present Melbourne, who spent some six hours a day with her on average as her constant adviser, mentor and friend, the queen was able to minimize her contact with her mother and had dealt Conroy's hopes the mortal coup she had long desired to deliver. While Conroy was still occasionally to be seen stalking the palace corridors on the Duchess of Kent's business, or visiting one of the duchess's waiting maids, Flora Hastings, in her private rooms, for the most part he was gone and his menace attenuated.

Victoria saw little of her mother, though courtesy required that the duchess be present at all court functions and that she join the queen for dinner and for whatever evening entertainment followed. Gradually Victoria stopped having breakfast with her mother, and spoke to her less and less. Dinners for thirty or forty people were common at the palace, and after dinner, the duchess customarily napped in her chair until a whist table was set up for her and play began. Victoria did not play; she sat with Melbourne, talking mostly with him and presiding over what Greville referred to as "the trivial, labored, and wearisome inanities of the royal circle."[14]

The duchess was aggrieved. She complained to Princess Lieven "that she had no future, and that she no longer counted for anything." For eighteen years, she said, Victoria had been "the sole object of her life, of all her thoughts and hopes," and now Victoria was taken from her.[15] She blamed Melbourne, and detested him, and she was envious of Lehzen, who at Victoria's request had been given a sitting room next to the queen's own while the duchess was relegated to a small suite of apartments some distance away. Her self-importance wounded, she protested, as she had once protested to King William, only now the object of her protests was her own child.

In public, however, the duchess did her best to appear to be on good terms with her daughter, and when in October of 1837 the diarist Thomas Creevey, a discerning if cynical observer of the court scene, sat next to the duchess at a dinner at Brighton Pavilion he was pleasantly surprised at how agreeable and "chatty" she was. He wrote in his diary afterward that he had been dismayed about having to be her dinner companion, but he found the experience quite tolerable. (After dinner, playing whist with her, was no pleasure at all, as he had had occasion to find out on earlier occasions.) It was Victoria, however, who captured all Creevey's attention.

"A more homely little being you never beheld," he wrote, "when she is at her ease, and she is evidently dying to be always more so. She laughs in real earnest, opening her mouth as wide as it can go, showing not very pretty gums."[16] The queen's eating habits were less than regal, Creevey noted; she "gobbled" her food, and ate like a horse. But her girlish charm more than compensated for her gluttony. "She blushes and laughs every instant in so natural a way as to disarm anybody," wrote the diarist. "Her voice is perfect, and so is the expression of her face when she means to say or do a pretty thing."

Victoria's visit to Brighton in October displeased her. The gaudy, overdecorated Brighton Pavilion, her Uncle George's favorite haunt, struck her as "a strange, odd Chinese-looking thing," a vulgar monument to the excesses of the previous generation. Times had changed; the exotic and the voluptuous were out, freshness and innocence were becoming enshrined in popular taste. Besides, though the Marine Pavilion was close to the ocean, from its windows one could see "only a little morsel of the sea." She was disappointed. She ordered her carriage and went home.

On the return journey, as the queen's carriage was passing along Birdcage Walk toward Buckingham Palace, she was startled to see through the carriage window a well-dressed man running toward her, his fist upraised, shouting that she had usurped the throne. So sudden was the assault that the soldiers of the queen's escort were taken off guard by it, and the man continued to spew out his menacing stream of insults for perhaps a minute or more, screaming that within a week he would force Victoria off her throne.

Overwhelmed by the soldiers and dragged off, his fierce cries diminishing, the mysterious attacker was taken to jail and eventually to an asylum. He was quite mad, convinced that he was the son of George IV and Queen Caroline.[17] Victoria, though shaken, was not seriously upset. But it must have disturbed her to learn later that this was not the first time the madman had struck. Six months earlier he had caused a commotion and forced his way into Kensington Palace, where he had to be subdued.

The carriage moved on toward the palace, past the wide expanse of sand and waste ground that ringed it and fanned out into the dark, narrow streets beyond. As she began to recover her calm, Victoria may well have pondered the meaning of her lucky escape, and wondered what further shocks and menaces might lie along those dark streets, just out of sight of the palace windows, where the real life of London began.

Chapter 6

THROUGHOUT THE SEVERE WINTER of 1838 the terror of London was Spring-Heeled Jack. Day after frost-filled day, as the river froze over and commerce came to a halt, reports reached the Lord Mayor of a monstrous character who sprang out at women walking in the street and made them faint from fright. The monster had many faces. Sometimes, as at Hammersmith, he was a huge baboon, glimpsed in the moonlight. Sometimes, as at Kingston or Hampton, he wore brass armor, with huge clawlike gauntlets. Sometimes he appeared in the guise of a bull, or a bear, or even wearing the sober blue uniform of a member of the Metropolitan Police.

Everywhere women shut themselves indoors, especially after the newspapers reported that Spring-Heeled Jack had assaulted an East End woman, "vomiting forth a quantity of blue and white flame from his mouth, his eyes resembling red balls of fire." Using his fearsome clawlike gauntlets he tore her clothes and pulled out most of her hair.

Pamphlets detailing the "extraordinary life, wonderful adventures and secret amours" of the London Monster sold well in the frost-filled days of February, and it was even said that Jack had been seen dancing at Kensington Palace, and climbing over the roof of the queen's green-houses.[1] All efforts to capture the elusive terror of the streets failed. Part joker, part fiend, he began to take on a mythic quality; then in April, just as the women of the capital were becoming resigned to staying indoors forever, he simply disappeared.

Vying with accounts of Spring-Heeled Jack for the attention of Londoners, as the cold receded and spring began, were the preparations being made for the queen's coronation. Never had London been so crowded, never had the streets been so choked with carts and carriages and omnibuses, drays and wagons, herds of animals and scurrying pedestrians. Debris from hastily remodeled buildings was strewn over wide areas, the din of carpentry rose into the sooty spring air on all sides while falling bricks were a hazard to passersby. Beyond the influx of visitors for the social season there were thousands more who came specifically to watch the coronation parade and to join in the weeks of festivities that preceded coronation day. Every day more people arrived, by coach and private carriage and even by the first fledgling railroad lines coming into the capital from Greenwich and Southampton and Birmingham. Lodging houses were packed, and every shop and house along the coronation route was rented far in advance, with the landlords making a shamelessly high profit.

There was so much to see and do: for the titled and privileged and other members of the *haut ton*, levees and concerts at Buckingham Palace and, on the queen's birthday, a ball with Johann Strauss leading his band; for the middle classes, Queen Adelaide's bazaar at the Hanover Square Rooms and the panorama of Canton displayed in Mr. Burford's Great Circle in Leicester Square, not to mention art exhibits, meetings of benevolent societies and excursions to the zoo and the museums. Between engagements, there were visits to dressmakers and tailors and hairdressers, trips to Thomas Hamlet's jewelry shop in the Oxford Street Bazaar and Howell and James's in Regent Street for silk, ormolu clocks and embroidered handkerchiefs. Women bought floral mantillas, men Rowlands' Macassar Oil and toupees—or "invisible ventilating perukes," as they were then called. Young women, eager to draw all eyes to themselves and frustrated with the unfashionable ruddiness of their cheeks, visited physicians who fastened leeches behind their ears to drink their blood and make them pale.

The queen, as her coronation day approached, was said by one observer to be losing whatever hint of prettiness her plain face had once held and had noticeably put on weight. Her mother spread the story that she drank too much wine, and though this was nothing more than a spiteful rumor prompted by the duchess's injured vanity, some people believed it. The queen herself, whose head ached from time to time from overwork, was worried about her eyes; the morning hours that she devoted to reading dispatches and signing documents taxed her vision and made her squint.[2]

Her face held a melancholy cast for she had lost "her earliest friend," the grandmotherly Mrs. Louis. The death of "dearest, faithful excellent Louie" was a severe blow. "I don't think I have ever been so much overcome or distressed by anything, almost, as by the death of this my earliest friend," she wrote to Leopold, and the combination of work, grief, and her mother's incessant needling tended to wear her down.[3] Even so, she turned a good face toward the world, impressing guests at the palace with her distinctive blend of dignity and unaffected charm. "She never ceases to be a Queen," Greville wrote, "but is always the most charming, cheerful, obliging, unaffected Queen in the world."[4]

The vast crowds that packed Westminster Abbey on the queen's coronation day were moved by the sight of the sovereign's diminutive figure, garbed in the Parliament robes of crimson velvet trimmed with ermine and gold lace, walking slowly down the aisle. Her immensely long train was held by Lord Conyngham and eight female attendants, their white and silver gowns sprinkled with roses. Victoria had not slept well the night before, and it was noticed that her face was flushed and her breathing ragged as she approached the altar. Still, despite the fumbling of the Bishop of Durham, who failed conspicuously in his duty of coaching the queen through the long ceremony, Victoria managed to perform each of the twenty-one separate sections of the coronation ritual without obvious mistakes. Melbourne was beside her much of the time, and she found his steadying presence and his kind, "fatherly" looks heartening.

The presence of "another most dear Being," "my dearly beloved angelic Lehzen," was also an encouragement, and the queen and her onetime governess exchanged smiles as the ceremony proceeded.[5] The Duchess of Kent, magnificently dressed in regal purple and weeping copiously, sitting just below Lehzen in the royal box, did not receive the accolade of a royal smile. One wonders where Sir John Conroy was on Victoria's coronation day, and what rueful pleasure it gave him.

Throughout the five-hour ceremony, with its robings and rerobings, its thunderous orchestral interludes and deafening choral anthems, its moments of high drama and rich pageantry, the little queen remained the center of all attention, drawing loud applause when the gleaming crown, its diamonds and rubies and sapphires flashing, was lowered onto her neatly coiffed small head. And when, robed in gold, she knelt in reverence before the high altar, the sight of her brought forth fervent whispers of prayer from even the most hardened worldlings.

The heavy crown gave Victoria a headache, but when at last she took up her orb and scepter for the procession out of the Abbey, and got into George III's exquisite golden coach, she felt surprisingly buoyant and energetic. The crowds that greeted her were, if possible, even larger than those that had shouted themselves hoarse earlier in the day. "The enthusiasm, affection, and loyalty were really touching," she wrote in her journal later, "and I shall ever remember this day as the proudest of my life!"6

She was indeed proud—but not overly so. Exalted, anointed, acclaimed she might be—but she still found time, between the disrobing and dinner, to give dear Dashy a bath.

For the next four days Londoners rejoiced. Hyde Park was given over to a vast fair, with hundreds of colorful tents and booths pitched on the grass among the trees. Huge gas-filled balloons rose into the sky, children rode ponies and donkeys and rowed boats on the Serpentine. Trumpets blared, gongs sounded and bands played while people strolled through the displays of cheap goods and watched magicians perform wonders and acrobats tumble and gyrate. Freak shows always delighted London audiences, and the displays at the queen's fair included two-headed children, headless beasts, "living skeletons" and giants and dwarfs. In the heat of the day there were cool ices for sale; later on, toward evening, fairgoers bought boiled beef, gingerbread nuts and pastries in the shape of kings and queens.7 Fireworks exploded in a thrilling display of color and noise each evening, and the dancing booths were "crowded to suffocation."

For a month and more following the coronation the capital continued to reverberate with pounding artillery as the Blues, the Lifeguards, and the Tenth Hussars passed in review. Buckingham Palace was host to more balls and grand dinners, while every night there were parties and receptions, affording entertainment to the elite guests and also to the casual onlookers who enjoyed watching the parade of carriages pass along the crowded streets of the West End. Not until August did the celebrating subside, and then, with the wealthy retreating to their country seats, and the oppressive stench of the Thames driving everyone who could afford it out of the capital, something like normality was restored.

Victoria had now been queen for over a year. She was nineteen, and fast approaching the dreaded age of twenty—and everyone knew that girls of twenty who were not engaged were doomed to spinsterhood. Her subjects told one another that she ought to marry, and joked that she might marry her Prime Minister, with whom she was said to spend virtually all of her time.

That William Lamb, Lord Melbourne was nearly sixty at the time of Victoria's coronation did nothing to countervail this gossip. For young women very often married much older men, and Lord Melbourne was popular, very rich, and available.

The truth of their relationship was far different from what gossip made of it. If Uncle Leopold was Victoria's "second father," then Melbourne was her third—and by far the most important and influential of the three. He was parent, teacher, and mentor to her, he was her protector and highly informative guide during the initial years of her reign. The gossips were right in one respect: the queen and Melbourne loved one another, but it was the tender, devoted love of parent and child, never the stormy, passionate stuff of romance.

Still handsome as he approached old age, with a fine head, thick black eyebrows and curling gray side-whiskers, and with an enigmatic, often wistful look in his dark eyes, the Prime Minister was a conspicuously soft and gentle man. Though he was leader of the Whigs, he made no secret of the fact that he found his office "a damned bore," and his political colleagues were of the opinion that he was too yielding, his personal indolence making him unfit to wield effective authority.[8] So physically relaxed that he seemed to melt into the sofa cushions, and so unconcerned with convention that he kept what hours he chose and infuriated his colleagues by his unpunctuality, Melbourne was a genuine eccentric, and Victoria found him captivating.

She liked to sketch the Prime Minister's face, tracing the lines of his often untidy gray-black hair as it fell becomingly over his broad brow, and she liked to listen to him read to her from official papers "beautifully with that fine, soft voice of his, and with so much expression."[9]

Elderly as he was, Melbourne was in some ways Victoria's beau ideal, as much the opposite of Conroy as it was possible for any man to be, and therefore approaching perfection. She filled her journals with records of her conversations with him, and listened attentively to everything he said to her when they met for their morning conference, when he rode with her in the afternoon, throughout dinner, when he always sat on her left, and during the long after-dinner hours of relaxed if dull conversation during which, to her annoyance, he often dropped off to sleep.

For his part, Melbourne set out to be an encouraging coach for the young queen, never letting her know how astonished he was at her naïveté and ignorance and working diligently, though always in his soft-spoken, amusing way, to correct the severe deficiencies in her education.

The Prime Minister had decided opinions, and conveyed them bluntly. He was an aristocrat to the core, and a deep-going snob; he liked and trusted those of his own class, and thought there was some good to be found in the lower classes, but middle-class people he despised as "all affectation and conceit and pretense and concealment." He had nothing but contempt for the do-gooders who had recently led the political fight to abolish slavery, and thought their crusade was nothing but "a pack of nonsense." After all, he told Victoria, most civilized countries have had slaves, and if the practice was not exactly laudable, it was probably inevitable.[10]

In an age of Reform, Melbourne was an anti-reformer, a skeptic who distrusted the mentality of improvement and betterment and those he called the "moral force men." "This damned morality will ruin everything," he said, and predicted that, with the return of religious piety, religious persecution could not be far behind. In disparaging religion Melbourne seemed to Victoria to be going too far.

"The world is very bad," she told him, and reminded him of the dissolute lives her uncles had led in their youth and middle age, their drunkenness and womanizing, their contempt for all the decencies. Times had changed, and for the better, she told him.

"I do not see anything so very bad," replied the Prime Minister, who had sampled all the louche pleasures of the Regency and emerged relatively unscathed. The royal uncles may have been dissolute, "but they were jolly fellows," Melbourne told the queen, adding "times have changed, but I do not know if they have improved."[11]

The dialogue between the monarch and her Prime Minister ranged broadly over many subjects, from the philosophy of government to the nature of Parliament, its proceedings and the party system to the personalities of the leading political figures. Melbourne taught Victoria how to size up the leading politicians and discover their strengths and vulnerabilities—a skill she would consider invaluable in the years to come. He discussed Shakespeare with her, he taught her history through his own experience ("I've been brought up with kings and princes," he remarked, and told her endless anecdotes about her predecessors). They talked not only of weighty matters but of trifles—the ugliness of pigs, Sir Walter Scott's bad ear for music, caps and bonnets, and fashionable milliners, all the "old duchesses" Melbourne had known.

No matter what he was discussing, Melbourne kept the same mild, mellow, commonsensical tone with Victoria, humoring her and often making her laugh. Wellington criticized him, behind his back, for joking too much with the queen, and "making her treat things too lightly, which are very serious."[12] But his detached drollery was a lesson in itself. In an era of serious-mindedness and earnestness, of clashing passions and grim purpose, the Prime Minister was a living monument to balance and moderation, and in this he served the impressionable young queen well.

He served her well, that is, for as long as his government was reasonably secure. In the spring of 1839 it began to totter, however, and the queen, who for some months had been displaying signs of a nervous crisis, went to pieces.

When the Prime Minister told her, on May 7, that the Whigs' majority in the Commons had dwindled to a handful and that he intended to resign she cried for days, clinging to Melbourne's hand—"that kind, dear hand of his"—and sobbing and begging him "not to forsake her." She felt forsaken already, and "cried dreadfully" throughout the coming days.

In truth she had been in crisis for some time. Her peremptory disposition had been much in evidence; she scolded her servants and lashed out at them following her unpleasant clashes with her mother. She wrote in her journal that she was "so spoilt" and began having apprehensive thoughts about her marriage to Albert, on which subject her relatives continued to press her. The prospect of a happy marriage to her Coburg cousin that had once raised her spirits had long since faded. She had changed. Now, she confided to Melbourne, she dreaded the thought of marrying at all. "I was so accustomed to have my own way," she wrote in her journal, "that I thought it was ten to one that I shouldn't agree with any body."[13] She knew, and it upset her, that some of the approbation with which she was greeted in her first year as queen was eroding. People were now saying that she was "lofty, high, stern and decided," and were criticizing her for being obstinate, pleasure-loving and self-indulgent—in short, for displaying all the arrogance, hedonism and hauteur of a queen.

In fact she was emotionally adrift, and often anxious. Terribly fearful of losing Melbourne, her solid emotional pillar and support, and enmeshed with Lehzen, whom she adored but who was jealous and possessive, and had to be placated, Victoria was afraid of being edged closer to marriage, which would mean being coerced by her husband. Lehzen had convinced Victoria that Leopold was eager for her to marry Albert so that, through Albert, he could control her and hence rule her realms.[14] She seemed unable to stand alone; therefore she must be certain that those on whom she leaned for support would not abandon or betray her. Worrying over this issue drained her, and her health suffered.

Significantly, Victoria complained that all her pleasures had lost their keen edge. She still stayed up late dancing, but with less elation. Her favorite quadrilles no longer thrilled her. Her afternoon rides were no longer exhilarating. She ate to the point of gluttony, and told Melbourne that she was always hungry. She took less satisfaction from the company of her pets, and the newest of them, a pet monkey, chose this awkward time to get sick. The work of ruling, which had once given her so much satisfaction, now seemed merely tedious. She complained petulantly to Melbourne that she "disliked to hear nothing else but politics and always politics," and he and others noticed that she seemed to veer between irritable boredom and an unnatural avidness that fixed itself on passing amusements. Privately, he may have wondered, as Stockmar did, whether the queen was showing early signs of the Hanoverian family disease.[15]

Just at this time, as the Whig government was collapsing, Victoria was confronting an imbroglio of a much more complex kind, one that revealed her immaturity and, for a time, eclipsed her better nature entirely.

Once again her mother and Conroy loomed as malevolent spirits that had to be exorcised.

The Duchess of Kent, feeling wounded and wronged, had stepped up her campaign of protest. She demanded higher status in the household, she wanted a larger suite of rooms, she deserved a larger allowance, and—here she touched the quick of Victoria's annoyance—she demanded that Sir John Conroy, who continued to manage her money, be formally invited to palace social functions and given marks of royal respect. Beyond that, she goaded Victoria with personal remarks and sent her vexing letters, remaining a perpetual thorn in her side.

It was more than Victoria could take. She knew that her mother was once again spending money she did not have, and borrowing heavily to pay her creditors. Conroy's mismanagement of the duchess's accounts had been exposed in *The Times*, but he was mounting a spirited (and expensive) defense, all the while continuing to frequent the palace, to Victoria a sinister, shadowy presence who spread evil in his wake.

Victoria thought she had discerned the evil. Her mother's lady-in-waiting Flora Hastings, whom Victoria had hated ever since Flora's company was forced upon her when she was fifteen, had drawn the queen's "quick and observant eye." Lady Flora's slim figure was noticeably thicker. There was only one possible explanation. She was pregnant. And there was only one possible father: Conroy, the "Monster and Demon Incarnate," as Victoria referred to him in her journal.[16]

The queen, who was just then enthralled with the thrilling performances of Isaac Van Amburgh, the American lion-tamer, at Drury Lane Theater, had no time for the sordid doings of the wicked Conroy and his paramour. She left it to Melbourne to deal with the scandal, and went on visiting the Drury Lane, where ferocious lions, cheetahs and leopards became as tame as kittens under the mesmerizing eye of Van Amburgh. After seven visits her fascination still burned bright, and she stayed after the performance ended to walk onstage and examine the huge beasts in their cages. "It's quite beautiful to see," she wrote of the lion-tamer's skill, "and makes me wish I could do the same."[17]

Though both the queen's physician James Clark and a respected specialist, Sir Charles Clarke, examined Flora and announced that she was a virgin, Victoria's suspicions did not subside, and a bitterly tense situation developed. Lady Flora continued to look and feel ill, the

Duchess of Kent loudly and tearfully demanded that her daughter apologize for her unjust suspicions, the queen's ladies erupted into petty warfare with the duchess's ladies, and inevitably the Tories began to use the scandal in the palace to attack the Whigs and bring discredit on the queen.

Meanwhile Melbourne's government fell on May 7, and Victoria, filled with dread, her nerves in shreds, was faced with having to summon Sir Robert Peel to form a new one. She disliked the cold, distant Peel, and inwardly she panicked. When Peel told her that it would be necessary for her to replace her Whig ladies with Tories, lest she appear to be acting in bad faith toward the new ministers, she was affronted. Summoning all her self-control, she told Peel, with "great firmness," that she could never consent. Further negotiation proved futile; the queen was adamant. The little soldier in her came forth, and stood her ground. The strength of her conviction was so great that it was Peel who became disconcerted and frightened. He backed down. Within days Melbourne was back in office, and people were saying that the spoiled little queen had caused a constitutional crisis by her childish recalcitrance.

But there was worse to come. Lady Flora, pale and wasted now, and clearly succumbing to a condition far more serious than pregnancy, had become a wretched invalid. And instead of realizing that she had made a mistake, and been led astray by her prejudices, Victoria did nothing. She continued to believe what she wanted to believe, which was that Flora Hastings was pregnant with Conroy's child, and that through Flora, Conroy's dark shadow was continuing to lengthen over her court.[18]

Victoria was badly in need of sane guidance, but no one offered it. Her naturally strong compassion was shut down. She was blind to the assault she herself had made against Flora's good name, and indifferent to Flora's genuine suffering. All the queen could see—all that she would let herself see—was that once again, she was caught in Conroy's snares, and that her mother (who, she told Melbourne, had never loved her) cared more for Lady Flora than she did for Victoria herself.

"I am but a poor helpless girl," Victoria wrote. Queen she was, but far from sovereign over her domestic circumstances. She might stand her ground with Peel, but with her own mother, and the Monster and Demon Incarnate, she was still vulnerable.

Finally, early in July, the emaciated Lady Flora died. To the end, Victoria was reluctant to see her, and complained to Melbourne that she found it disagreeable to have a dying person in her household. Her callousness was seen as repugnant, all the more so after the corpse of the wretched lady-in-waiting was opened and the surgeons discovered, not a baby, but a hugely swollen liver. Flora's honor was intact.

The newspapers trumpeted forth the sad demise of Lady Flora, a martyr to royal persecution. The queen dropped still more in public estimation. Readers of the Tory *Morning Post* and *John Bull* shook their heads over the heartlessness of the shallow young Victoria. There was much head-shaking as well over the summer's great social event, a mock-medieval tournament held at Eglinton Castle in Scotland in which many young lords and ladies took part. The young people were reported to have spent thousands of pounds on gowns, arms and armor, and the details of their extravagant feasting and spurious jousting were widely reported. Victoria had no more substance to her than the superficial, pleasure-loving revelers at Eglinton, people said; her shabby treatment of Lady Flora left no doubt of that.

Dispirited and at a low ebb, defensive (though perhaps inwardly remorseful) about her role in the Flora Hastings debacle, tired of the business of ruling and unsure where her reign was heading, Victoria did not know where to turn. She could take some small satisfaction in the fact that in June, Conroy had resigned his office in her mother's household and left England, but she did not allow herself to believe that his voluntary exile would be permanent. As for the duchess, she had sworn to remain by her daughter's side until she married—and as Victoria dreaded marrying, it seemed as if she would be there forever.

In the long, warm summer afternoons the queen went out riding, her attendants fanning out beside her, following her around the park and along her favorite narrow lanes where, she once wrote, "one could fancy oneself two or three hundred miles from London."[19] Riding invigorated her, and, for a few hours at least, helped to keep at bay the "dull, flat" mood that so often afflicted her.

But even on the sunniest afternoons clouds seemed to gather. Unpleasant prospects loomed, and she could not stave them off forever. For the time being Melbourne was back by her side, but Peel was waiting in the wings—and Victoria knew that it was only a matter of time before the Whigs fell once again. She had written to Uncle Leopold telling him in no uncertain terms that "no engagement" existed between her and Albert, but Leopold was arranging for Albert and his brother to visit her in the fall, and she knew that eventually she would have to make up her mind to marry. Now listless, now irritable, the twenty-year-old queen lurched toward her future, her mouth set in a resolute line, her guard raised. Whatever happened, she was determined not to be taken unawares.

Chapter 7

―――――∞―――――

W HEN THE TWENTY-YEAR-old Albert of Saxe-Coburg-Gotha
contemplated marriage to his cousin Queen Victoria, he
groaned inwardly. He had met her, of course, and had not
disliked her—or if he had, he had been too discreet to record his dislike.[1] But that had been three years earlier, before she became queen,
before stories began to circulate about her ruthless treatment of Flora
Hastings and, far more serious, about her precarious sanity.[2]

Now that she was queen, so he understood, she had become impossibly self-willed, with an obstinacy that drove away all her better
instincts, and a hot temper, and a lamentable fondness for what he
called "court ceremonies, etiquette and trivial formalities." To Albert,
who detested social artifice and was above all a lover of nature and the
outdoors, his cousin's enthusiasm for dances and parties and frivolous
pastimes was deeply distasteful. He knew that, if he was to please her,
he too would have to lower himself to enter society and adopt its triv-
ialities, and the thought appalled him. "These are gloomy prospects,"
he told his tutor, and he meant it.

Victoria, for her part, was fighting the idea of marriage for all she was worth. She told Melbourne in July of 1839 that "the whole subject was an odious one," and that she wished it were possible for her to remain single, like her great predecessor Queen Elizabeth. She had a deep dread of childbearing, and a fear of being controlled, as her mother and Conroy had once controlled her.[3] Even though Albert was the best of the available princes—and she and Melbourne had gone over them all—still she drew back from seeing him, sensing that to see him and visit with him would be to commit herself.

If only she could put off all thought of betrothal for three or four years, she told her Prime Minister. Yet three or four years with her mother hovering ever near, pecking away at the fraying edges of her life, seemed a torment. And her mother would stay on, an unwelcome duenna, until she married.

Albert and Ernest were to arrive in England in mid-October, and as the time approached, Victoria became nervous. She couldn't sleep, she was "sadly cross" to Melbourne, she fretted about a visit from Queen Adelaide, whose presence she expected to be "a severe trial." Her fears rose up en masse, and would not be stilled. On the very morning of the day her cousins were due to arrive, October 10, stones were thrown through the windows of Victoria's dressing room at Windsor—an omen, if she chose to look on it as such, of shattered times ahead.

But then her cousins drove up into the courtyard, and were ushered in, and Victoria caught her first glimpse of Albert, looking up at her from the bottom of the staircase with his beautiful, soulful blue eyes, his broad-shouldered figure both manly and graceful, and her heart began to pound. This was not the sweet, agreeable boy she had met three years earlier; this was a strong, capable man, a protector, not a lord and master. "It was with some emotion that I beheld Albert," she wrote in her journal, "who is beautiful."[4]

Victoria was enchanted. Even though Albert was pale and ill from the dangerously rough Channel crossing, he seemed to her perfection, and she embraced him warmly. Later that evening, Albert sat across from her on a sofa and she basked in his attractiveness ("he is so handsome and pleasing" she wrote in her journal), asking Melbourne coyly whether he saw any cousinly likeness between them.

Over the next four days her admiration grew into adoration. She and Albert talked for hours, they rode together, played games, went to church together—in short, they tested their companionship, and the test went extraordinarily well. On Monday, October 14, Victoria went to visit Lady Sandwich and her "darling baby." It is tempting to think that this visit made her thoughts turn with sentimental longing to having Albert's children, for that very afternoon she announced to Melbourne that she had "made up her mind" about marrying Albert.[5] If she had any doubt about his willingness, she did not express them to the Prime Minister, instead they went on to discuss a tentative date for the wedding.

The following day Albert and Ernest spent the morning hunting, "charging up the hill at an immense pace" after their quarry. Early in the afternoon Victoria sent for Albert.

"He came to the closet where I was alone," she wrote afterward, describing the scene, "and after a few minutes I said to him, that I thought he must be aware why I wished them to come here, and that it would make me too happy if he would consent to what I wished."[6] In these roundabout words, she proposed to him. "We embraced each other," she went on, "and he was so kind, so affectionate." She told Albert that she was "quite unworthy of him," and that it was "a great sacrifice" for him to give up his independence to marry her. He denied the sacrifice, and said happily that he would be more than content to spend his life with her. Overwhelmed, she took his "dear hand" and kissed it again and again.

She then swore him to secrecy—only Albert's father, his brother, Stockmar, and Uncle Leopold were to be let in on the secret for the time being. He went to fetch Ernest, who congratulated them both, saying "he was the only loser by it, as his brother had been everything to him." "I feel the happiest of human beings," Victoria wrote, and it was an understatement.

In a way that seemed to her miraculous, the emotional balance of Victoria's life had been restored. Her recent depression and irritable ennui vanished. She felt not only loved, but renewed; the depth of Albert's affection "made up for all she had suffered and endured" in the past.[7] All at once it seemed to her that there was a grand economy at work in her life, replacing what had been taken away, healing what had been broken; only the language of the supernatural could contain her rapturous response. "Oh! to feel I was, and am, loved by such an Angel as Albert was too great to describe!"[8]

The Angel himself was far less carried away. "Victoria is so good and kind to me," he told his brother, "I am often at a loss to believe that such affection should be shown to me."[9] He felt privileged, but he was not in love. Nor had he lost sight of Victoria's flaws and weaknesses. He was well aware that, as her husband, he was certain to face trials and hardships. "My future position will have its dark sides and the sky will not always be blue and unclouded," he told Ernest. "My future lot is high and brilliant, but also plentifully strewn with thorns."[10] He could foresee that he would miss his home, that he would never become accustomed to English food or English ways. He knew, for Victoria lost no time in telling him, that a virtual state of war existed between herself and her mother; he could not avoid being drawn in. And there was Lehzen, whose jealousy was transparent and whose enmity was to be reckoned with. Significantly, neither the Duchess of Kent nor Lehzen was informed of the secret engagement.

But if the bridegroom was not in love with the bride, and if there were sure to be thorns in the path of the royal couple, still they were drawn together by strong bonds. Both were emotionally vulnerable, though Albert hid his sensitivity behind a mask of decorum and punctilious reserve. Both had had sad childhoods, deprived of love. Both were romantics, she melodramatic, he high-minded, given to inner suffering and noble self-sacrifice. Both loved music, and Albert played the piano and organ well and wrote songs. (Shortly after their engagement he presented her with a book of his published songs, inscribed, in German, "to my dear Victoria from her faithful Albert.")

Finally, they complemented one another in that, beneath her enthusiasm for pleasure and entertainment, Victoria yearned for the seriousness she so admired in her husband-to-be. Albert offered her a model of worthy living, and she wanted very much to be able to follow his example, to set aside the life she had been leading and set her feet on a higher path.

When it was officially announced that the queen would marry her Coburg cousin Albert, the public reaction was mixed. Though many people accepted the match, and wished the queen well, some objected. Albert was sneered at as another in the long list of "lucky Coburgs," like his aunt the duchess and his uncle Leopold, fortune-hunters who married far above their station. Street singers poked cruel fun at the bridegroom. "He comes to take, for better or for worse, England's fat Queen and England's fatter purse," went one satirical ballad. Lady Holland called Albert the "soi-disant prétendu," or "self-styled pretender"—a slur on his ambition.[11]

"Everything is always made so uncomfortable for Kings and

Queens!" Victoria burst out when her wedding arrangements were being discussed, and difficulties addressed, in December. Albert had gone back to Coburg to settle his affairs, and she missed kissing him, missed leaning on "that dear soft cheek, fresh and pink like a rose." She was losing weight, and once again sleeping badly. Her nervousness flared up, and to Melbourne's dismay she was showing a marked disinclination for going out in public.[12]

One great victory was gained, however. After some struggles, the Duchess of Kent was made to understand that in consequence of her daughter's forthcoming marriage she would be moving out of the palace, and giving up her rooms at Windsor. A house in Belgrave Square was rented for her; a month after the wedding, "the enemy in the house" was gone.

Torrents of rain beat down on the muddy waste ground around Buckingham Palace on the royal wedding day, February 10, 1840. The thousands who had gathered in the park were soaked and miserable, their umbrellas turned inside out by violent gusts of wind that threatened to topple the great leafless trees and tear the roofs off half-built houses. By the time the queen's carriage appeared, to convey her the short distance to St. James's, they were too dispirited and waterlogged to cheer her, but they applauded and smiled before scattering for shelter.

Albert was waiting inside the chapel, flanked by his brother and his tall, handsome father, when a blare of trumpets and a blaze of heralds and pursuivants in gaudy uniforms proclaimed the arrival of the queen. Preceded by her numerous aunts, uncles and cousins, and by the aging Melbourne bearing the Sword of State, Victoria came in, small but stately, her round face framed with orange blossoms and her eyes swollen from crying. Twelve young attendants, all in white with white roses, bore the long train of her white satin gown, and she sparkled with diamonds as she moved down the aisle.

"The Queen's look and manner were very pleasing," wrote Lady Lyttelton, who as one of the bedchamber ladies was a member of the procession. Despite her tears, her face showed "great happiness," and "her look of confidence and comfort at the Prince as they walked away as man and wife was very pretty to see."[13]

After the ceremony, Victoria and Albert had a quiet talk in her dressing room, then joined their guests for the wedding breakfast, the principal feature of which was a three-hundred-pound cake adorned with cupids and satin love knots and a large figure of Britannia blessing the bride and groom. Later, Victoria put on a white silk gown trimmed with swansdown for the journey to Windsor, where they were to spend their brief honeymoon.

All along the route to Windsor damp crowds waved and called out good wishes, delaying the arrival of the coach until nearly eight in the evening. By this time Victoria had developed a "sick headache" and had to lie down on a sofa. "But, ill or not," she wrote in her journal, "I never, never spent such an evening." It was, she wrote, "bliss beyond belief." As for the wedding night, she confided to her journal only that "we did not sleep much," and that when dawn broke, "and I beheld that beautiful angelic face by my side, it was more than I can express!"[14] Many years later, writing to her daughter Vicky, the queen alluded to the "shock" of "the marital act" and to her sufferings and upset at the outset of her marriage, but if her initiation into sex was mortifying, it was also ecstatic, for Victoria was quite lost in Albert's beauty and comforted by his tenderness.[15]

A few days before the wedding, Victoria had bought a new dog, a bluish-gray Scottish terrier that she named Laddie, and had it sent to Windsor. With Laddie, her favorites Islay and Dash, and Albert's beloved greyhound Eos at their heels, Victoria and Albert strolled along the terrace, accustoming themselves to their new status as husband and wife. The morning after the wedding, one of the ladies of the bedchamber, the Duchess of Bedford, noted that although Victoria appeared to be "excessively in love" with Albert, he seemed to be "not a bit" in love with her. He gave the impression of "not being happy," the duchess thought, and indeed he was not feeling well, and had to spend the afternoon lying down, recovering from the previous day's tensions and the previous night's ardors.[16]

After three days at Windsor, Victoria returned to London to take up her duties once again, but hardly a week had passed when she began to feel queasy and often sick to her stomach. Her "aches and sufferings" increased; soon she realized that she was pregnant.[17]

She was furious at having been "caught," as she put it, but like it or not, she was in an "unhappy condition," and her physical state now dictated what she could and could not do. She found the restriction all but intolerable; she could enjoy nothing, her stomach heaved, her head ached, she was always having to rest—though the pressures of work remained as they had always been. To soothe her restlessness, she kept a bottle of camphor lozenges by her bed, and before long she discovered that she couldn't get to sleep without them.

Though utterly enraptured by Albert, Victoria kept a line firmly drawn between her blissful personal life (now clouded by her pregnancy) and her position as sovereign. Albert discovered, to his chagrin, that Victoria did not confide in him on matters of politics or governing; this came as a great shock, since one of his principal motives in marrying her had been his conviction that his position as her husband would give him an opportunity to exert a positive influence in public affairs. He had thought that she was offering him a rare opportunity for a meaningful and effective life; now that opportunity seemed blocked, and he complained.

Tension arose between the spouses. Ernest noticed it, and commented that his brother and the queen "could not yield to each other." Though at her wedding Victoria had vowed to obey her husband (she had not wanted the word "obey" omitted from the ceremony, even when asked about it), still it was she who gave orders to him, not the other way around—and he resented it.[18]

Stockmar, always an astute observer of court politics, was convinced that Lehzen was to blame. Victoria, he wrote, "is influenced more than she is aware of by the Baroness."[19] And indeed the baroness, as Lehzen was now called, was clearly jealous of Albert, as she had been of Melbourne, as she would be of anyone who threatened to come between her and the queen. Having been unsuccessful in preventing Victoria's marriage to Albert, she was now attempting to subvert it.

Victoria was blind to the machinations of her "adored Angel Daisy," but others saw clearly enough what was going on. Though she had refused any official position (a tactic that made her invulnerable to being officially removed from office), in actuality Lehzen all but ran Victoria's household and managed her privy purse. Beyond that, she was a sort of mother figure to the maids of honor, and acted as Victoria's private secretary. She had wielded inordinate influence during the Flora Hastings affair. From the start of the reign she had been constantly at Victoria's side during her waking hours, tactfully leaving the room when ministers were present but returning the instant they were gone. When of necessity away from the queen, she watched her through the palace windows, with what one observer described as "her usual half-anxious, smiling, fixed look"—a look that betrayed both her shrewdness and her insecurity.[20]

Privately, Albert was convinced that Lehzen's interference was malicious, yet he saw how devoted Victoria was to her onetime governess and protector and was astute enough not to precipitate a quarrel with her. Wisely, he kept his peace, knowing that Victoria adored him and perhaps believing that, over time, her love for him would outweigh her loyalty to the baroness. He was patient with his irritable, often ill wife, sitting through the insipid concerts she enjoyed and doodling on the printed program (he preferred the "ancient" music of the Renaissance and baroque periods), deferring to her when she objected to his plan to bring outstanding scientists and scholars to the palace. Night after night he sat beside her on a sofa, arranging prints in albums and making sketches of Eos and the other dogs, creating for her the atmosphere of cozy intimacy that made her happy and calmed her nerves. He composed songs for her, they played duets and sang together, and all the while, week after week, she grew larger until, in her doctor's words, she was "more like a barrel than anything else."[21]

One evening in June, as Victoria and Albert were driving in a small carriage into Green Park, Albert caught sight of a small, furtive-looking boy only a few feet from the carriage, holding something out toward them. He heard the loud crack of the gun before he realized what it was, and for an instant he was stunned. The horses shied and the carriage came to a halt. Albert put his arms around Victoria, but before anyone in their party, or among the spectators, could react, the assassin stooped, took careful aim with a second pistol and fired, still at very close range.

By a miracle the shot went over the heads of the queen and her husband and embedded itself in a garden wall. Now dozens of onlookers, drawn by the shots, rushed toward the little man with the pistols with shouts of "Kill him, kill him!" Albert called to the postilion to drive on, and the carriage lumbered forward.

When he asked Victoria how she felt, she only laughed; she had been assaulted before—though never shot at—and she took it in stride. She even had the presence of mind to order the carriage to drive to her mother's house so that the duchess would not worry about her daughter's safety.[22]

It was customary for women to conceal their pregnancies as much as possible, and for as long as possible, but the short, hefty Victoria could not hide her distended belly. She was uncomfortably aware of being "stared at" at drawing rooms and levees, where she had to sit for hours on display. Albert gallantly noted that, large as she was, she was nonetheless "lovely to look at" in a low-necked gown, with a bunch of roses tucked between her swelling breasts, but her doctor considered her shape to be "most extraordinary" and confided to a friend that he expected her to become "very ugly and enormously fat" as she got older.[23]

In mid-September, with the baby's birth expected in a little over two months, a diplomatic crisis arose and Victoria was reported to be greatly alarmed. Palmerston, Melbourne's bold and aggressive Foreign Secretary, was pursuing a policy in the Middle East that brought England and France into antagonism and threatened to lead to war. Others in the Cabinet were on the verge of resigning in protest, but the secretary blithely held to his dangerous course. Melbourne was beside himself, struggling to hold his government together, eager to prevent war and nearly as eager to prevent Victoria from either becoming ill over the issue or attempting to take over the Foreign Office herself.

After several tense weeks, and much skillful maneuvering on Melbourne's part, the belligerence of the French Prime Minister, Adolphe Thiers, was checked and the crisis averted. Victoria settled down to prepare for her delivery.

She summoned Dr. Charles Locock, a celebrated obstetrician, and in plain terms discussed the forthcoming birth with him. Would the pain be very great, she asked him. No doubt she would bear it well, he answered.

"Oh yes," the queen told him, "I can bear pain as well as other people."

Tradition dictated that royal childbirths be attended by dozens of official onlookers, from household officers to government ministers; for centuries queens had given birth in airless rooms amid noisy crowds. Victoria would have none of that, she told Dr. Locock firmly. Official witnesses would be tolerated in an adjoining room, but in the birth chamber itself she would permit only the doctor himself, the monthly nurse Mrs. Lilly, and her husband.

Dr. Locock was put off by Victoria. She lacked delicacy, he thought. She was disturbingly earthy and open about the physical aspects of her pregnancy, and immodest besides. Overall he was "not a little disgusted with the Queen's manner."[24]

When her pains began, very early in the morning of November 21, the queen was taken by surprise. It was weeks too early, and the nursery was not yet ready. Even the baby clothes, the lace-trimmed gowns and embroidered caps and monogrammed pillows on which the next king would lay his tiny head, were not yet completed.

The very sleepy Albert, the ever vigilant Lehzen, and Dr. Locock, nominally in charge, could not agree about how the queen would be cared for during her labor. Albert tried to send the meddling Lehzen away, but she stood her ground, a mother hen petulantly protecting her chick, and the doctor, clearly baffled, and unsure how to treat his important patient, was nearly as uncomfortable as the queen.[25]

After twelve hours of pain, with Albert in all but constant attendance, the baby was at last born.

"Oh Madam," Locock said in dismay, "it is a Princess."

"Never mind," the weary queen replied. "The next will be a Prince."

Chapter 8

THE NEW BABY, PRINCESS Victoria Adelaide Mary Louise, was barely three months old when the queen became pregnant once again. She had been in very low spirits ever since giving birth, weeping and sad, complaining that tiny Vicky was much too heavy for her to carry, often calling for Albert to soothe and entertain her. The discovery that she was about to begin the whole painful, inconvenient and mortifying process of pregnancy once again made her furious. Albert was just then reading Goethe to her, *The Sorrows of Young Werther*. It must have seemed as though Werther's sorrows were nothing compared with hers, doomed to nine months of headaches and nausea, embarrassment and distasteful intervention by what she called "those nasty doctors."[1]

Once again she had to keep her camphor lozenges by her bed, and take elaborate precautions against harming herself or the baby, denying herself the pleasures of riding and dancing and subjecting herself reluctantly to the stares of her guests at drawing rooms and assemblies.

In one important respect motherhood had been a benefit. Victoria's popularity soared. The critics who had condemned her for her callous and unjust treatment of Flora Hastings now approved her as a devoted wife dutifully fulfilling her role in producing royal children. In the popular view, she had gone from headstrong girl to model matron, and her subjects were pleased.

Her officials too were pleased, for it seemed to them that marriage and motherhood had settled her and made her more steady. Proof of the queen's greater equanimity came later in the year when Melbourne's government fell and the consequent General Election gave the Tories a majority. Sad at the loss of Melbourne but resigned to working with Peel, Victoria weathered the crisis, even agreeing to part with three of her bedchamber ladies with no argument or bad feeling.

The queen's officials were right: she had changed, and the reason was not far to seek. "I suppose no one was ever so completely altered and changed in every way as I was by dearest Papa's blessed influence," Victoria wrote some years later, looking back at the early days of her marriage. "I owe everything to dearest Papa. He was my father, my protector, my guide and adviser in all and everything, my mother (I might almost say) as well as my husband."[2] Never having known unselfish love, she now experienced it in full measure, and it made all the difference.

Yet it also made her dependent on Albert as she had never been dependent on anyone. He became her private secretary, her teacher (when he read Goethe to her, it was not merely to amuse her, but to instruct her), her counselor and caretaker. He no longer felt excluded from her confidence on issues of governance; on the contrary, she now came to him for advice, and asked him to be present when she conferred with her ministers. They worked side by side, at adjoining desks, and when her headaches and queasiness became too severe for her to go on working, she relied on Albert to do what was necessary in her absence.[3]

In the battle for preeminence in Victoria's affections, Albert had won. But Lehzen did not give up easily. At fifty-seven, she had earned the right to retire, yet she clung to her twenty-two-year-old mistress, and to her dwindling duties, with the tenacity of a much younger woman. Knowing that Victoria would be emotionally torn by Lehzen's departure, and not wanting to upset her while she was pregnant, Albert endured Lehzen's constant meddling and interference—and her manipulative efforts to estrange Victoria from her husband—without bringing matters to a head. But he was convinced that she was "a crazy, stupid intriguer" and he complained to Melbourne, before the latter's departure from office, about the "constant state of annoyance he was kept in" by her intrusiveness.[4] At least once he had tried to order the baroness out of the palace, but she insolently defied him, telling him that "he had not the power to turn her out of the Queen's house." Later she complained to Albert's private secretary, George Anson, that Albert had "slighted her in the most marked manner and she was too proud not to resent it."[5]

Victoria's sick headaches became worse as her pregnancy advanced, and her dependence on Albert increased. He had to be on call to lift her from her sofa to her bed, "coming instantly when sent for," many times a day. She fretted when, on rare occasions, they were separated for many hours. In June, Albert went to Oxford to receive an address at Commemoration. He left Victoria at Nuneham, "to her great grief," for some hours. It was "a trial" for her; the following day she was indisposed and could transact no business.[6]

Throughout the rainy, foggy summer she clung to him, relying on him to support her during the sad changeover from Melbourne to Peel, following him in her carriage when he went shooting or hunting for a few hours at midday. In the autumn, when storms battered the coast and the Thames overflowed its banks, drowning low-lying areas of London, she grew so large that she was all but immobile, her burden heavy within her. This time, she and Albert hoped, the baby would be a boy, a brother for the thin, wiry, precocious "Pussy" who was now nearly a year old but who in recent months had been sickly. Several times she thought her labor had begun, only to discover that it was a false alarm. Dr. Locock, ill at ease as usual, offered professional competence but no reassurance, while Lehzen attempted to give orders and take charge, offending everyone.

Finally, on November 9, the queen was seized with strong pains and entered an agonizing labor. It was much worse than her first time; she suffered acutely while Albert sat beside her, holding her hand, mopping her brow, murmuring comforting words. When she finally "shook off her burden," as she put it, Dr. Locock told the queen that she had a fine son. The boy that she and Albert had been so eager to produce had finally arrived. A prince, who would one day be king.

Londoners rushed out into the streets when they heard bells pealing and artillery booming a salute to the heir to the throne. The news spread rapidly, and soon cheers of "God save the Prince" filled the air.

No one could remember the last time a royal prince had been born—and in fact two generations had passed since George III's queen had laid a son in the royal cradle. The only objection to the new baby came from his sister Pussy, "still the great pet amongst us," Victoria noted, who looked down at her blue-eyed brother and scowled.[7]

The following month the general rejoicing turned to mourning when reports reached the capital that a large British force sent into northern India had been massacred by Ghazi and Afghan warriors amid horrifying suffering and brutality. Only one man survived to tell what happened to the thousands of others, including many women and children, who were hounded to their deaths in the terrible snow-filled mountain passes near Kabul. It was a blow to British honor, and a setback to imperial expansion—and a spur to further endeavors undertaken to redeem the tragedy.

Victoria did not write extensively of the Kabul disaster in her journal. Instead she was preoccupied, once again, with conflict in the palace, this time between herself and her Angel Albert.

The occasion of the quarrel was Pussy's sickliness. Albert had become deeply attached to his bright little daughter and she crowed with delight whenever her papa came near. It pained him that she was becoming thin and pale—and he blamed the nurse and the doctor, James Clark, who was giving her too much calomel, and above all Lehzen, who was attempting to take charge of the nursery. Yet when Albert, having chastised the nurse, attempted to talk with Victoria about the situation she was so "hasty and passionate" that she shouted him down, adding ugly accusations that he was suspicious of her, envied her authority, and was ambitious to take over from her. Finally, all restraint forgotten, she threw up her hands and told her husband that as far as she was concerned, he could murder Vicky, and that she was sorry she ever married.

Seething, the prince managed to avoid replying in kind but had to leave the room.

Later, mastering his anger, he informed his wife in writing that she had starved Vicky and Dr. Clark was poisoning her. "I shall have nothing more to do with it," he wrote imperiously. "Take the child away and do as you like and if she dies you will have it on your conscience."[8]

Behind the harsh words was the shadow of Lehzen, who, Albert was convinced, was feeding Victoria lies about him, coloring her perception of him and misrepresenting his every act. Lehzen had to go;

Stockmar arranged her departure, and she left for the Continent, with the queen's thanks and an annuity. Her exit brought an immediate change for the better. Before long harmony was restored, Pussy improved and Victoria and Albert were on good terms once again.

That spring a dire prophecy, said to have been made by a medieval monk, was repeated widely in London:

> *In eighteen hundred and forty-two*
> *Four things the sun shall view;*
> *London's rich and famous town*
> *Hungry earth shall swallow down;*
> *Storm and rain in France shall be,*
> *Till every river runs a sea;*
> *Spain shall be rent in twain,*
> *And famine waste the land again;*
> *So say I, the Monk of Dree*
> *In the twelve hundredth year and three.*[9]

No earthquake shook the city, but there were tremors of social upheaval. On May 2, sixteen burly men carried a huge petition—a mammoth scroll—up to the door of the House of Commons and tried to squeeze it through the narrow entrance. Frustrated, they divided it into sections and finally deposited it before the astonished Members. The scroll contained well over three million signatures, gathered primarily from the industrial districts, of subscribers to the People's Charter. The anguished voice of England's poor was demanding to be heard.

The Charter itself brought the condition of Victoria's subjects into stark relief. The vast majority of working people, it said, labored under inhuman conditions—and for wages too low to provide bread for their children and a roof over their heads. Yet while they toiled for pennies a day, the queen and her husband received hundreds of pounds—a wasteful extravagance. The people, the Charter said, were governed by an overpaid few, who were elected by a privileged elite. But that must change: every man must be able to vote, and Parliament must meet every year, a Parliament made up of paid Members chosen by secret ballot from electoral districts of equal size.

Years of bad harvests, low wages, and extreme industrial distress were creating pressure for further reform. In the decade since the Reform Bill of 1832, Britain's population had grown enormously, swelled by immigration from Ireland. The burgeoning industrial cities, their overcrowded, disease-ridden slums sprawling outward in a chaotic jumble, were home to an increasingly distressed and disaffected population, always on the verge of starvation and lacking the means to improve their situation. To such a population, the Chartist program offered a voice, and an opportunity for betterment.

Through Chartist orators such as Feargus O'Connor, the movement gave vent to widespread hatred and resentment of all privilege—and especially of the aristocracy. "You, gentlemen," O'Connor thundered during one speech, "belong to the big-bellied, little-brained, numbskull aristocracy. How dare you hiss me, you contemptible set of platter-faced, amphibious politicians?"[10] The "numbskull aristocracy" was not only bloated and foolish, many believed, but willfully indifferent to the sufferings of others, and wickedly extravagant in the face of the nation's want. Flamboyant excesses such as the Eglinton Tournament reinforced this belief, and drove a wider wedge between the people and their rulers.

Barely a week after the People's Charter was presented to Parliament, Victoria presided over yet another display of aristocratic exorbitance. The throne room of Buckingham Palace was fitted up with "Gothic tracery" and medieval furnishings, with huge emblazoned shields of England and France, embroidered in gold on purple velvet, lining the walls. A thirteenth-century gilded throne had been specially built to replace the queen's customary throne. Gorgeously clad dancers in period costume—some of the men wearing suits of mail—danced the "Crusaders' Quadrille" to a band of musicians in spangled jerkins, while on a raised dais, bathed in pinkish light, sat Victoria and Albert costumed as Queen Philippa and Edward III.

For the first time in three years Victoria was able to enjoy the Season, as in the past she had been in misery from the aches and pains of pregnancy. She was determined to enjoy her medieval ball. Yet one observer noticed that she looked "hot and oppressed," in her stiff embroidered mantle of cloth of gold, the heavy fabric weighing her down. She was a glittering icon in her gem-studded, gold-embroidered jacket and ermine-trimmed red velvet skirt; even her high-heeled red silk shoes sparkled with gold and diamonds. On her head she wore a crown made to resemble the one Queen Philippa had worn, with red velvet lappets added that hung down over her plump cheeks. Beside her sat Albert, magnificent in a robe of Garter blue with large gold flowers and a red velvet cloak trimmed in lace and pearls. He too gleamed with gems, and as usual, with his handsome features and tall, narrow-waisted figure, Albert drew more admiration than his wife.

The royal couple descended from their dais and attempted to dance a quadrille, but Victoria's heels tripped her up and made her clumsy. Still, she loved to dance, and continued to make the effort, dancing also with her cousin George and watching with pleasure while her courtiers glided past in their antique finery.[11] Not until two-thirty in the morning did the queen take her departure, clearly satisfied with the outcome of her medieval ball.

Predictably, the newspapers reported every detail of the glittering gala at the palace, and equally predictably, there was a public outcry at the wastefulness it represented. The queen's costly gown was displayed in Hanover Square, and drew criticism, and when it was reported that during the evening Albert had lost a very large and valuable jewel from his belt, people speculated bitterly on how much that lost gem was worth, and how much food and warmth its value might have provided to those in want.

Ironically, Victoria had intended that her fancy dress ball would provide work for the silk weavers of Spitalfields, who made the elaborate costumes. But any praise she might have earned for this gesture was lost amid the chorus of reproach. The magnitude of Britain's social ills was far too great, and far too unmanageable, for anyone at court to comprehend.

The one man who did make an effort to comprehend it was Albert, who let it be known that in his view everyone ought to rise above his own petty quotidian concerns and attempt to be cognizant of the age in which he or she lived. The 1840s were proving to be a time of intense self-scrutiny; newspapers and journals were calling their era "Victorian," and the term was becoming associated with decency, modernity, a humane and progressive spirit, and mechanical advance.

To be "Victorian" was to be up-to-date—and Albert was nothing if not contemporary. In addition to his grasp of political and social issues, he kept himself informed of the newest scientific discoveries, trends in architecture, engineering and farming, progress in medicine and important cultural movements. His active mind was often restless; he would have liked to read and study in his leisure hours but was forced to spend the long, dull evenings at court in idle social pursuits instead. He occupied himself playing double chess (he disliked cards), an elaborate game requiring four players. When particularly bored, he played against himself, though this too soon palled.

The more Albert became absorbed in understanding the age, the less interest Victoria took in her public duties. No doubt this was partly because she had two children to occupy her attention—and became pregnant a third time in the summer of 1842. But there was now an exceptionally capable woman in charge of the nursery, Lady Lyttelton, and Victoria had always deplored what she called "baby-worship" and was certainly not guilty of it herself. In fact her dislike of political life antedated her marriage. "I cannot bear women mixing in politics," she told Melbourne in 1839. There was something distasteful about it, something unnatural. It did not fit the prevailing view of women, a view that could not help but affect the queen.

Besides, there was Albert, so capable and dutiful, so ready to relieve her of the endless tasks of rule. More and more, during 1842 and 1843, she turned over to Albert the chore of reading dispatches—she gave him a key to the dispatch box, a signal mark of trust—and preparing replies, which she then approved or rewrote. She looked to him to continue her education in public affairs, and read the things he gave her (including his own copious memoranda), and listened to his opinions about individuals in government and the best way to deal with them. Thanks to Albert she became more comfortable with the stiff, shy Peel, whose fidgeting annoyed her, and in time grew to like him and admire his ability.

There was no more conflict between the spouses, Victoria no longer accused Albert of suspiciousness or envy or overmuch ambition. Now that Lehzen was no longer there to instill doubt and distrust, the marriage regained harmony and a division of labor came into existence that gave Albert sweeping responsibilities. The queen presided, consulted with her ministers (with Albert present), appeared at all public functions and made all final decisions. Her "large searching eye, open anxious nostril, and firm mouth" were the image of monarchy.[12] But it was Albert, as her alter ego, who in small ways and large, often guided the helm of state.

To be sure, it was because their basic views were congruent that Victoria could delegate so many of the essentials of her task to Albert. Yet, as she told him, "it is you who have entirely formed me," and if this was an exaggeration—for her own experience, and her years with Melbourne, had formed her too—still in important ways she was as

much Albert's student as he was her subject. It seemed to Greville
that Albert had become "so identified" with his wife "that they are one
person, and as he likes and she dislikes business, it is obvious that
while she has the title, he is really discharging the functions of the
Sovereign. He is King to all intents and purposes."[13]

So it seemed to a shrewd observer, but it must not be forgotten
that all the men at Victoria's court were inclined to see the man as the
dominant partner in any relationship, and believed implicitly that
women were less intelligent and less capable than men.[14] All Victoria's
contributions were minimized, all Albert's magnified, by the precon-
ceptions of the men surrounding the queen. Yet the same prevailing
biases that affected Greville affected Victoria herself, and inclined her
to demur to Albert's leadership.

From the start of her reign, Victoria had heard Melbourne make
slighting remarks about women's minds. "No woman should touch
pen and ink," he once said, deploring women novelists and adding that
women had "too much passion and too little sense."[15] Learning Greek
as well as Latin was a good thing for a man, he said, but "unnecessary
for a woman"—even a queen. One of Melbourne's heroes was Henry
VIII, no friend to women, who beheaded two of his six wives, divorced another, and abused two of the remaining three. In the Prime
Minister's view, King Henry was "a very great, good-natured man,"
who was terribly "bothered" by women. "It's always the woman's
fault," he observed, when a marriage goes sour. But then, in his view,
"the happiest marriages are those where the woman's taken by
force."[16] In subtle and unsubtle ways, Melbourne had trained Victoria
to look to men for guidance, his tender yet patronizing tutelage
preparing her less for independent rulership than for continued tutelage—by others.

Melbourne's precepts echoed current belief. "Nature, reason and
religion declare," wrote Arthur Freeling in 1839, in *The Young Bride's
Book*, "that men should be vested with the controlling power. When
two persons differ upon a subject which must be decided, one must
give way. You have in your marriage vow sworn to obey. . . . It is useless to attempt an evasion of this duty, by assuming to yourself abilities
superior to those of your husband." [17] A very popular and widely read
writer, Mrs. Sarah Ellis, went even further in deifying the male gender.
"One important truth," she wrote in *The Wives of England*, "is the superiority of your husband simply as a man." Men of fine character,

Mrs. Ellis said, approach "the nature and capacity of angels," and deserve the same degree of admiration and respect as angelic beings. Submission, subordination, reverence: these were the marks of a good wife, and in retreating, to a degree, from her monarchical role Victoria was merely following a well-worn path.[18]

The queen's third pregnancy was much easier than her first two. Her health remained robust and she did not have to spend many hours languishing on a sofa. In her sixth month she joined in the dancing at several New Year's parties, and told Uncle Leopold in a letter that she was "very merry." When her time came, late in April of 1843, she put on the same shift she had worn when Pussy and Bertie were born and stoically underwent her labor. The baby was a girl, "pretty and large," who was given the names Alice Maud Mary.

With Alice, who, the queen predicted, would be "the beauty of the family," and Pussy, who at two and a half was active and already speaking distinctly in both French and English, and the infant heir, Bertie, "sadly backward" but very like his father in looks, the royal ménage was shaping up nicely. Victoria was not quite twenty-four. A portrait of her painted by Franz Winterhalter shows a womanly maturity in the large blue eyes, much pride, allied to a romantic softness. Marriage and motherhood had given Victoria new depth, and if her conception of her public role was changing, her private life was giving her the greatest happiness she had ever known.

Chapter 9

———— ⌘ ————

SOMETHING HAD TO BE done about the drains. The ancient cesspits under Windsor Castle were overflowing with muck, and the drainage at Buckingham Palace was so faulty that even the workmen complained that the structure "reeked with filth and pestilential odors."[1]

When plumbers installed a water closet in a room above the queen's bedroom, she complained that its contents leaked onto a ledge under her dressing room windows, and caused a terrible stench.[2]

The Department of Woods and Forests, which was responsible for keeping the royal residences in repair, was informed that much work needed to be done to restore "the safety, salubrity and comfort" of the queen and her family. But the antiquated department was glacially slow, months turned into years and nothing was done.

It was not only the drains, it was the cold. Albert complained that at Buckingham Palace "we are almost freezing to death," and when the east winds blew, the children shivered and even Victoria—ever an advocate of cold rooms and fresh air—put on several layers of shawls and moved closer to the fire.[3] Windsor was even worse. Cruel cold winds whistled down its ancient corridors, drafts swirled around the ill-heated rooms, and servants sneezed and sniffed their way through their duties from late fall to early spring.

If Windsor and Buckingham Palace lacked proper plumbing and warmth, they also lacked privacy. Londoners passing the palace could see directly into the queen's bedroom in the evening, distinguishing furnishings and pictures and figures in the room by candlelight.[4] Security was impossible; several times intruders entered the royal apartments by stealth, made themselves at home, and were not discovered for days. Victoria felt beleaguered by sightseers, newspaper writers, and others who gathered at the gates of the royal residences, eager for a glimpse of any member of the family, insatiably curious and avid for tidbits of information. When she and Albert drove outside the grounds, they were "followed and mobbed," and each year brought another attempt at assassination. Because of threats against the children, Albert kept the key to the nursery in his possession at all times, and slept with it under his pillow.

Victoria longed to have "a place of one's own, quiet and retired." In June of 1845, work began on just such a place.

Out of their own funds, the queen and Albert bought Osborne House, a three-story mansion above the village of East Cowes on the Isle of Wight. The house had a magnificent view of the Solent, with its parade of ships, of Southampton Water and Cowes Roads, and of the naval anchorage at Spithead. It also had nearly 350 acres of private grounds—so very private that there was little foot traffic on the high road, and the family could go out walking without meeting anyone. Adjacent to the house was a large working farm, planted in wheat, oats and barley, with piggeries and a flock of six hundred South Down sheep. Best of all, there were pleasant woods to stroll through and secluded bathing beaches, with the sea so "blue and calm" that Albert said it reminded him of Naples. In all it was "a perfect little Paradise," as Victoria wrote to Peel, and provided "the greatest benefit, pleasure, and satisfaction."[5]

Albert and Thomas Cubitt, builder of Belgrave Square and Eaton Square, collaborated on the design of a new house for the site. It resembled a Mediterranean villa, with Italian-style towers, porches, and formal gardens, yet its ultra-strong, fireproof construction was as modern as any structure in Britain. A basement furnace supplied hot water for bathing, and the bathrooms had toilets—which made the house exceptional indeed. Inside, tall marble pillars, chandeliers, costly fitted carpets and ornate tilework gave the house grandeur, while dozens of life-size statues and large paintings satisfied the connoisseur in Albert.

Not everyone admired the style of the new Osborne House; the Horn Room, in which all the furniture—even the chandeliers and candlesticks—was constructed of the horns of stags, was an acquired taste. But the elaborately landscaped grounds, which occupied Albert and several dozen gardeners over a period of years, were universally prized. Camellias, orange blossoms, roses, and jasmine mingled with rhododendron and beds of colorful annuals on the terraces and along the carefully laid out walks. Albert planted hundreds of trees, and grapes and other exotic plants were grown in heated greenhouses.

In the fall of 1846 the family moved in to Osborne House, though it would be many years before it was complete in every detail. By this time Pussy, now called Vicky, was nearly six years old, a confident, often obstreperous child whose "odd tricks" of standing on one leg and laughing loudly and bolting her food exasperated her mother and led her governess, Lady Lyttelton, to tie her hands behind her back and make her stand in a corner until she calmed down. "Insubordinate and unequal-tempered," Vicky was also unarguably an intellectual prodigy; encouraged by her doting father, she absorbed quantities of information and excelled at her lessons in French, English history and reading. Vicky's adult observations delighted her mother as much as her obstinacy aggravated her—but Vicky was Albert's favorite, and she knew it, and what Albert favored, Victoria heartily endorsed.

Bertie, at four and a half, was so far below his sister in ability that his parents could not help but be disappointed in him. Victoria had seen him as "sadly backward" almost since his birth, and now that he had begun his lessons, he was proving to be a reluctant student and a slow learner. No doubt his gifted sister's teasing and mockery made him shy and defensive, and ill at ease in the presence of his parents. Just after his fifth birthday Victoria noted in her journal that Bertie "is a very good child and not at all wanting in intellect, but he is awkward, and does not do himself justice."[6] Until he resembled Angel Albert in every respect, Bertie would never please his mother.

At three years old the third royal child, Alice, was plump and relatively placid, and adored by her brother. And now there were two more children: two-year-old Alfred and infant Helena, always called Lenchen, who was born the day after the queen's twenty-sixth birthday and whose birth had been exceptionally arduous and painful. At her birth Albert was worried about the baby. "She came into this world rather blue," he wrote to his brother. Soon enough, however, Lenchen became pink and rosy, and slept peacefully in the seventeenth-century German cradle that all Victoria's children had been laid in.

Five children—and none lost. In an age when so many infants did not survive their first year, the health of the queen's sons and daughters was remarkable. Their nursery governess, Lady Lyttelton, kept them dosed with calomel and rhubarb and wrapped them in flannel petticoats against the chill. No doubt the superior hygiene in place at Osborne House contributed its share to their well-being. They ate heartily, got plenty of exercise (they were taught manners, but were allowed to run and jump and shout in joyful bedlam) and lived well-regulated lives. Every evening each child in turn visited mama, beginning with the oldest and going on to the youngest. She scrutinized them, asked them questions, and, no doubt, tempered her kindly but frank criticism with affection. None of Victoria's children felt overlooked or left out.

The queen was a conscientious parent, but Albert was a truly fond father, never happier than when he was turning somersaults in the haystacks on the Osborne farm so that Bertie could learn to do them, or constructing an oceangoing wooden "floating bath" in which the children could learn to swim, or giving them rides on his back or getting down on his knees to play with them on the rug. "He is so kind with them," Victoria wrote, "and romps with them so delightfully, and manages them so beautifully and firmly."

Once again, Albert excelled. In every sphere, it seemed, he was destined to know more and do better—to be a model to others. Parenthood was no exception. Yet despite his pleasure in his children, and in the overall harmony of his marriage, as he entered his late twenties Albert was disquieted.

"I am beginning to look at the accumulating years with mixed feelings," he confided to his brother at the end of 1846. He wrote to Ernest often, and treasured his replies, which he kept in a special book with a lock. He also wrote very frequently to his younger cousin Pedro of Portugal, Uncle Ferdinand's son, and until the latter's death in 1844, to his father. To his grandmother Albert had once written that he would "never cease to be a true German, Coburger and Gothaner."

After six years in England, he remained true to his word; he was still the German among Englishmen, the outsider. His high if ill-defined rank, his increasing influence, great ability, and Adonis-like handsomeness would have set him apart had his fidelity to German ways not done so. As it was, he was inevitably ill at ease in the place he could never truly call home.

When he had first come to England he wrote sadly to Ernest that the only familiar faces surrounding him were those of his valet Cart and his favorite dog Eos. Now, six years later, Cart was still there (as was another personal attendant, Rudolf Löhlein, who was all but Albert's twin in looks and who many people believed was his illegitimate half brother), but Eos was dead, along with the little bullfinch he had brought from Coburg that whistled a favorite tune, "How peaceful art thou, good world." [7]Efforts to bring other friends to England had not succeeded. He had befriended Peel, and his secretary George Anson, but he had no "inner circle" of male friends, and the only person with whom he could reminisce about Germany was "Aunt Kent," Victoria's mother.

"Really, when one thinks of the very dull life, and particularly the life of constant self-denial, which my poor, dear Albert leads," Victoria wrote to Leopold in 1847, "he deserves every amusement in the world, and even about his amusements he is so accommodating that I am deeply touched by it."[8]

The dull life was phenomenally productive. Besides the ongoing work of government, and his labors on Osborne House, Albert was chairman of the Royal Commission to redecorate the Palace of Westminster, took charge of concerts of Ancient Music, wrote songs and choral anthems, made alterations at Windsor Home Farm, where he had a prizewinning herd of white Windsor pigs, was an enthusiastic member of the Royal Agricultural Improvement Society and, as Chancellor of Cambridge University, took an interest in reforming the curriculum. His projects in the fields of fine art, architecture and engineering were multifarious, and he took a keen interest in the army, even going so far as to design a new hat for the infantry to take the place of the Waterloo-era shako.

Unfortunately, Albert's new infantry hat—a high cone with a wide brim—lent itself to ridicule, and the hat, and its designer, were both lampooned and bitterly criticized in the newspapers. Albert's stiffness, his dislike of high society and his adherence to a high moral code—

one that most others were unable to attain—brought on him accusations of aloofness and prudery. Criticism concentrated on his two observable weaknesses: he was a poor shot, and he rode indifferently. There was much "impertinent sneering" over this, as Victoria put it. To counteract the sneering, Albert went out riding with the Belvoir Hunt, and tore off across the fields, risking life and limb, taking suicidal jumps that would have made Victoria's blood run cold had she been there to observe them.

The other members of the Hunt watched, open-mouthed, as Albert outrode them. In their eyes, he was vindicating himself. They forgave him much for the sake of that daredevil ride, which caused a sensation and was written up in glowing terms in dozens of newspapers. The sneering was over—for a time.

Two weeks after Albert's unforgettable ride, Victoria noted in her journal that "tomorrow momma gives us a dinner."[9] It was an unprecedented notation, and an indication that, at long last, a rapprochement was under way between Victoria and her mother. With Lehzen and Conroy gone, and with Albert on comfortable terms with his aunt the Duchess of Kent, Victoria was beginning to see her mother in a different light. Being a mother herself may have made her more empathetic toward her own mother—and no doubt she wanted her children to know and enjoy their grandmother. Yet real warmth was still lacking, on both sides.

The duchess, at sixty, was arthritic and complained of perpetual drowsiness, but otherwise was aging well. She now occupied the London house her old enemy William IV and lived in, Clarence House, and at Windsor was mistress of Frogmore House. At last she lived like royalty, and still spent like royalty on flounced dresses and coalscuttle bonnets with plumes. A new controller now managed her finances, but though she trusted him, she was reluctant to allow him to examine Conroy's financial records, which remained a closed book.

Late in February, 1848, shocking news arrived from France. The seventy-four-year-old king, Louis Philippe, widely thought to be a just and able ruler, was overthrown in a sudden coup, and had fled Paris.

For days people talked of little else. "So astounding has the event been, so awful and surprising, from its inconceivable rapidity and the immensity of the operation, that every mind has been kept in a restless whirl and tumult," Greville wrote.[10] A strong king, with an immense army, protected by a fortified capital, had been ousted overnight and forced to run like a fugitive. Fresh reports and rumors, many of them false, swept through London every hour. People said it was a worse disaster than the Revolution of 1789, and that the horrors attendant on a popular takeover were only beginning.

Victoria was as amazed as anyone. She had met the king and his family—his daughter was Uncle Leopold's wife, and there were other family connections—and had always believed, with the majority of her subjects, that his throne was secure. Soon word reached her that he had come to England seeking asylum, and she installed him, along with his large entourage of relatives and servants, at Claremont. When the former king and his wife came to Buckingham Palace to visit her, she was taken aback by how "beaten down" they looked, shorn of jewels, fine clothes, and, above all, of rank. A shudder of insecurity passed through her, and intensified when during London riots, lamps were broken by Chartists demonstrating in front of the palace.

Victoria was at the end of yet another pregnancy, her child was expected in a matter of weeks. It was no time for alarms or upsets. But as it turned out, the shocking news from France was only the first link in a chain of fearful messages from the Continent. Day after day the dispatch boxes brought word of more governments in collapse. Hanover, where elderly Uncle Ernest ruled, Bavaria, Prussia, Hungary, and a host of dukedoms and principalities—including Leiningen, ruled by Victoria's half-brother Charles—all succumbed to popular rebellions. A tidal wave of violent unrest seemed to be sweeping across the face of Europe, and all those who attempted to resist were left foundering in its terrifying wake.

Albert, deeply apprehensive over events on the Continent and concerned about his brother in Coburg, was overworked and overtired, yet he carried his pregnant wife from sofa to bed to desk a dozen times a day, and did his best to calm her fears. When her labor began he took his place at her side, and endured with her the worst ordeal she had yet undergone. No doubt tension and dread made her suffering more acute, as did the large size of the baby. When she was born there was a shadow of disappointment, as both parents had wanted a boy.

Victoria worried that the newborn girl, christened Louise Caroline Alberta, might be marked for life by the circumstances attending her birth. Indeed she was barely a week old when more royal refugees arrived in England—this time the Prince of Prussia and his retainers—and moved into Buckingham Palace to await events.

"I feel grown old and serious, and the future is very dark," Victoria wrote in her journal on April 4. She was depressed, and her nerves, as always following childbirth, were unsteady. One day she felt strong, the next tearful and shaky. What she described as "these awful, sad, heart-breaking times" wore her down, and she felt certain, as many did, that there was much worse to come.[11]

She had good reason to be anxious, for the government, led by the diminutive, elderly John Russell and the brash, aggressive Henry Temple, Lord Palmerston ("those two dreadful old men," Victoria called them), commanded only a small majority and the ministers faced extreme difficulties.

Britain was once again struggling with a severe economic depression. Dozens of firms had failed, including a number of banks, and as a result, countless thousands of laborers were out of work. Perhaps a quarter of the population was in want. Bread was dear, shelter in the teeming slums of the industrial cities dangerously vile. Though the majority of the destitute were loyal to the crown and the ministers, some desperate men and women, emboldened by the success of popular revolutions in France and elsewhere, were contemplating the use of force against the government if their demands were not met.

Compounding the grave situation was the disaster in Ireland, where for the past three years the potato crop had failed, leaving the population to flee or starve. Many starved; many more, weakened by malnutrition, died of typhus and dysentery and recurrent fevers. Those that could, went to America or to England, where by the spring of 1848 some half a million Irish immigrants had found a haven of sorts in the swollen slums.

The government, firm and sincere believers in self-help, were tragically slow to realize that only public intervention on a massive scale could alleviate a human disaster of unimaginable proportions. Peel sought to remove a weighty barrier to the importation of grain from the Continent in sponsoring the repeal of the Corn Laws (laws that, in force for a generation, had kept the price of British grain high, to the benefit of aristocratic landowners)—and wound up dividing and weakening his Tory party as a result. Yet many political opponents of repeal, profoundly ignorant of Ireland and its woes, scoffed that the talk of famine was a hoax, designed to bring pressure for unwise economic reforms. Finally, early in 1848, some direct aid was sent; soup kitchens were set up and army officers sent to aid in the distribution of food. But by then, the famine and distress in Ireland had merged with the hardships in England to strengthen the Chartists, who were once again clamoring for reform, and threatening rebellion.

Chartist leaders announced that a mass meeting would be held on April 10 on Kennington Common, to bring pressure to bear on the government. No one knew how many tens of thousands of people would attend, or what mayhem might ensue. It had been just such a gathering that had brought down the French monarchy. Immediately steps were taken to protect the city, with the thin, elderly Wellington, chalk-faced and top-hatted, brought in to supervise the defenses.

London was in a state of alarm. Fears of an armed uprising, fears of chaos and violent unrest, even fears of invasion by a hostile power kept tensions high as volunteers from the countryside were brought in to keep order. It seemed to Greville that every gentleman in the capital was sworn in as a special constable, and every bridge was defended, every road protected by artillery and police. Warming up for their meeting, bands of Chartists paraded, carrying banners and singing, to the tune of the "Marseillaise," "March on, march on, All hearts resound to Liberty or Death!"

After four days and nights of anxiety it was decided to send Victoria out of the capital before the mammoth meeting took place. She disliked giving the impression that the "wanton and worthless men" who were going to demonstrate had frightened her into leaving, and she wanted her subjects to believe that she was courageous. But the very real danger outweighed all other considerations, and on April 8 she left by train for Osborne.

Dark clouds threatened rain on the morning of April 10. From various parts of the city, processions of Chartists made their way toward Kennington Common, each procession hundreds strong,the faces of the marchers resolute. A cart carried a petition stating the Chartist demands, bearing over five million signatures. The protesters marched through streets that were all but deserted, for all places of business had been ordered to remain closed and the glut of riders, carriages, omnibuses, carts and herds of animals that normally choked the main thoroughfares were not in evidence. Instead, thousands of constables stood quietly in position, unarmed yet prepared, should the need arise, to call for help from armed troops.

The Common began to fill with people, yet by midmorning it was clear that their numbers were relatively few. Hundreds of thousands had been expected; no more than fifteen or twenty thousand made their appearance. There was no turmoil, no ugliness, no rabble-rousing speechifying. All was polite and orderly. By noon the rain-drenched crowd had begun to disperse.

The queen's relief, when she heard what had happened, was immense. Perhaps Britain would avoid the fate of the continental states after all.

"Great events make me quiet and calm," she had written to Uncle Leopold a few days earlier. In truth she had known little calm for many months, and Albert, who had been frantic with overwork for six weeks, had had all he could do to soothe her. For the first time she realized that, the state of society being what it was, she might not go on being queen forever. Her subjects had been loyal so far, but there was no certainty in monarchy any more. Only she herself, her uncle in Belgium, and the Czar of Russia still occupied their thrones; the rest of the sovereigns of Europe had been toppled.

She thought of her children, and realized that Bertie might not one day be king. Her bright little Vicky, her shy, good Affie, her affectionate Alice, pretty Lenchen, still in her cradle—what sort of world would they inherit? And Baby Louise, the large, placid infant only three weeks old who was the newest addition to the nursery, what of her? The season of turmoil into which she had been born would be certain to leave some mark upon her. Surely, the queen thought, Louise would be "something peculiar."

The baby slept on, and her mother, feeling safer than she had in months, settled into her sitting room at Osborne, listening to the rain, thankful for the house her husband had built her, her oasis of security amid the tumult of a confused and anxious age.

Chapter 10

T HE GREAT GLASS BUILDING shimmered in the sunlight, multi-
colored flags flying from its rooftop, a gleaming fairylike palace
whose airy brightness cheered and dazzled the thousands of
spectators who crowded Hyde Park hoping for a glimpse of the queen.
They had come, on this opening day of the Great Exhibition, to catch
sight of Her Gracious Majesty and to marvel at the beauties of the
Crystal Palace, a structure unlike any ever seen, and to see the thousands of exhibits on display there from all over the world.

The morning of May 1, 1851 was fine and clear, with only the occasional passing cloud to obstruct the brilliant sunlight. When near noon
the nine state carriages arrived from Buckingham Palace, and the
queen and Albert alighted with their two oldest children and entered
the sparkling glass cathedral, a blast of trumpets greeted them, and the
thousands of people seated in the galleries burst into cheers and applause. The queen, holding nine-year-old Bertie by the hand, took her
place under the huge high nave, a crystal fountain behind her, and behind it, a leafy tree, its topmost branches reaching almost to the
domed glass ceiling.

All at once a choir of six hundred voices broke into the "Hallelujah Chorus," with a full orchestra and a pipe organ. Yet so deafening were the cheers of the crowd, the queen wrote in her journal afterward, that the music was all but lost.[1] For this was a day of royal triumph— and not the queen's triumph alone, but Albert's. It was Albert who had planned and brought to fruition the great "Peace Festival" being celebrated on this day, Albert who had commissioned the Crystal Palace, and arranged for the vast array of exhibits within it, Albert, standing erect and handsome in his scarlet uniform beside his wife, who now gave the order to declare the Exhibition open.

This was Albert's day of days, and as he strolled down the long exhibit hall and through the nineteen acres of mechanical displays and statuary and agricultural implements, he must have felt considerable satisfaction. Only three years earlier, the states of the European continent had been convulsed in revolution; now, with many of the rebel governments overturned, order had been restored once more. And England, proud, safe England, which led the world in wealth and productivity and ingenuity, was looking to the future, and the arts of peace that would flourish there.

Thirty-four nations had sent their goods to be displayed at the Crystal Palace, but it was the British goods that drew the most admiration. Steam engines, models of bridges and buildings, "patent freezing machines," plows and reapers, revolvers and infantry helmets and rabbits carved from fruit pits (the contribution of Albert's brother Ernest): these were the marvels that drew the most attention—apart from the quantities of nude statuary. A gigantic block of black coal, weighing twenty-four tons, was prominently displayed, as was a fountain from which spewed pure eau de cologne. There were quantities of items of clothing, not only fur stockings and boots and "bootakins" but silk corsets, corsets for sleeping in, and corsets embroidered with the royal arms. Vicuña gloves, feather boas, men's high silk hats and "smoking caps" and unpickable pockets received a good deal of attention from the onlookers, as did such rarities as the Koh-i-Noor diamond and the exhibit of bonnets made by Australian convicts from palm leaves.

All the London papers described the Great Exhibition in glowing terms, and hardly anyone had a word to say against it—except Victoria's ever-critical Uncle Ernest in Hanover, who referred to it as "Albert's rubbishy exhibition" and the evangelical Earl of Shaftesbury, who objected to the nude statues and demanded that they be decently covered. Day after day, for nearly five months, thousands of spectators poured in from all over Britain, many arriving by special trains, to take in the spectacle, until by the time the Exhibition ended, some six million people had paid their shilling to see it, and as there was so much to see, many people came more than once.

It was so reassuring, the sight of such a wealth of goods, such rich evidence of the abundance with which a provident God had showered Britain. A new wave of prosperity washed over the realm as the new decade opened, bringing hope that at last there would be an end to the periodic economic crises that had disrupted so many lives and caused so much misery and uncertainty. The same beneficent Providence that was blessing the realm with prosperity was opening more and more of the world to British goods and British ways. Traders, missionaries, governors and administrators were being sent to every corner of the expanding empire in an effort to spread the Protestant faith, manufactured products, and the values of civilized life—values that they confidently assumed were superior to those of the indigenous peoples—throughout the world.

It was a noble, if narrow and self-serving, mission, fueled by a vision reinforced in thousands of Gothic churches every Sunday, where stirring hymns proclaimed the might of that God who greatly favored the British, as he had once favored the Israelites. A new ethos was coming into being, one that defined the British as a nation destined for greatness, leadership, wealth and moral and cultural superiority. Under the banner of rectitude, buoyed by an unshakable faith, Britons saw themselves as thundering forth to rule the world.

So Victoria's subjects strode with assurance into the 1850s, with many of their earlier worries in abeyance. Chartism, and the deep fear of social chaos that it represented, had melted away. The solid materialism with which upper and middle-class Britons were surrounded helped to assuage earlier worries that rapid industrialization would wreck the social order. The queen was on her throne, her heir was thriving, God was in his heaven, and all was right with the world. The anxious serious-mindedness that had characterized religious belief was giving way to something less febrile and more resolute: a deep-seated faith in progress. Were not hard drinking and blood sports on the decrease? Were not church building and church attendance on the rise? Was not every respectable home furnished with an abundance of upholstered settees and Brussels carpets, inlaid pianos and plush-draped tables and glowing paraffin lamps? Such comforting thoughts were surely adequate to damp down any lingering worries over the fate of the realm.

But, of course, they were not adequate. Not for everyone, and not all of the time. For despite the faith in progress in evidence in Albert's shimmering crystal cathedral, deep fissures were developing in the solid, comfortable bedrock of Victorian life. Even as the ethos of national greatness and moral supremacy was taking shape, other forces were rising that threatened to shatter its complacent optimism and challenge the Victorians' view of themselves and their future.

Faith itself was under assault. Though divines continued to write books on the inerrancy of the Bible, the discoveries of science about the great age of the earth and evolutionary changes in its geology and, in particular, the development by historical scholars of critical textual analysis made it increasingly difficult for educated people to believe that the world was only a few thousand years old, as the Bible taught, or that the Bible itself was anything other than an inspired collection of ancient texts flawed by the inconsistencies and limitations of their human authors.

As religious orthodoxy became more rigid, liberal thought galloped ahead. Doubts crept in; hymns of complacent certitude gave way to hymns of embattlement, meant to offer comfort amid the shocks of an increasingly secular world. To be sure, the very urgency of religious debates proved that belief was still a central issue—probably the central issue—to Victoria's subjects. But it was no longer unexamined belief, and it had begun to fray around the edges.

Thoughtful people wondered why, in such a season of divinely appointed plenty, so many continued to be in want. It was, wrote the novelist and politician Benjamin Disraeli, as if Victoria reigned over two nations, not one; one nation was prosperous, the other desperately poor. And the two nations were profoundly ignorant of one another, as if occupying "different zones, or inhabiting different planets." While the wealthy gorged on seven-course dinners with many dishes at each course, the poor gnawed on crusts and yearned for an end to their misery. Periodic cholera epidemics swept the capital and other cities which, at their height, carried off thousands of people each day.[2] Babies and young children died in vast numbers. Indeed death, with its ostentatious panoply of paid mourners, ornate hearses, ostrich plumes and sable-draped horses had become a distinguishing feature of Victorian life. Mourning shops were as much a fixture on the streets of London as greengrocers or chemists, and as the death of even a distant relative required that women wear somber black from head to toe for months at a time, a large part of the population was always clad in respectful weeds.

Ostentatious mourning was a symptom of another disturbing sign of the times: its emphasis on appearances. People went to increasing lengths to maintain a public image of decency and respectability—which meant hiding anything shameful and hushing any breath of scandal. Denial, duplicity and escapism were the inevitable result. Not only were there two nations in Victoria's Britain, for many people there were two selves—the silk-hatted, frock-coated public self and the unkempt, unbuttoned private self, with its secret desires and surreptitious underground life.

Night after night, when the long, duty-filled workdays of middle-class men were over, they slipped quietly away to the streets near the Haymarket, to Sam's or Bigwell's Cafe or The Burmese, supper rooms open all night where naked or near-naked women posed on stage and where prostitutes in every price range made themselves available for hire. Secret, well-guarded passageways led to plush-lined, silk-upholstered brothels where champagne flowed freely and young girls were ready to serve every sexual taste—including sadomasochism and other "unnatural" desires. Outside in the street, less expensive women in great numbers trolled for custom, while in the dark alleyways or under the trees in the park, the poorest and least desirable of the streetwalkers carried on their desperate trade.

The traffic in sex, astounding in its volume, was even more astounding in its cynicism. Mothers offered their young daughters for rent or sale, white slavery flourished, and the cynical seduction and abduction of young girls by brothel owners—for demand always seemed to exceed supply—had become a cottage industry. Parts of London were rapidly becoming a wasteland of debauchery and furtive vice, and the society that tolerated such sordidness was becoming more hypocritical (and more guilt-ridden) with each passing year.

Victoria, safe in her haven at Osborne, knew little of this. She was well aware that the world contained much wickedness and vice, as well as much wretchedness, yet in her day-to-day life she kept it all at a distance. During the worst of the Irish famine, for instance, she gave instructions that her household consumption of bread should be limited to one pound a day per person, lest she and her servants be seen to squander food while others were going hungry. Yet the sufferings of the famine victims did not preoccupy her; her letters and journal entries are by and large silent concerning them, and when it was suggested that a "Day of Fasting" be observed in Britain, she responded negatively.[3]

"I love peace and quiet," the queen wrote. "I hate politics and turmoil." More and more she left all the politics and turmoil to Albert, who was "so wonderfully fit for both—such perspicacity and such courage," while she got on with the business of living. "We women are not made for governing," she noted, "and if we are good women, we must dislike these masculine occupations." She added, significantly, that "there are times which force one to take interest in them *mal gré bon gré*, and I do, of course, intensely."[4] She did not abdicate her governing role, she merely let Albert carry much of it, retaining ultimate authority herself.

She was happiest when at Osborne, sitting under the huge trees, sketching dog roses or cornflowers, or watching her children running on the lawn, chasing butterflies. Lady Lyttelton, whose appointment as nursery governess ended in 1851, left an evocative description of the family at Osborne. One afternoon she glanced out her window at the lawn where Albert and his sons were playing. "Such merry voices sounding from all over the lawn in at my window," she wrote, "and a pretty sight to see and think of. Old Count Mensdorff [husband of the Duchess of Kent's late sister Sophie] recovering from his gout in a wheeling chair drawn by a tiny pony, the Queen standing by, attentively taking care of him. The Prince and his two boys noisily and easily managing Prince Alfred's new kite which is unrivalled in soaring ambition . . . "[5]

Of such was the life of Osborne made, and Victoria's happiness there, supervising her children's development, writing to her many relatives, spending as much time as she could with Albert, was very great. In 1851, the year of the Great Exhibition, she was thirty-two, with seven children (a third son, Arthur William Patrick Albert, had been born the previous spring) under the age of twelve. She sketched them all, one summer when their cousins, Feodore's children, were visiting from Schloss Langenburg; they had all gone to visit the Duchess of Kent on her birthday, and the queen made them line up in order of their age, like stair steps, so that she could record how they looked in her sketchbook.

Such cataloguing of the children was typical of her style as a mother. The inner recesses of her children's personalities eluded her. "Severe in her manner," according to Lady Lyttelton, and "a strict disciplinarian," Victoria was both conscientious and affectionate, training her "quick and observant eye" on all her children, but especially on the boys. [6] Albert chided her for thinking that "the function of a mother is to be always correcting, scolding, ordering them about and organizing their activities." [7] Transgressions were noticed and promptly punished, eccentricities noted and, if possible, corrected, evidences of goodness eagerly searched for and cherished, for Victoria so wanted all her children to be good. The boys, she hoped , would be exactly like Albert, the girls, better versions of herself. ("I am very often sadly dissatisfied with myself and with the little self-control I have," she confessed in her journal.[8])

The children were a source of pride and pleasure, certainly, yet Victoria's emotional connection with them was far less intense and deepgoing than her profound closeness to Albert. She relied on him entirely, and almost exclusively, for emotional support; she looked to him for everything, and became more and more dependent on him. It had long since become a habit, this excessive dependency; separation from him was genuinely painful for her, and she dreaded it. It was as if she had lost herself in Albert—willingly, yet to her harm. He had once remarked that "a married couple must be chained to one another, be inseparable, and they must live only for one another." [9] Victoria had indeed become chained to her remarkable husband, and while this emotional fusion gave her a degree of security she had never had with anyone else, it also threatened her well-being, for without Albert, she hardly knew how to proceed with anything, and anxiety threatened to engulf her.

This was more than an exceptionally close intimacy between loving spouses; it verged on pathology. When Victoria told her daughter Vicky some years later that she "did nothing, moved not a finger, . . . didn't put on a gown or bonnet if he didn't approve," she was describing with accuracy her degree of willed helplessness. Her life had become conditional on his, without his patient wisdom to guide her, his arms to embrace and carry her and his voice to soothe her fears, above all, without his comforting presence to give her reassurance in her every act and word, she felt all but lost.

At times she felt, as the decade of the 1850s opened, that she had lost Albert to his preoccupations. If he wasn't going out to hear the geologist Charles Lyell lecture on "antediluvian raindrops," he was looking after his prize pigs, or attending agricultural fairs, or working at the new system he had devised for filing papers in the royal archives.[10] "Albert grows daily fonder and fonder of politics and business," the queen told Uncle Leopold in February of 1852. Two weeks later, in a letter full of emphatic underlines, she told her uncle "Albert becomes really a terrible man of business; I think it takes a little off from the gentleness of his character, and makes him so preoccupied. I grieve over all this, as I cannot enjoy these things, much as I interest myself in general European politics."[11]

Albert was becoming anxiously concerned over the future of Britain and the continental states. First had come the alarming revolutions of 1848, then, late in 1851, France underwent yet another upheaval when Louis Napoleon, nephew of the great Napoleon who had conquered Europe, seized absolute power and proclaimed himself Emperor of the French. Affairs in the German states were also in ferment, with Prussia predominant among them. ("I do not like to write about Germany," Albert declared in a letter to his brother. "Involuntarily, I make a fist and this prevents me from writing."[12]) Throughout Europe, groups with aspirations to govern themselves were threatening to rise against foreign rulers, and there was always a danger that one of those risings might lead to a wider war.

After the death of Wellington in September of 1852, Albert felt that, to a degree, he had inherited Wellington's mantle—an assumption most highborn Britons would have scoffed at—though he had the common sense not to attempt to assume formal command of the armed forces.[13] In his own mind Albert saw himself as the architect, if not quite the guardian, of Britain's security, and as such it was up to him to undertake, as Wellington had, to prepare reports on England's defenses. He was aware that the advent of steam transport made England vulnerable as never before to naval attack, particularly from France. At the same time the army, which had not seen battle in a generation, was no longer composed of seasoned veterans but untried recruits and time-serving older men lacking experience.

With these and other concerns weighing on him, Albert worked like a demon, not stopping for lunch but munching something at his desk, always hurrying, never getting to the bottom of the hillocks of papers that sprouted all around him as he worked. Every foreign crisis doubled his paperwork; in 1848, by one estimate, well over twenty thousand separate dispatches had come to the palace. Victoria saw his fatigue, and took note that his pulse was always "week and feeble."[14] Lady Lyttelton, who was in a good position to observe the royals at close range, commented that at times, she saw a look of sadness in Albert's eyes, an abiding melancholy that implied disappointment, yearning and a wistful nostalgia for his Coburg past.

Or perhaps it was a yearning to be rid of Palmerston, the ebullient, disconcertingly assured Foreign Minister who had been a thorn in the side of the monarchy ever since the beginning of the Russell ministry in 1846. Palmerston had been a fixture of Victoria's circle from the start of her reign, a senior statesman whose experience in government stretched back a decade before she was born, when he had been Tory Foreign Minister during the later years of the Napoleonic Wars. Now a Whig, albeit an idiosyncratic one, Palmerston enthusiastically went his own exuberant way, unhampered by party loyalty and untroubled by any felt need to accommodate his sovereign—which caused Victoria and Albert enormous "anxiety and worry" and kept the crown and government in a perpetual state of tension.

Palmerston's position gave him enormous power, as Britain was the strongest, richest and most feared country in the world and he directed her influence worldwide. If he chose to order in the British navy whenever, in his view, British interests were threatened in any manner, he went ahead—without consulting Victoria. ("Diplomats and protocols are very good things," Palmerston declared, "but there are no better peace-keepers than well-appointed three-deckers."[15]) If he decided that a foreign revolutionary leader should be encouraged in his plotting against an oppressive regime, he offered his protection—and his personal hospitality. If he wanted one man as ambassador to Paris and the queen wanted another, then he simply went ahead and appointed his own candidate, after assuring the queen that he would follow her preference.

Palmerston was often disingenuous with Victoria, and Victoria, who hated deceit in any form, and who was apprehensive lest the Foreign Minister's reckless belligerence lead Britain into war, was outraged. She complained to the beleaguered Lord Russell that she could "hardly go on" with Palmerston, and had no confidence in him. He made her very uneasy, she said, with his constant tergiversation and his bitter, caustic messages sent to foreign courts—messages she was constantly seeking to soften. "No remonstrance has any effect with Lord Palmerston," she told Russell. She wanted him out, and a more cooperative, obedient and reasonable man put in his place.

That the Foreign Minister contrived to ignore Victoria's strongly worded suggestions and emendations in his documents, and to ignore Albert's sage advice, was bad enough. That he authorized his clerks to open and read private letters she sent to her relatives in Europe was intolerable. But that Palmerston, whose morals were those of the freer, more lax and even louche Regency, should presume to assault the honor of one of the queen's own ladies, Mrs. Brand, was unforgivable.

According to the indignant Albert, some years earlier Palmerston had entered Mrs. Brand's room at night and locked the door; only her screams and "miraculous efforts" had prevented him from "consummating his fiendish scheme by violence."[16] Moral paragon that he himself was, Albert could not stomach any sort of sexual impropriety, and in his eyes Palmerston was little short of a demon of depravity. In actuality, Palmerston was indeed a man of the world and no stranger to sexual intrigue (his nickname was "Cupid"), but his unfortunate encounter with Mrs. Brand was nothing more than a mistake; Palmerston had blundered into the wrong room, and the occupant had screamed in terror before he was able to make his exit.[17]

In the constant clashes between Palmerston and the court the larger clash between Regency worldliness, now at its last gasp, and Victorian moral rigor was playing itself out. But there was another, more significant dimension to the conflict. To Palmerston, the queen's role in Britain's constitutional government was an advisory one; her right to look over any documents he and the other ministers issued was essentially a formality, for Parliament, not the queen, was sovereign. He, Palmerston, served Parliament, and through it, the British people. To Victoria, on the other hand, all the members of the Cabinet were obliged to recognize and defer to her authority, and if they flouted it, or ignored it, as Palmerston repeatedly did, they were guilty of not only the grossest sort of ill-mannered impropriety but something akin to treason.

It was precisely this issue—the scope and legitimacy of monarchical authority—that had led to the revolutions of 1848 and that was still causing conflict throughout Europe. Just how limiting ought to be the limits on monarchical power? Perhaps because he was not a monarch, Albert was able to see this issue from the point of view of political philosophy, and to acknowledge that, in any clash of views, Victoria was obligated to defer to the government then in power. But Victoria, who tended to see most things from a personal perspective, had no taste for such abstractions. To her, Palmerston was "an unprincipled man" who was evasive, deceitful and downright disobedient. He was mocking her authority—and like her mother before her, Victoria held her own authority in exceptionally high esteem. Palmerston had misbehaved, and like one of her wayward children, he had to be reprimanded severely. And if the reprimand failed to take effect, he had to be ejected from the Cabinet. ("And made to stand in the corner until he thinks better of his misdeeds," she might have added, for such was her attitude.)

Toward the end of 1851 Palmerston was removed from office by Lord Russell, but before long he was back again, and more popular with the people than ever. Clearly there were some things that Victoria simply could not control, and would have to learn to live with, if she was to maintain her equilibrium. She could not control all of her ministers, all of the time. She could not prevent Albert from being, at times, "a terrible man of business," and abandoning her for his work. She could not prevent her children from misbehaving. And, as she was soon to discover, even in a season of prosperity and optimism, she could not prevent the advent of a very grave, very personal tragedy that struck at the heart of her domestic peace and threatened to disrupt it forever.

Chapter 11

HAVING GIVEN BIRTH TO seven healthy, flourishing children, in April of 1853 Victoria went into labor with her eighth child. This time her labor was eased by the administration of chloroform, applied to a handkerchief and held over her nose. Overcoming the strenuous objections of many doctors and clergy, who argued that the agonies of childbirth were God's curse on women and that to interfere with those agonies would be sinful, Victoria had decided to request relief from her pains as a small but growing number of women had been doing for half a dozen years.

The results were more than satisfactory. Dulled by the anesthetic, the sharpest of the pains were relatively easy to bear, and the queen blessed the drug, her doctor and Providence. Her fourth son, Leopold George Duncan Albert, came into the world a large, ugly baby, and was said to look just like his mother.

But unlike her other children, this son did not flourish. He lost weight, he could not digest his wet-nurse's milk, he cried for hours at a time and the queen, who was very worried about him, lost sleep, her nerves perpetually on edge. The arrival of this eighth child, which had begun uncommonly well, was turning out to be an emotional ordeal.

The wet nurse was replaced, and Little Leo began to accept the new nurse's milk. Yet he remained thin and undersized, and his incessant crying was heartrending to his mother, who blamed herself for giving him a bad start in life. She sensed that something was wrong, and no doubt she dreaded that, after defying the odds seven times, she might lose this child.

Her fears were confirmed as the squirming, lively Leo learned to crawl, then to stand. His knees and elbows were constantly swollen and there were livid bruises on his thin arms and legs. His urine was often pink with blood, and when his teeth began to come in, he screamed incessantly, as if in exceptional pain. To be sure, Little Leo's wails were often lost in the din of Alice's tantrums and Vicky's strident backtalk and Bertie's violent and combative struggles with his tutor, but the queen, distressed and full of dread for her son, made sure that she was kept informed of his difficulties and his development.

When baby Leo tried to walk, and huge purple bruises appeared on his legs, there could no longer be any doubt that his sufferings were the result of a grave disorder. Several doctors examined him, and confirmed each other's opinions that he was a "bleeder," a victim of hemophilia. His blood lacked a vital clotting factor, making him liable to hemorrhage. Leopold would not have anything approaching a normal life, the doctors told Victoria and Albert. He would have to be constantly watched for signs that his dangerous condition had put him at risk. He could not exert himself, for even the slightest exertion could cause him to bleed internally, perhaps fatally. He did not dare cut himself, for even the smallest cut could bleed for days. Even if he lived the most guarded life possible, he would not necessarily escape harm, for hemophiliacs commonly began to bleed spontaneously, for no observable reason, and most died young, often in infancy or childhood.

Both parents were dismayed to realize that at best their son would always be, to an extent, an invalid; both had to live with the sad knowledge that his life could end at any time. This mortal threat hung over their family, shadowing its happiness and making the queen even more edgy and nervous than she already was.

In the months following Leopold's birth she became impossible to live with, displaying that side of herself that made her unlovable. She exhausted the patience of everyone but Albert by her complaints and demands for sympathy. In her misery she became self-obsessed, and

attacked the long-suffering Albert for "want of feeling, hard heartedness, injustice, hatred, jealousy, distrust" and a dozen other shortcomings. Childbirth invariably reminded her of her often reiterated view
that men were selfish, uncaring beings and women were the suffering
vessels they exploited. And no matter how often Albert reminded her
that sex was sacred and its consequences, however painful for women,
were divinely ordained, she continued to be bitterly indignant.[1]

Victoria's frequent quarrels with Albert followed a depressingly
repetitious pattern. A chance remark would send her into a furious
tirade, during which she frequently became violent. At this, Albert
would leave the room "to give her time to recover herself," which
would only infuriate her further. She would storm after him, following
him from room to room as he tried to escape her barrage of accusations
and insults, knowing that the more he evaded her, the more she would
blame him for his want of feeling. He would not engage with her,
matching his rage against hers; he saw his restraint as necessary and, ultimately, the wisest course, but to Victoria it felt cold and unloving. Ultimately she left him alone—after an hour or more of shouting and
one-sided confrontation—and the dispute was continued in written
form. After a day or two a semblance of harmony was restored—to be
shattered all too soon by a repetition of the bruising cycle.

His iron sense of duty prevented Albert from losing control during
his wife's harsh scenes, and he invariably assumed the role of the benevolent, understanding parent who could unravel the cause and course of
the quarrel and wait patiently until the erring child returned to her
senses. Yet, as he once wrote to Victoria candidly, "you hurt me desperately."[2] Year by year, he was paying a price for always burying his own
rage and for bearing his own pain and disappointment unaided. At
thirty-four, he looked at least ten years older; still handsome, he had
nonetheless put on weight and was losing his hair. His expression, once
full of boyish romanticism, had darkened, and his features betrayed his
constant struggle with overwork, deep concern over the direction of
British and European politics, and wounding domestic upsets.

Once again Albert had undertaken the large and daunting task of
designing and overseeing the building of a home for his family, this
time in Scotland. Five months after Leopold's birth work was begun
on a new castle on the Balmoral estate the queen had bought the previous year. With the aid of an Aberdeen architect, Albert planned a
comfortable mansion with seventy rooms (and fourteen water clos-

ets), capable of accommodating a staff of a hundred people plus a large number of visitors and guests. A colony of workmen had to be imported to the Deeside property, and housed in temporary wooden barracks, to construct the thick stone walls. Once these were completed, work began on the interior, whose "cheerful and un-palace-like rooms" were warm with maple and birch woodwork, hunting pictures, cozy chintzes and tartans. Silver wall sconces in the form of antlers, guns or game bags carried out the theme of the house, which was more that of royal hunting lodge than anything else. As at Osborne, the initials *V* and *A*, interlocked, were prominent in the decor, as were Scottish thistles and the special Balmoral plaid—designed by Albert—of lilac, red and black on a gray background.

The castle, as it took form over several years, had a rustic, homely charm—though sophisticates from London who visited Balmoral ridiculed its stuffy, overtartanized quaintness—but it was the estate itself, with its forests and clear streams, its sparkling air and dramatic vistas of mountains and lochs that made Balmoral the royals' favorite residence. Time and again, in her journal and in letters, Victoria referred to "the dear Highlands, which I feel I love,—I fear more than matter-of-fact un-poetical England."[3] At Balmoral the family lived, not only privately, but like ordinary well-to-do gentlefolk; the queen, to be sure, was very much the lady of the manor, and none of her tenants ever forgot it. Yet one suspects that she was more herself—her best self—when she went out alone to visit the old ladies in their cottages on the estate than at any other time.

She got to know her Scottish tenants, brought them gifts, enjoyed watching their children grow. The austere, harshly simple yet wholesome lives of the Highlanders, their blunt forthrightness and apparent lack of guile won Victoria over completely; she admired and trusted them far more than she trusted her English courtiers and servants, and they returned her trust with a touching devotion.

Two things dominated life at Balmoral: family expeditions and Albert's sport. With the boys dressed in kilts and sporrans, and the girls and even the queen in tartan gowns, the family went out on long walks or rides to pick raspberries, or to catch Scotch Argus butterflies in the woods or to find specimens of the tree orchid called Creeping Ladies' Tresses to take back to Osborne. Walking with the children, Albert pointed out the distinctive bird life, the whimbrels and siskins and oyster catchers. Taking them fishing in the streams, he taught them to spear the swift salmon as they swam upstream or to run after the large, strong Highland foxes with a pack of greyhounds and terriers.

Scrambling up and down hillsides, sliding into wet ravines and across slippery screes, children and parents alike were invigorated; Victoria happily tore her crinolines and muddied her boots following Albert, who in turn followed the gillies to secluded glades where picnics were laid. Often, mounted on small, sturdy Highland ponies, they all went up the nearby mountain of Lochnagar in a daylong journey. Victoria and Albert occasionally went out alone, traveling incognito, to outlying villages and had the rare pleasure of being left entirely to themselves, an unexceptional middle-class couple on a holiday.

But such excursions were rare, for Albert was eager to pursue his sport, and was never happier than when "creeping" after stags for eight or nine hours at a time. One reason the Balmoral site had been chosen was that it offered an abundance of fauna. Hungry deer came right into the castle gardens, and stags could often be seen from the upstairs windows. Albert blasted away at them, often in vain; his shooting continued to be poor, though with time and after a number of visits to Balmoral, he got better.[4]

Albert greatly admired the Highlanders for their "honesty and sympathy," and chose one of them, a blond, blue-eyed young man with a "vigorous, light, elastic tread" to be Victoria's particular servant. Johnnie Brown was in his early twenties, strong and alert, very "handy," according to the queen, when she needed someone to carry her across swollen streams or to lead her pony Arghait Bhean along the steep mountain paths. Victoria sketched the handsome Johnnie, and put her sketches in the albums she and Albert made of Balmoral, along with Albert's watercolors and the works of artists Victoria commissioned to paint the estate and her family.

While the royals were at Balmoral, the Duchess of Kent stayed at Abergeldie Castle, near enough to permit her to spend time with her grandchildren yet far enough away so that Victoria would not feel burdened by her company. Elderly and arthritic, she passed her days in reading, and did not play more than a marginal role in her daughter's life. Victoria and her mother had been on cordial, if not intimate, terms ever since Lehzen's departure, and in the early 1850s two important events brought them closer. First, the full extent of Conroy's gross financial mismanagement came to light, forcing the duchess to acknowledge the painful fact that the man she had trusted and relied on for so many years had deceived her and stolen from her, as he had from Victoria's great-aunt Sophia. Then, after Conroy's death in 1854, the duchess wrote Victoria a contrite letter of apology.

"I allowed myself unintentionally to be led to hurt you, my dearest child," she told her daughter, "for whom I would have given at every moment my life!" She blamed herself for being gullible and naïve in Victoria's early years, and confessed that she had suffered a great deal in consequence. "God be praised that those terrible times are gone by," she wrote, "and that only death can separate me from you My beloved Victoria."[5]

Though nothing could ever entirely heal the wounds Victoria carried from her childhood and girlhood, her mother's heartfelt confession moved her, and in her generosity she undertook to support Conroy's widow and children—even the once-hated Victoire.

In the fall of 1853 a restless, antagonistic mood swept England. The newspapers were full of accounts of Russia's sinister designs against the territories of the Turkish Sultan, and British and French efforts to keep the Russian Empire from expanding at the expense of the Turks.

Of all the powers on the European Continent, the Turkish Empire was the weakest, yet to Britain perhaps the most important, for a strong, intact Turkey was an essential buffer between Russia and the states of Western Europe. The immense bulk of Russia, incomprehensibly vast in its territory, murky (to Europeans) in its semi-Asiatic culture and autocratic to a degree repugnant to freedom-loving Britons, posed a constant threat to European stability. Now that stability had been upset by the czar's order to his troops to invade Turkish territory along the Danube. Further encroachments were certain to come, the papers said; it was only a matter of time before the Russian bear was in Constantinople—and the Russian fleet was on the high seas, challenging the supremacy of the British three-deckers.

This patriotic Britons could not allow. When they learned, early in December, that Russian ships had sailed out of Sebastopol and, in a merciless and unprovoked attack, sunk the Turkish fleet at Sinope, they protested with marches, rallies and angry demands that the government take immediate action to support the Turkish underdog. "Turkish Independence" was the rallying cry. By this time, Russia and Turkey were at war, and the bellicose mood was spreading. Never mind that a generation had passed since the British army had actually fought a war. Never mind that all the senior officers were old men, unfit for command; Palmerston was an old man, and when it came to championing the cause of liberty against oppression, he was the most vigorous and vociferous of all.

Send in the fleet! Send out the troops! The clamor grew louder and louder, and officers from the fashionable regiments, especially the elite cavalry regiments, suddenly found themselves lionized. These dandified elegants, with their elaborately long whiskers, corseted waists and affected speech (they called the queen "Victowia" and the nation "Bwitannia" and professed themselves to be "vewy patwiotic"), symbolized the might of British arms. No army, it was thought, could stand against the onslaught of their perfectly trained, perfectly coordinated mounted troops—certainly not the ragtag army of Russia.

Victoria was nonplussed by all the war furor, but became "enraged and indignant" when it led in a painfully personal direction. Albert came under attack in the press.

First the *Morning Advertiser*, and then the Tory *Morning Herald* and *Standard*, began running articles, maligning Albert for exerting undue influence over the queen, sitting in on all her meetings with ministers (which he did), writing documents on her behalf (which he also did), carrying on a private correspondence with British diplomats abroad and attempting to pervert the natural course of foreign policy—the natural course being, to the war-eager public, the Palmerstonian, anti-Russian course. Albert was German, the press sneered, and no German could be a true Englishman in his "sentiments and principles." He was not only German, he was known to be pro-Prussian, and the Prussians were allied with Russia. Therefore if Britain was hesitating in aiding suffering Turkey, it must be Albert's fault.[6]

Day after day, the articles and letters in the papers became more virulent, until the assault on Albert reached the level of hysteria. Extravagant rumors spread, the most outlandish of which was that Albert was a Russian spy, subverting the monarchy. The spy had been taken to the Tower of London, people said, and imprisoned there. And the queen had chosen to go with him. They were shut up together in the ancient fortress, awaiting their doom.

In the frosty days of January, 1854, huge crowds gathered in the narrow streets around the Tower compound, hoping to hear something about the fate of the queen and her perfidious consort. They would not listen to reason; they were certain that the royals languished behind the gray stone walls, and that before long they would be dealt with as their treachery deserved.

In mid-January Albert was the chief topic of conversation; by early February, when Parliament opened, "nobody thought of anything but the coming war," Greville wrote, and when Victoria and Albert attending the opening of Parliament—giving the lie to the extravagant story of their imprisonment—they were enthusiastically received. In a matter of weeks it had become clear that Britain was indeed moving rapidly toward hostilities with Russia, and popular opposition to the queen's husband was forgotten in the larger issue of imminent war. Albert was eulogized in the Commons, his loyalty and entire devotedness to the welfare of the nation praised. Ironically, it would be Albert, as Victoria's secretary and virtual co-ruler, on whom the extra burden of wartime paperwork would fall most heavily.

And fall it did, as war was declared in March and the telegraph office in the basement of Osborne House began to be swamped with messages.[7] Orders were sent out, regiments mustered. Victoria watched with pride as the men she called "our beautiful Guards" and "my noble Troops" marched in review on their way to embarkation for the Black Sea.

The public, expecting a short and glorious war, cheered them on, confident that the combined British and French forces would assault Sebastopol, oust the Russians, and sail back home triumphant. But months were to pass before the troops were assembled in the Crimea in full strength, and by then the soldiers had begun to succumb to cholera and fever and general weakness brought about by malnutrition and exposure. War correspondents telegraphed dispiriting messages: not only were there no glorious victories to report, but the men were dying in their thousands from sickness and want.

"I feel so proud of my dear noble Troops, who, they say, bear their privations, and the sad disease which still haunts them, with such courage and good humor," Victoria wrote in October of 1854. The truth was being kept from her. Courageous the men certainly were, and some were good-humored. But for many the Crimea was not a scene of glory but of suffering—and needless suffering, the result of inept commanders, inefficient provisioning and general chaos.

When battle was finally joined, at Alma, Balaklava, and Inkerman, the combined British and French won Pyrrhic victories. The cost in lives was immense, and still Sebastopol was not taken. The queen was "bewildered and excited" to read of the gallantry of her "dear Troops," especially the cavalry brigades who had ridden, steadily, expertly and suicidally, into the very mouths of the Russian cannons. "I regret exceedingly not to be a man and to be able to fight in the war," she told Princess Augusta of Prussia. "There is no finer death for a man than on the battlefield."[8]

Death on the battlefield was one thing, but death amid the filth and ordure of a military hospital was another, and despite the efforts of Florence Nightingale and her band of nurses, most of the wounded in the Crimea perished. Reports of ghastly slaughter, of the tragic and unnecessary waste of brave lives, of battlefields littered with human and animal corpses, of hundreds of costly cavalry horses going mad in the heat and having to be destroyed, of exhausted men, living on moldy bread and green meat, tramping through mud, sleeping on the icy ground with no blankets led to criticism of the officers in charge and of the government that continued to support them.

By the end of 1854, with the campaign season over and little real progress made, the mood of the public had shifted. "Almost everybody is in mourning," Greville wrote, "and grief and despair overspread the land." The joyous anticipation that greeted the outbreak of hostilities in the spring had been replaced by a sense of futility. "The end of this year sees us deploring the deaths of friends and relatives without number, and our army perishing before the walls of Sebastopol, which we are unable to take, and, after bloody victories and prodigies of valor, the Russian power [is] hardly as yet diminished or impaired."[9]

"My whole soul and heart are in the Crimea," Victoria wrote to Uncle Leopold.[10] She and her daughters were busy sewing blankets and knitting mittens and scarves for the troops, but there was little else she could do. The reports in the newspapers made her weep, while the behavior of her cousin George, Duke of Cambridge, exasperated her in the extreme. Given command of a division, the duke had shown himself far less than heroic under fire and, succumbing to "low spirits and desponding feelings," had left his men and gone away for a rest cure.

As winter closed in Albert was wrestling with recurring colds and with the stomach pains that had attacked him frequently during the previous half year. "Lately I have not felt very well," he wrote to his brother, "and this makes intellectual work difficult." [11] Difficult or not, he kept at it, filling volume after volume with lengthy memoranda,

handwritten and full of detail, working long hours at his desk, labori-
ously reading the contents of every dispatch box and attending every
ministerial meeting. The incompetence of those in charge of feeding
and equipping the army preoccupied him, and he bombarded the Prime
Minister, Lord Aberdeen, with insistent demands for improvement.

Worried about Albert, dismayed over the state of the war, her
nerves on edge, Victoria was faced with fresh difficulties as the new
year 1855 began. Aberdeen's government faltered, then fell, and after
a "very trying" two weeks she discovered she had no choice but to
summon Palmerston to form a new one.

"Altogether, affairs are very unsettled and very unsatisfactory," she
told Uncle Leopold at the end of February. She had just been to visit
wounded veterans of the Coldstream Guards, speaking to each man
personally, thanking each for his sacrifice and acknowledging his brav-
ery. They were a pitiful sight, pale, thin amputees, men disfigured or
blinded by head wounds, men without legs. Some were mere boys, all
were damaged for life.

"I cannot say how touched and impressed I have been by the sight
of these noble brave, and so sadly wounded men and how anxious I
feel to be of use to them," the queen wrote in her journal. They would
all have their photographs taken for an album she was preparing, and
each would receive the new medal she had recently commissioned,
delivered by her own hand. But there were so many other things to
think of, finding them employment, increasing the tiny pensions the
army paid them, ensuring that their wives and children were provided for.

The burden on the queen's heart was heavy that spring, as she prepared to go with her family to Osborne. She could not look after all
the wounded men, but she could at least learn their names, and in a
few cases, give them pensions out of her own income and keep herself
informed as to their welfare. Let Albert look after the larger issues of
the conflict—she would carry in her mind's eye images of her "dear
Troops," lying mutilated on their cots, their faces turned to their queen
in piteous devotion.

Chapter 12

O N APRIL 16, 1855, a day of brilliant sunshine and mild spring breezes, the Emperor of the French and his beautiful and stylish wife Eugenie arrived in London, to be met by huge crowds and a magnificent reception. Londoners were eager to see this nephew of the great Bonaparte who, against heavy odds, had seized power and then proclaimed himself Emperor Napoleon III. They were equally eager to see his consort, for by all accounts she was a woman of rare loveliness and charm with exquisite taste in dress.

Short and nondescript, with a "mean and diminutive figure," according to Greville, the emperor was almost a comic figure; absurdly long mustaches and a tiny "imperial" beard drew attention to his oversize head. But Eugenie, tall, slim and auburn-haired, was as captivating as her husband was unprepossessing, though it was noticed that she trembled with apprehension as she went to meet Victoria.

Two things had prompted Palmerston, now Prime Minister, to arrange the state visit of the Emperor of the French. First, the recent death of Czar Nicholas and the accession of his peace-loving son Alexander marked a shift in Russia's intentions that was likely to shorten the war. And second, Emperor Napoleon had expressed eagerness to go to the Crimea and take command of the allied French and British forces himself—a dangerous mistake, in Palmerston's judgment. It would be Victoria's task to dissuade him from this plan, while befriending him and applying her personal diplomacy to cement relations between the two realms.

She had not at first welcomed the task that the Prime Minister had thrust upon her. Believing as she (and Albert) did in the importance of maintaining legitimate dynasties on the European thrones, she was highly dubious of this Napoleonic upstart, and distrustful of his attitude toward England. Only two years earlier there had been fears that he would land troops on her south coast, and though he professed nothing but amity toward Britain his ultimate aims could not be discerned.

And she had another, more personal reason to distrust him. He had repeatedly proposed to her niece, Feodore's daughter Adelaide of Hohenlohe, and though his proposal had not been accepted, Adelaide had been inclined to accept it. But while still formally in negotiation for Adelaide's hand, he had suddenly proposed to Eugenie, a gross breach of both personal and diplomatic etiquette.[1] Clearly, Victoria thought, Napoleon III was not a gentleman.

Yet as she greeted him at the entrance to Windsor, embracing him as she would an anointed sovereign of the blood royal, she was struck by his magnetism and charm, and in the following days her favorable impression of him deepened. He seemed to know everything about her, even details of her life from the time she was a little girl, and she felt flattered by his interest and attention. They were, after all, equals, in rank if not in birth, and there ought to be a special empathy between sovereign rulers.

And Eugenie, with her cool, elegant, classic beauty, enhanced her odd little husband's stature. Her sleek Grecian hairstyle, the "coiffure à l'Impératrice," so different in its dramatic simplicity from the fussy girlish ringlets and matronly "penny bun" Victoria wore, her beautiful gowns of rich white silk and Ottoman satin in the fashionable colors of "London Fog," "Spanish Raisin" and "Siberia," appealed to Victoria's aesthetic sense. Though Victoria often complained that she "hated being troubled about dress," in fact she delighted in pretty clothes, and she and Eugenie found common ground in talking of fashion, and even exchanged gown trimmings.[2] Victoria wrote to Uncle Leopold that Eugenie was "very pleasing, very graceful, and very unaffected, but very delicate." An affection grew between the two women in a short time.

What Napoleon and Eugenie really thought of their English hosts can only be conjectured, but others in the French imperial circle were not reticent in recording their views of the English queen. When in the hot August of 1855 Victoria and Albert visited Paris, Marshal Canrobert set down his observations about her. His first impression was how dowdy she was in her dress, with an enormous white flounced gown that emphasized her stoutness, a massive silk bonnet (bonnets had gone out of style) with streamers that hung down her back and an excessive display of marabou feathers, an unmatching mantle of crude green cloth and an outsize purse—"like those of our grandmothers," Canrobert thought—of white silk on which was embroidered, in gold, an absurd fat poodle. Her clothes seemed to smother and stifle her.

"The Queen seemed very small to me," Canrobert noted, "but of a most amiable appearance; above all, in spite of the shocking toilette, I was struck by her dignified air."[3]

That evening at dinner he noticed her green silk gown trimmed with lace and roses, the green of the gown clashing with the violets in her elaborately looped hair with its crowning diamond aigrette. Her plump hands, he observed, were weighted down with rings on every finger and both thumbs. One of the rings bore a flashing ruby "of prodigious size," and the jewels so encumbered her small hands that she had difficulty using her knife and fork and could hardly get her gloves on. Victoria's complexion was coarse, and her features commonplace; her mildly bulbous eyes, reddish nose and ever-open mouth were more fishlike than anything else.[4] Yet an American observer, Benjamin Moran, who saw her at about this time thought her "very pretty." "Her manner is wonderfully natural," Moran wrote, "and sometimes she turns up her eyes with an expression of girlish simplicity extremely captivating."

Girlish she was at times, and captivating she could be, yet she was also a scold, with a caustic tongue and an imperious manner. Self-obsessed, demanding, spoiled, she expected and usually got her way; though it was perfectly true that, as she told Vicky later, she hardly put on a bonnet or tied a slipper without Albert's approval, it was also true that she often turned on him, accusing him so harshly of coldness, hard heartedness, hatred and jealousy that it wounded him deeply.[5] She was utterly dependent on him yet quite independent enough to make his life a torment—not constantly, but all too frequently.

She complained incessantly that her nerves were frayed, on edge, and that she was often "a great deal worried and knocked up." She did not take it well when Albert opined that women's nervous suffering was nothing but lack of self-control. Still, she did engage in what she called "the hard struggle for self-control," and congratulated herself when she achieved it, even for a few weeks.

Her edginess made her restless and interfering. Albert complained to her about her "fidgety nature," which, he told her, "makes you insist on entering, with feverish eagerness, into details about orders and wishes." This constant agitation and intrusiveness, combined with her imperious manner, caused much disagreeableness and disharmony— which in turn set her nerves on edge even more.[6]

Albert, for his part, had developed a set of habits and an outlook that constrained him severely yet allowed him to endure the jars of his marriage while accomplishing what he had originally come to England to do. He had shackled himself to his work, and he worked almost without ceasing, producing volume after thick volume of handwritten memoranda on the war, the organization of the army, the proper role of the British in European affairs. Twenty-five volumes on the Crimean War alone had poured from his pen by the summer of 1855, and twenty-five more would pile up before the conflict ended. [7] Albert's "noble, genial expression" continued to charm and impress those who met him, and he was very handsome despite his balding head and paunchy stomach, but it was his devotion to the public good that marked him most. Indeed he had earned the sobriquet "Albert the Good"—something that pleased his wife no end—and his aura of self-sacrificing devotion made him seem almost too good to be true.

Work was his solution to the riddle of life, and self-abnegation the philosophy that undergirded the work. "Man is a beast of burden," he wrote to his brother, "and he is only happy if he has to drag his burden and if he has little free will. My experience teaches me every day to understand the truth of this more and more."[8]

Convinced of the correctness of this self-denying view, he did his best to train his oldest son to imitate it. But Bertie, who in the summer of 1855 was not yet fourteen, was developing a quite different philosophy of his own. He had accompanied his parents to Paris, and he was enchanted with the glamour, verve and sparkle of the French capital. Paris was a city after his own heart, a city where celebration and laughter appeared to be valued more than obligation and grim toil, and he begged Napoleon and Eugenie to let him stay on with them rather than return to dull England where he had to endure irascible pedagogues and stern lectures from his parents.

"Life is composed of duties," Albert told Bertie, "and in the due, punctual and cheerful performance of them a true Christian, true soldier and true gentleman is recognized."[9] Albert preached in vain; Bertie would never see life as composed of anything other than opportunities for enjoyment, and in fact when Bertie observed his father's life—which he rarely did, for he was not analytical—he could not help but notice that Albert's continual devotion to duty and neglect of self were making him ill.

Albert was managing to drag his burden, but it was becoming heavier year by year. He was sick every winter. Painful rheumatism in his right shoulder, so severe he could not sleep, attacked him frequently. He was often doubled over with stomach pains. "I have endured frightful torture," he wrote in his diary in the year he and Victoria visited Paris. "I continue to suffer terribly."[10] Exhaustion was robbing him, not only of his well-being, but of his ability to fend off disease. He might extol the duty-bound life to his son, but he was a walking recommendation for the opposite course.

A month after the royal visit to Paris news reached Victoria, then at Balmoral, that Sebastopol had at last fallen to the British and French. This long-awaited, bitterly hard-won victory loosed a torrent of rejoicing. Though the messenger carrying the news arrived late at night, after dinner, Albert insisted that a celebration take place at once. He led all the men of the household, flanked by all the servants, keepers, gillies, and the population of the nearby village, up to the top of the nearest hill where a huge bonfire was lit. As it blazed, the villagers, delirious with joy, and mightily fortified with whisky, danced and shouted and cheered "in great ecstasy." Bertie, Affie and Arthur were awakened and allowed to scramble up the hill after their father. Not until midnight did the entire crowd come down again, still singing, bagpipes playing, guns firing, to stand under the windows of Balmoral and cheer for the queen and Albert and "the downfall of Sebastopol."

It was a glorious and long-remembered evening, and the peace celebrations that followed nine months later were extravagant and
thrilling. Fireworks exploded in Hyde Park, Victoria Park and on Prim-
rose Hill. All the public buildings, clubhouses, and shops were brightly
lit and shoals of visitors—one estimate put their numbers at over a
million—came in by train to watch the spectacular display. The Crystal Place, which had been dismantled and moved to Sydenham, drew
immense crowds for its newest attraction, the "Great Fountains."
Frothy streams, cascades, two enormous high waterfalls, plus innumer-
able fountains on the terraces and throughout the grounds sent up
showers of sparkling spray that made the thousands of visitors gasp
with pleasure and exclaim that London had at last exceeded Versailles
in splendor.

The queen, with Albert and their two oldest children, came to
Sydenham to officially open the waterworks, and as the nearly twelve
thousand jets began to spout forth, and with a thunderous noise torrents began rushing over rocks and splashing down on temples of gold
and glass Victoria "seemed highly delighted" at the magical effect.[11]

More sobering was the parade of Crimean troops the queen reviewed at Aldershot, among them the sad remnant of the Eleventh
Hussars, heroes of the Light Brigade, only some twenty-five officers
and men ("few and faint, but fearless still," in the words of a contemporary magazine), who rode gallantly past, sunburnt, their chests covered in medals. Victoria had given out so many medals, with her own
hands, to men sadly broken by the war and its attendant privations.
She wrote to Uncle Leopold about how moved she was at the reac-
tions of the soldiers when she handed them their medals personally.
"Noble fellows! I own I feel as if they were my own children; my heart
beats for them as for my nearest and dearest," she told him. "They
were so touched, so pleased; many, I hear, cried—and they won't hear
of giving up their medals, to have their names engraved upon them,
for fear they should not receive the identical one put into their hands
by me, which is quite touching."[12]

To Florence Nightingale, who had brought some measure of order
and hygiene to the disorder and filth of military hospitals, Victoria
gave a special medal inscribed "Blessed are the Merciful." And to
Palmerston, now in his early seventies and so deaf people had to shout
at him to make themselves understood, she gave the Order of the

Garter. She rewarded him, but she withheld her regard; years after-ward, she confided to her daughter, "I never liked him, or could ever the least [sic] respect him."[13]

The peace celebrations concluded, the royal family went to Bal-moral, as they did each August. The new castle Albert had designed was now complete, the many rooms fully tartanized and cluttered with ornamental and decorative objects. High winds and pouring rain made it seem more like winter than fall, and as Victoria forbade the lighting of fires, on principle, during the summer months everyone caught cold. Children, visitors, and ministers alike sneezed over the dinner table, with the windows flung wide to the frigid air. Albert sneezed over his ruined sport. Lord Clarendon, who had the ill luck to be in attendance during that chill August, complained that "it is very cold here, and I believe my feet were frostbitten at dinner, for there was no fire at all there, and in the drawing-room there were two little sticks which hissed at the man who attempted to light them."[14]

Victoria was adamant—and prickly. She was pregnant yet again, against the advice of Sir James Clark, who had warned her that an-other pregnancy might cause her so much nervous strain that she would suffer serious harm. Sir James was in fact less worried about the queen's body than her mind, for her tantrums and outbursts of violent irritation revived his old concerns for her sanity. Ill and irascible, she made Albert miserable with her complaints; she felt degraded, she was in a disgusting condition, her sufferings were intolerable and he, an in-sensitive man, had put her in this unenviable state.

He had heard it all before: eight times before. He responded in his usual grave, rational way. When she shouted and looked around wildly for something to throw, he withdrew. He fled, she followed. Finally, evading pursuit, he sat down to write her a response.

"If you were rather less occupied with yourself and your feelings . . . and took more interest in the outside world, you would find that the greatest help of all."[15] Self-control, outward-directed attention, above all deeper relationships with her children were what Victoria needed, in Albert's view, and when she had recovered her composure he told her so—in front of the children.

Their oldest and most promising child, Vicky, now nearly sixteen and Albert's special favorite, was far from fully grown yet for years her bright mind and adult insights had made her seem her parents' peer.

Beyond being intelligent, Vicky was vivacious, "full of frolic and fun," as an American who met her in 1856 remarked, "and a heart as big as a mountain."[16] Her charm, her bright smile, her ability to converse on any number of current topics, made her stand out among the Protestant princesses of Europe.

A year earlier, in 1855, Vicky had fulfilled her parents' long-desired wish that she become engaged to Prince Frederick William of Prussia ("Fritz"), nephew and heir of the reigning king. She would one day be Queen of Prussia, cementing an important dynastic link, and to help prepare for her role she was acting as Albert's secretary. She was also spending many hours with Fritz, and Victoria was put out that so much of her own time was spent chaperoning Vicky and her Prussian fiancé, who though nine years older than his bride-to-be was "so much in love," the queen remarked, "that, even if he is out driving and walking with [Vicky], he is not satisfied unless he can have her for an hour to himself, when I am naturally bound to be acting as chaperon."[17]

Though she found the role of chaperon irksome, the queen was in fact drawing closer to her daughter as the time for the latter's marriage approached. Despite Albert's taunt that Victoria was "thankful to be rid" of Vicky, in truth she was discovering an unprecedented affinity with her precocious child. Where before Vicky had been Albert's daughter, like him in her acuity and wide intellectual grasp, now, as she contemplated marriage, she was becoming as much her mother's daughter as her father's, finding common ground with Victoria on matters of dress and wifely duties and the prospect of children.

Victoria was already planning Vicky's trousseau, taking great pains to ensure that she would go off to frigid Prussia with enough warm flannel petticoats and plush pantalets and a complete assortment of gloves, shawls, hats, gowns and the wide, full crinolines that had recently made every movement a delicate and even dangerous maneuver for women.

What may have been exacerbating Victoria's crotchetiness was fear about the baby she was carrying. Would it be a normal, healthy child, or another bleeder, like Leopold?

At three and a half, Leopold was Victoria's "Child of Anxiety," as she called him. He clambered around the nursery in his ungainly way, following Arthur, three years his senior, wherever the latter went and jabbering in his high-pitched voice. Covered with bruises, he often had to be kept in his bed, and his keen, restless mind resisted the inactivity. It was already apparent that Leopold was intellectually gifted, as his older sister Vicky was, but his precocity was overshadowed by his physical condition; he had to be watched constantly and guarded from harm, and Victoria fretted over him and quarreled with Albert over how he ought to be managed.

Now she and Albert were tempting fate by bringing another child into the world. Her troubled pregnancy was marked by a season of grief. Her much older half brother Charles of Leiningen died, and even though he had never been more than a peripheral figure in her life, she plunged enthusiastically into mourning for him. Mourning was good for her, she declared; it gave "relief" to her overwrought emotions.

Her swelling bosom and ballooning abdomen swathed in dozens of yards of black bombazine, the queen presided over court functions throughout the winter, enduring, though never willingly, the ebullient Palmerston with his endless dodges and feints when presented with monarchical authority. She had a particular request, that Parliament would at last acknowledge Albert's position by granting him the title "Prince Consort." Constitutional difficulties prevented this, but she persisted, until she entered the final month of her pregnancy and had to put aside her campaign on Albert's behalf and to lighten her workload considerably.

During the final weeks of her pregnancy, Albert, or when he was unavailable a strong footman named Lockwood, carried Victoria from her bed to her couch and back again many times a day. Albert was often away, attending lectures or meeting with officials of the many charitable societies he helped to sponsor, and Victoria suffered in his absence.

One brisk day in late March he and Bertie went to open the Golden Lane school for poor children in a London slum. Some £18,000 had been raised through charitable subscriptions to build new buildings for the school, which offered instruction from nine in the morning until ten at night for over two thousand children. Flanked by the Archbishop of Canterbury, the Bishop of London and a cluster of other dignitaries, Albert delivered a long and wordy address, assuring his hearers "of the deep interest which the Queen takes in the wellbeing of the poorest of her subjects."[18] The speech concluded, thunderous applause broke forth and the children, after singing a hymn, shouted and clapped for Albert and Bertie until the latter's carriage disappeared into the rainy dusk.

Victoria's baby was overdue. March turned into April, day after fine spring day passed, and still the labor pains did not begin. The birthing room was ready, the monthly nurse on call, night and day. The old, yellowing shift Victoria had worn for each of her deliveries—her lucky shift—was freshly laundered and laid out ready to be put on.

At last, early in the afternoon of April 13, she began to feel unwell and soon the doctor was called. At once Albert was beside her, "mothering" her in his usual tender way, calling her his "dear little wife" and reassuring her. The pains became intense, lasting for hours, and the queen was given chloroform to ease them. She was brave, and once again immeasurably grateful for the comfort of the blessed drug, yet the baby was slow to make its appearance. Suppertime came and went, and early evening, and by now Victoria lay exhausted against her pillows, her lucky shift stained with perspiration.

Everyone in the birth room was becoming apprehensive. Had Dr. Clark been right, had it been a mistake for the queen to try to give birth once more? In the corridor outside, messengers waited to take bulletins to the Cabinet and the newspapers. There were whispered conferences out of earshot of the royal patient. What if she should be unable to expel the baby? What if she should die, as her cousin Charlotte had died in childbirth in 1817? Many women did not survive the rigors of birthing, particularly after the age of thirty. What if the baby was dead or dying in her womb?

On into the night the pains continued to come and go, severe at times but never bringing ultimate relief. Prayers were offered, in German and in English, silently and out loud. Victoria held Albert's hand but lay almost motionless against the banked pillows, her face white and strained, her tired eyes closed as she tried to rest between contractions. The household staff, expectant and on alert all afternoon and evening, prepared to go to bed.

Then, a little before two o'clock on the morning of April 14, the queen experienced the onset of a new wave of pains, stronger than before, and more chloroform was dripped onto the handkerchief held over her nose. Another half hour of intense labor and at last, to everyone's immense relief, the baby came into the world, red and screaming, a fifth daughter.

"It is a fine child, and a girl!" Albert exclaimed. The messengers were informed, word spread quickly among the household servants, and within minutes all the Tower guns were firing a salute. Londoners awakened to the reassuring news that their queen had once again passed through the dangers of childbirth successfully, and that another royal princess lay in the nursery.

"She kept us waiting at the door for thirteen hours before she would come in," Albert wrote jokingly in a letter describing his new daughter's birth. It was like him to make light of the ordeal, after it had passed, but the queen could not transform her arduous experience into humor so easily. Her recovery was slow and punctuated by periods of depression. On her birthday, at the end of May, she was heartened by the sight of her flower-bedecked present table at Osborne, with wreaths and bouquets and piles of carefully wrapped gifts—drawings from the children, portraits and art objects from Albert, handmade crafts from the servants and a special dinner and concert to follow. But her lighter mood was fragile, and temporary. She was feeling the first uncomfortable pangs of approaching middle age.

At thirty-eight, she had fulfilled the role Uncle Leopold had once imagined for her, that of "mother of a numerous family." Nine children, and only one of them, it appeared, at risk of failing to survive. Motherhood preoccupied her, but not happily. "Children are a terrible anxiety," she would tell Vicky some years later, "and the sorrow they cause is far greater than the pleasure they give."[19] What pleasure there was to be found in life came not from children, of that she was certain, but from a devoted marriage. And much as she adored her husband, Victoria was aware, as she approached forty, that her marriage had begun to founder.

Chapter 13

THERE WAS NO DENYING it: Victoria's marriage was no longer the joyous union it had been. Albert had changed. He was often "very trying—in his hastiness and over-love of business." He spoke harshly to his wife. He walked quickly, bolted down his food while sitting at his desk, was eternally preoccupied with the condition of the realm, the condition of the army, the condition of public and private morals. Badly drafted dispatches irritated him and upset his stomach, and Victoria dreaded to show them to him.[1] He was often, perhaps even usually, unavailable to Victoria, for when he was not working or attending public functions or shooting or hunting he had to rest, or to spend time with the children, or recuperate in his study, nursing his painful shoulder.

Loving and solicitous at times, Albert was nonetheless undemonstrative, correct, reserved. As he aged, he retreated into rigidity—retreated, so it often seemed, to a place where his passionate wife could no longer reach him. She could not really fault him (though she did so, vociferously), for he was a man of spectacular virtue, as everyone agreed; the Liberal Gladstone praised his "ready, watchful mind," the

Conservative Disraeli announced that Albert was "the best educated man he ever met," even the servants in the palace had nothing but good to say about him. (When he passed maids scrubbing floors he always greeted them pleasantly, raising his hat politely and muttering, "Don't mind me. I am sorry to trouble you."[2])

Even so Victoria was disgruntled, and deep down she knew that nothing was as it had once been between them. It was very apparent that when Vicky married Fritz in January of 1858, and left England for Prussia, her departure "left a deep void in his heart," as Albert told his beloved daughter in a letter.[3] Victoria could not fill that void, nor could any of the other children, not even the baby, Beatrice, who liked to watch her father as he dressed in the morning and who crawled up into his lap while he played the organ.

Vicky, Albert's gifted, astute, charming daughter, their firstborn and his wife's appropriate successor, had she only been a boy, had been sent off to a difficult foreign court where she would be consigned, like all royal wives, to childbearing and dutiful wifely subordination. This was as it should be, given her gender, but what a grave wrong! For, as Albert and Victoria knew only too well, the heir to the throne possessed none of Vicky's special qualities and was proving to be more and more of a burden with each passing year.

And most of the burden fell on Albert. For even though Victoria tried to form her son's moral character, reading sermons with him and chiding him when he misbehaved, it was ultimately left to Albert to determine the course of his upbringing and to try to find a way to shape the highly unpromising boy into a future King of England.

Unpromising Bertie certainly was. He bullied and mistreated his siblings, threw stones in his tutor's face, grimaced grotesquely and swore and spat and became violent when anyone tried to control him. Albert called in a phrenologist—an expert in the then fashionable "science" of reading people's traits from the contours of their crania—who detected large bumps on the Prince of Wales's head indicating combativeness and destructiveness.[4] When Albert tried to teach him anything, Bertie refused to pay attention and sat stupidly, letting nothing penetrate his thick skull. Only the prospect of pleasure galvanized him into action—pleasure, or excess. Too often he ate too much (his friends called him "Tum-Tum"), or stayed up too late, or pushed his somewhat ungainly body past its limits; then he got sick headaches, which incapacitated him and disgusted his parents.

Victoria condemned her son as idle, weak, and dull. He had no depth, no self-control, no taste or charm. Lazy and shallow, he had not even the benefit of good looks. ("Handsome I cannot think him," Victoria wrote to Vicky in Prussia, "with that painfully small and narrow head, those immense features and total want of chin.") In short, he was a complete disappointment, and all but incorrigible.[5] Contemporary periodicals might compliment the prince as "a manly, frank open-faced lad, and a great hand at cricket," but his parents knew the truth. Bertie was a practical joker who enjoyed squirting his friends with soda water and putting dead seagulls in their beds and, when his jokes turned malicious, burning their hands with a lit cigar.[6]

It was his tendency to lash out hurtfully, coupled with his soft, self-indulgent streak that disturbed his parents most. Everyone, even his friends, was afraid of Bertie's temper, which erupted whenever he lost at croquet or felt bored or thwarted. He bellowed like a rhinoceros and made a shambles of his room, inducing "a state of speechless terror" in the servants.[7]

To civilize him, and broaden his horizons, Albert sent Bertie traveling abroad. But the effort backfired. Classical ruins left him cold. ("You look at two mouldering stones and are told it's the temple of something," he wrote home.) And when the prince and a party of young companions and chaperons visited the Rhine Valley, the results were disastrous.[8] Gladstone, whose son was one of Bertie's acquaintances, learned that the young men were guilty of a "squalid little debauch"—probably involving wine and women—and had to chastise him severely. Had Albert been informed of what had happened, his anger and exasperation would have been boundless. But Gladstone did not tell Albert about Bertie's escapade, and chances are he did not find out.

To distract themselves from Bertie's waywardness, Victoria and Albert devoted more time to their younger children—Alice, withdrawn and easily intimidated, but thoughtful and self-sacrificing; Albert's favorite son Affie, shy, with an "amiable, happy, merry temper" and mechanically inclined; plain, tomboyish Helena, or Lenchen, phlegmatic and robust; Louise, the child of the Year of Revolutions, moody, artistic, and very pretty; Victoria's favorite son Arthur ("This child is dear, dearer than any of the others put together, [after Albert] the dearest and most precious object to me on earth," she wrote[9]) strikingly like his father in looks, obedient and even-tempered; ugly, monkeylike Leopold, spreading anxiety wherever he went yet clever and winning; and plump, lively Beatrice, called Baby, with her satiny skin and huge blue eyes, everyone's darling.

For the younger children Albert designed and built a dairy on the grounds at Windsor, a fairy-tale place of white marble and stained-glass windows, colorful tiles and Wedgwood jars to hold the milk. Lenchen, Louise, Arthur and even Leopold took turns turning the crank on the barrel churn to make butter, as Victoria looked on, pleased at their interest and relieved that they were not all like Bertie.

Victoria had now been queen for more than twenty years, and much as she complained that because of her gender, she was really not suited to her role ("I am every day more convinced that we women, if we are to be good women, feminine and amiable and domestic, are not fitted to reign,"[10]) she was well able to manage the work she was called upon to do, and because so much of the actual labor was delegated to Albert, she was also able to make time for various restful pursuits. She embroidered waistcoats for Albert, she made cushions and plaited paper bonnets, and when, to her dismay, Vicky announced that she was pregnant, the queen made a quilt for the baby. "With the exception of the marking and joining the long stripes I have done every stitch of [it] myself," she announced proudly.[11] She was rarely idle, for idleness bred discontent; productivity, productivity and constant enterprise, were after all the keys to a contented life.

Victoria had done all she could to adjust that "reversal of the right order of things" that her marriage to Albert represented. She was his sovereign, yet he, in her phrase, "did everything."[12] Albert had been granted the title "Prince Consort" officially in June of 1857, an elevation that did nothing to improve the regard in which he was held by the British public. (He was still widely disliked, and a pamphlet circulated in the year he attained his new title called him "the most unpopular man in these isles."[13]) Yet doing everything, as a working partner, he did not do enough, as a husband. And so, the marriage had indeed changed, and for the worse.

The times, too, had changed, and not for the better.

Everywhere Victoria looked she found reason for alarm. Dominating popular magazines and songs was the disturbing phenomenon of the "Fast Girl." "Yes, Sir! I can waltz! I can flirt! I'm out of the schoolroom at last!" went one such tune. "Pa says I'm a romp, Ma says I'm a pert, I say, I am fast! I am fast!"[14] Out went decorum, maidenly modesty, the shy, retiring girl that had been the early Victorian ideal. Bonnets gave way to wide-brimmed round hats (condemned by conservatives as "fast and bare-faced"). Girls adopted such masculine styles as the starched collar, leather belt, and boots with military heels. Bold plaid plush pantalets peeked out from under wide skirts. The "fastest" of the young women actually smoked—not cigars, but the newer, Turkish cigarettes that came to England after the Crimean War.

All fashionable women, not only the fast set, wore the wide, circular crinoline that had to be held stiffly away from the body by wire hoops. So bulky were these vast swinging structures that it took only a few of them to fill a drawing room; a sofa was barely wide enough for one woman and her spreading concentric yards of silk or crape. Never since the days of Marie Antoinette had well-dressed women taken up so much space, or announced themselves so emphatically. They floated like heavy balloons across dance floors, down wide lawns, across stone-laid street crossings swept free of refuse by crossing sweeps.

Victoria considered the crinoline to be an "indelicate, expensive, dangerous, and hideous article," a symptom of social degeneration. Her own daughter Vicky had accidentally set her crinoline on fire and nearly burned herself to death.[15] Hooped skirts "put an immense division between the sexes," wrote George Meredith, and smothered social interchange. Preachers fulminated against the indecencies of the crinoline from their pulpits; doctors, many of whom were already fighting a losing battle against the tightly laced corsets that pinched and squeezed women's internal organs, now tried to talk their female patients out of wearing overly wide skirts. Female shoplifters discovered in the inner pockets of their crinolines an ideal place to conceal purloined goods, and even respectable women could not resist the temptation offered by the yards and yards of fabric to make off with trinkets and bijoux from the better stores.

It was not only young women who were perceived to be subverting morals. Men too were rebelling against somber dress and restrained conduct—though "softness," or effeminacy, met with revulsion and was broadly defined; any man who took a warm bath in preference to a more healthful icy-cold one would have been despised as effeminate.

Still, men began wearing beards, and curling them with special curling irons. Some rouged their cheeks. Many affected tight trousers, huge cravats, toothpick-slim canes and shirt collars that reached almost to their ears. Borrowing the mannerisms of the cavalry, they displayed perpetual ennui and spoke with a slow drawl. ("Oh Lord! What a horrid bore!" was the standard response of the Fast Set.)

As ubiquitous as the crinoline was the tall chimney-pot hat with a narrow brim, which poked its black nose up into the sooty air and offered a tempting target to street urchins armed with clods of filth. Men wore top hats everywhere they went, even indoors. Gentlemen's clubs were forests of black stovepipes. Clerks wore their top hats when helping customers. Cricketers played with their hats on, and even at the seaside, where men bathed in the nude, they kept their tall hats nearby, ready to put on again once they emerged from the ocean.

Along with the disturbing alterations in manners and dress went even more disturbing changes in the currents of thought.

Ever since the later eighteenth century educated people in the West had begun to approach all human knowledge from a fresh and naturalistic standpoint. Reason was being brought to bear on everything from politics to social norms to the physical world. Biblical scholarship was bringing long-unchallenged religious truths under the scrutiny of logic and a new view of history, one that recognized the radical differences that separate past from present.

The creation story as told in Genesis, along with much else in the Christian scriptures, was increasingly being regarded as myth, not as a factually accurate account of how the world and its inhabitants came into being, and in particular biblical chronology, which if strictly calculated put the age of the earth at some six thousand years in the past, was set aside as no longer reconcilable with scientific understanding.

These shifts in perception brought in their wake wide cracks in the granite foundations of Victorian faith. If the earth was tens, or even hundreds of thousands of years old, and if, as the scientists who studied the earth were beginning to assert, its features were in a constant state of metamorphosis, then the entire concept of creation became moot. Furthermore, if, as Thomas Malthus claimed, the growth in the earth's population was fast outstripping the growth in the food supply (which seemed incompatible with the belief that a providential God was overseeing the beneficent unfolding of human history), then humankind was clearly headed for catastrophe, not the glorious Second Coming of Jesus.

The devout dismissed these apparent contradictions between advancing knowledge and biblical revelation as ultimately inconsequential, and urged those who were becoming uneasy in their beliefs to rededicate themselves to the fight against godlessness. But the men of learning kept on discovering evidence that the world was not as the ancient Hebrews perceived it. A humanlike skull found in the Neander Valley in Germany in 1856 added to the growing debate over whether humans evolved from animals, and educated and uneducated people alike now spoke of the "missing link" and looked for evidence of it. In 1857 Londoners flocked to Piccadilly to see the bearded "baboon lady," a grotesquely hairy woman with a simian face, whose existence seemed to bear out the theories of the scientists about where humans came from.[16]

The queen's frequent attacks of nervousness found a resonance in the nervous malaise of the age, with its ever-increasing haste and bustle, its maddening pace and frenetic aspirations, its omnivorous greed and seemingly inexhaustible lust for gain. Trains hurtled through the once placid countryside, men of affairs strode ever more rapidly along the narrow lanes of the City, collisions between carriages and omnibuses, drays and wagons seemed to multiply as speed became an end in itself. Railway passengers consumed enormous quantities of Brockeden's Compressed Bi-Carbonates for their heartburn, and Eno's Fruit Salt ("The Study of the Stomach is the Study of Morality," Eno's posters read) for bilious headaches.

It was as if the entire world was running as fast as it could to outpace disaster—and yet disaster was coming ever closer. Every year the bankruptcy lists published in the *Gazette* grew longer and longer. Cholera swept through the capital at increasingly short intervals. Misery and crime multiplied with the swelling population—the population Malthus had predicted would soon starve—and in the bleak, cheerless poorhouses of the London slums, more and more thin, pale men and women lay in coffinlike wooden boxes, shivering and in despair.

In the fall of 1857 Britishers were horrified to hear of disaster on a much larger scale. In the Indian subcontinent, native troops, or sepoys, in Bengal had mutinied and were pouring into Delhi and surrounding towns, burning and looting and forcing British civilian colonists to flee for their lives. Every two weeks, with the arrival of the mail ship from India, news of fresh horrors spread: of the heartless massacre of the heroic British garrison troops at Cawnpore, hundreds of women and children shot, stabbed and mutilated by vengeful Indians; of the siege of the Residency at Lucknow, where nearly a thousand men, women and children took refuge behind makeshift defenses and withstood constant attack from a much larger Indian force, suffering agonies in the blistering heat and dying horribly of untreated wounds and disease.

As the ghastly stories spread the rage of the British public mounted, heightened by the exasperating six- to seven-week delay in receiving messages from faraway Bengal. Rumors fed the mood of outrage, accounts of further massacres, widening danger, ever more fearful insurrections. *The Times* was full of personal letters received from survivors, telling grisly tales of the merciless slaughter of British captives and the harrowing deaths of small children at the hands of brutish rebels. Accounts of atrocities, many of them invented, spread like the cholera through the London streets: of English women raped and mutilated before being killed, of parents forced to eat their children's flesh, of gallant husbands cut down before their wives' weeping eyes.

The sheer barbarity of the scene, as relayed to a horrified public by the sensationalizing press, rocked the nation and led to a storm of questions about the nature and value of empire, the security of Britain's global supremacy, and the competency of the government.

No one was more concerned about these issues than the queen, who as soon as she received word of the mutiny, urged that no time be lost in sending troops to shore up Britain's weakening military presence. As in the time of the Crimean War, Victoria's heart was rent by the accounts of suffering of the "poor ladies" caught in the web of violence and she wrote Lady Canning, once her lady in waiting and now wife of the Governor-General of India, that she "could not bear to hear more" about the vile treatment of British victims. "A woman and above all a wife and mother can only too well enter into the agonies gone through of the massacres," she wrote, adding "I cannot say how sad I am to think of all this blood shed in a country which seemed so prosperous—so improving and for which, as well as for its inhabitants, I felt so great an interest."[17]

Finally in mid-November the glad news arrived that troops loyal to the imperial government had relieved Lucknow and captured Delhi.

Londoners indulged in a frenzy of celebration, but for the queen, who was receiving reports of the terrible reprisals being inflicted on the rebels, the joy of victory was tarnished by her awareness that so many Indians were suffering. Mutineers were hacked to pieces, blown out of the mouths of cannon, hanged and spitted and tortured by the thousands. Entire villages were destroyed in an orgy of annihilation that surpassed anything the mutineers had carried out against the British.

Victoria lamented the destruction—and when in August of 1858 she took over direct political control of India from the East India Company she expressed her "horror and regret" at the misery created by the civil war and vowed to rule in a spirit of toleration—particularly religious toleration—and to work for the material betterment of her millions of Indian subjects.

The hot August of 1858 was made more oppressive by the stench off the river. Tepid from the unusual heat, and churning with filth, the Thames meandered odoriferously between its banks, driving people away from the city and forcing the House of Commons to end its sessions. Victoria and Albert went to Deptford to see the huge new ship *Leviathan*, a twenty-three-thousand-ton monster vessel that represented the newest technological marvel, but soon retreated, "half poisoned," the queen wrote to Vicky, "by the dreadful smell of the Thames—which is such that I felt quite sick when I came home."[18] The smell made her headaches worse, and threatened to bring on the neuralgic pains in her face that had become a problem in recent months.

Stress always brought on the queen's chronic pains, and she was very distressed indeed about Vicky's pregnancy. Vicky herself was quite happy, and wrote to her mother of her "pride of giving life to an immortal soul."[19] But this high-minded philosophical attitude fell on deaf ears; Victoria knew from her own experience how during pregnancy "our poor nature becomes so very animal and unecstatic," more like a cow or a dog than a human being with a soul, and she blamed Fritz for putting Vicky at risk for so much suffering and potential danger.

Victoria's annoying tendency to interfere and try to control everything, even from a distance, was affecting her relationship with her daughter. She wrote Vicky long letters and sent telegrams and generally bombarded her daughter with demands for information about her life in Prussia. What dress had she worn when she landed? What bonnet had she worn with it? How large were her apartments? What furnishings were there in her sitting room? Why did she have to have her maids dress her hair, couldn't she keep a hairdresser at the palace? On and on, page after page, the queen's inquisitive questions spilled out, and when Vicky's responses were insufficiently detailed, Victoria complained. She knew that there was a chance their correspondence would be opened and read by postal spies, so she sealed her letters with silver paper (to make any tampering obvious) and tried to send particularly private letters by messenger.

But when it came to Vicky's pregnancy, letters were insufficient. A visit was required, to permit discussion of those delicate matters which only married women could discuss face to face, and which, as Victoria knew, were badly managed in Germany.[20] Vicky would need all the careful advice Victoria could give her, especially if, as Victoria suspected, the baby was likely to be lost through miscarriage.[21]

The queen and Albert set out for Berlin by train, with the heat still oppressive and with Victoria's neuralgia and Albert's stomach trouble and rheumatism making them both peevish. Albert blamed Victoria for making Vicky ill with her hectoring letters, and she in turn was irritated with him, though she tried to moderate her irritation when he was in pain.[22] She was apprehensive about Vicky, and furious at the press, which had been spreading a rumor that both she and her daughter were in "an unhappy condition" at the same time.[23]

As the train arrived at Hanover, Victoria's mood darkened. Only a few months earlier she had been forced to send to this insignificant kingdom many of her most prized crown jewels, the result of a lengthy dispute between the Hanoverian crown and the British crown, since 1837 two separate entities. It was galling to have to part with her handsome pearls and diamonds, especially when the recipients were to be the heirs of her late Uncle Ernest, the Wicked Uncle whose menacing presence had troubled her childhood.

And in Hanover Victoria had a fleeting glimpse of another presence from her childhood. Her old governess Lehzen, who had been living abroad for many years, stood on the platform as the queen's train passed through and waved vigorously at the royal carriage. Victoria may or may not have known that Lehzen would be there, but in any case, the sight of the old woman did not elicit from her any but the most formal and dignified response. No nostalgic sentiment tugged at her, no long-buried tears came to her eyes. Victoria had long since arrived at a mature and dispassionate view of Lehzen, as an intriguer who had estranged her from her mother. She gave orders that Lehzen was "not to be encouraged" in her greeting and that the train was to proceed on to Brandenburg, where Vicky was waiting, without further delay.

Chapter 14

———— ✺ ————

B Y THE TIME SHE reached the age of forty-one Victoria was a grandmother, not once but twice over. Vicky had given birth to a son,
Frederick William Victor Albert, early in 1859 and then a daughter, Charlotte, the following year. Being a young grandmother gave the
queen pleasure, though she worried over Vicky, particularly in the days
just after William's birth, when Vicky lay between life and death and the
doctors and midwives shook their heads in tacit consensus that she
would not recover.

Hovering at the edges of Vicky's life, dreading every part of her
daughter's initiation into the pains and trials (somehow Victoria saw
only the pains and trials) of sex and motherhood, the queen wrote
Vicky endless letters admonishing her not to "give in to baby-worship"
and sewed cushions in "English colors" for her ailing back. When
Vicky's replies were slow in coming, Victoria sent her telegrams. She
wanted to know whether Vicky's doctors were still treating her with
leeches for her bad cold; she wanted word about grandson William's
poor little withered left arm, which hung uselessly and did not grow;

she wanted to know all about both children, particularly the "wild-spirited" William, whom Vicky called her "bit of quicksilver."[1]

Victoria had long since begun to plan for her other children's marriages. Alice, who was nearly eighteen in the winter of 1861, was engaged to Prince Louis of Hesse-Darmstadt, a very minor but entirely acceptable figure with a modest income. Vicky had helped to find a potential future wife for Bertie, the Danish princess Alexandra, but no definite engagement had yet been formalized. Alfred, sixteen but short for his age, and still in some ways childish (Uncle Leopold called him "a dear little rogue"), was too young yet to be the object of any matchmaking; he had only recently returned from a South African cruise, his trunk full of "splendid horns of all those wonderful animals," as his mother noted. Victoria continued to shelter Lenchen, Louise and the younger children from everything to do with sex, keeping them, in her words "carefully kept and guarded," against their wedding days to come.

It had been a bitterly cold winter, with deep snow in the north and killing frosts in many parts of England. Londoners had endured below-freezing weather for an entire month, and many had died of cold and deprivation. Victoria passed the long dark winter afternoons playing Wagner's *Lohengrin*, currently her favorite piece of music, over and over, and by reading the newspapers, with her favorite dachshund, "dear old Dacko," following her every move with his melancholy brown eyes.

She was worried about France. Napoleon III, who had charmed and impressed her only a few years earlier, now loomed as a dangerous enemy once again. His armies had defeated the Austrians in Lombardy, and he was building ironclad ships to challenge the British navy. Victoria complained bitterly about the French emperor and the menace his vaulting ambition represented; according to the foreign secretary, Lord Clarendon, Victoria and Albert's resentment of Napoleon III "embittered their lives and conversation." It seemed as if there was no true escape from the daily cares and burdens of the queen's high office, and when political crises were at their worst she dreamed of turning her back on it all and fleeing.

"I am sick of all this horrid business—of politics and Europe in general," she wrote to Vicky, "and think you will hear some day of my going with the children to live in Australia, and to think of Europe as of the moon."[2]

But of course she could not go to Australia, for Albert would not have gone with her, and she needed Albert desperately.

Over the years their lives had become so entwined that she lost herself in him; to act or think or make decisions on her own had become alien to her. She often shouted at him, and made harsh accusations, but her anger and frustration only revealed the depth of her bond. In her mind she developed an image of her husband as Albert the Great and Good, a superhuman being of infinite capabilities and exquisitely developed humanity. This Albert, the one that lived in her mind, was far different from the real prince, a valiant but sad character who, to less idealized eyes, was losing his battle with overwork and ill health. The real Albert often scowled, barked at his wife and wore ridiculous long underwear with fitted feet to bed, but Victoria's Angel Albert was a semideity whom she revered as father, protector, adviser, and lover. "How miserable and . . . lost I am without my master," she wrote to Vicky when the prince was away from court.[3] Nothing was the same when Albert was away. Life paused, and would not resume its course until his return.

The return of her wedding anniversary always made Victoria sentimental, and on February 12, her twenty-first anniversary, she wrote of that day long ago "which had brought us, and I may say the world at large, such incalculable blessings." Few wives were as fortunate as she was, to have a husband who after more than two decades "is not only full of the friendship, kindness, and affection which a truly happy marriage brings with it, but the same tender love of the very first days of our marriage."[4]

Though Albert's illnesses curtailed his activities more and more, he and Victoria had nonetheless managed to climb a four-thousand-foot peak near Balmoral the previous October, and he could still join her from time to time in dancing reels. Victoria relished the few times when she and Albert, with only a few attendants, traveled incognito deep into the Scottish countryside, where no one knew who they were and they could pretend to be English aristocrats (with German accents) on holiday.

Victoria told herself that all was well, that she was fortunate and blessed in her marriage, but whenever she looked at Albert she had to acknowledge that all was far from well. His handsome face was haggard, his expression alternately tense and sour. Everyone who saw him was struck by how ill he looked. Two months earlier he had had an exceptionally severe attack of what he called "the real English cholera," with a high fever, chills, and general weakness that hung on for the better part of a month. And shortly after celebrating their wedding anniversary he was laid low by yet another attack of his chronic stomach pain, and he lay shivering in his bed, violently ill, for five days. He had hardly begun to recover from that when a painful toothache worsened and his cheek and gum became so swollen that a surgeon had to puncture the gum—not once but twice.

March brought a particularly heavy load of "tiresome and annoying business," which roused Albert from his sickbed and made him sleepless with worry. Victoria was worried too, not only about the state of affairs on the Continent but about her seventy-four-year-old mother.

The aging Duchess of Kent had been a semi-invalid for several years, and Victoria had begun to devote more time to her, taking her along on outings and keeping her supplied with cloaks and shawls. Two years earlier the duchess had suddenly been taken ill, and the seriousness of the attack had come as a terrible shock to her daughter. "I hardly myself knew how I loved her, or how my whole existence seems bound up with her," Victoria wrote afterward, "till I saw looming in the distance the fearful possibility of what I will not mention."[5] That her mother was coming closer to death weighed on Victoria, and forced her, at some level, to begin to come to terms with her feelings for her.

It was not easy. Despite the surface rapprochement Victoria had achieved with her mother early in her twenties, her ambivalence toward her ran very deep, and Victoria had never fully recovered from the painful, often desperate alienation she had experienced throughout her early years. In Victoria's adulthood the duchess had never been anything other than a marginal figure in the life of the royal family. Victoria's immense correspondence and lengthy journals contain only sparse and infrequent references to the duchess. By 1861, however, their cordial, tentatively affectionate yet distant relationship had grown warmer, and Victoria's solicitude and increasing concern were often evident.

Albert was convinced that Victoria's renewed attention to her mother had had a salutary effect on his wife's character, making her softer and kinder. And indeed she felt increasing compassion for the old lady whose world had shrunk to a bedside table covered with medicinal powders and pills and whose few remaining pleasures were

corroded by illness. As the duchess sank toward her final illness, her relationship with her daughter was more loving than it had ever been.

Early in March, 1861, the duchess had to have surgery on her arm to remove an ulcer. But the procedure did not go well, and she developed a severe infection. On March 15 a messenger came to Buckingham Palace with word that the elderly duchess had suddenly become much worse and was not likely to survive for more than a few hours. A train took Victoria, Albert and Alice to Windsor, where they went immediately to Frogmore. Victoria went in and found her mother in a semicomatose state, and breathing with great difficulty.

"I knelt before her, kissed her dear hand and placed it next my cheek," Victoria wrote in her journal afterward. "But though she opened her eyes she did not, I think, know me. She brushed my hand off, and the dreadful reality was before me, that for the first time she did not know the child she had ever received with such tender smiles!"[6] Sobbing, the queen left the room. She spent the night on a sofa, "in silent misery," getting up three times to tiptoe into the sickroom, lamp in hand. The duchess's lady-in-waiting Augusta Bruce saw the queen kneel by her mother's bedside and kiss her hand, whispering "mama" in a tender yet urgent voice, "as if the sound might rouse her."[7]

There was another sound in the room, the loud ticking of the Duke of Kent's old tortoiseshell repeater watch, which still, after more than forty years, kept time by the duchess's bedside. The sound of the repeater striking the quarter hour, Victoria wrote, "brought back all the recollections of my childhood," and this flood of memories, sad and happy, plus the sight of the tearful Albert and Alice, made Victoria feel "truly orphaned." Early in the morning she went to sit on a footstool by the dying duchess's bedside, holding her hand, "feeling the end fast approaching" as her mother's breathing became more and more labored and faint. The agony of the deathwatch was very great, and in that agony Victoria did not turn to Albert for comfort, though he offered it. She faced her momentous loss alone, having withdrawn deep within herself.

At nine-thirty on the morning of March 16 the duchess died, quietly and without regaining consciousness. Fearing that his wife's mental health might give way under the strain, Albert picked her up and took her out of the room, calling on Alice for help in keeping her calm. He did well to anticipate an emotional storm. The queen "clung to the dear room" in which her mother had died, cried copiously and suffered terribly ("the outbursts of grief are fearful and at times un-bearable," she wrote in her journal), and became even more with-drawn and at the same time exceedingly nervous. All loud noises alarmed her, even those incident to a houseful of children. For weeks she kept to her room, taking her meals alone, weeping and nursing her grief, her constant crying "a comfort and relief." Another comfort was to return to Frogmore and sit in the death room, in the silent house, and go through her mother's things.

She saved every memento she could find, every flower, every bit of hair, every letter and sentimental keepsake. There were letters from the father she had never known written to her mother at the end of his life, and there was a heartrending little diary in which the duchess had written down her own sad, loving thoughts following his death. Baby books from Victoria's own babyhood ("they show such un-bounded tenderness!"), more documents indicating clearly that Lehzen and Conroy, in separate ways, had worked to estrange Victoria and her mother, and other revealing records came to light.[8]

Her grief made Victoria feel twenty years older, she told Vicky. Now she, and not her mother, was the head of the family, no longer a young grandmother but simply a grandmother, with all the solemnity and weight of that status. "I feel everything so differently since that dreadful sixteenth of March," Victoria told her daughter. Her grief did not lessen with the passing weeks, but grew deeper, and with it came a diffuse anger that was, inevitably, directed toward Albert.

Once again, in the aftermath of his Aunt Kent's death, Albert had to manage everything, overseeing the winding up of her tangled busi-ness affairs, doing his own work and Victoria's, above all attempting to tame and soothe his distracted wife and guide her back into the main-stream of life and onto the path of ruling.

It was essential that Victoria give at least the appearance of resum-ing her duties as sovereign; by mid-April there were rumors in London that her grief had brought on the dreaded Hanoverian madness, and that soon the queen would have to put away. But whenever Albert cautiously suggested that Victoria rouse herself from her mourning by taking a trip or involving herself more in the lives of others—for ex-ample, in looking after eight-year-old Leopold, with his bruised legs and lively mind—she grew stony, or shouted him down. How dare he try to play the role only her mother had played, she demanded. No

Victoria as a child of four,
by S. P. Denning

Victoria at eleven years old,
after R. T. Lane

Queen Victoria, aged eighteen,
at her first council meeting

Victoria in 1838, aged nineteen,
by R. T. Lane

Victoria as an adolescent, with her mother, by Hayter

Victoria at thirty-six, in all her usual finery

Victoria and Albert with their nine children at Osborne

*Victoria, with her dog, at Balmoral in 1867, wearing
her perpetual mourning black*

Victoria with four of her grandchildren

Victoria in her mid-fifties

Victoria at seventy-two, working on her papers

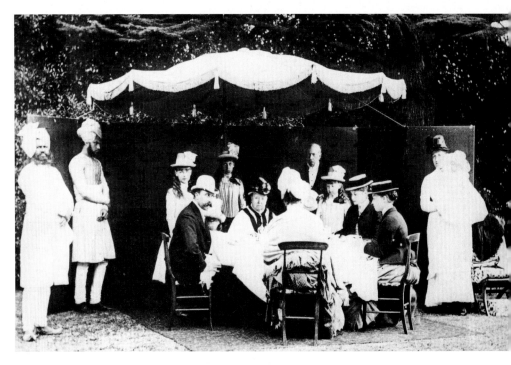

The queen dining alfresco with family members, Indian servants in attendance

Victoria with her great-grandson Prince Edward, the future Edward VIII, c. 1900

mere man could take her mother's place, her kind, tender mother, who had, after all, always loved her!

A bleak summer arrived, with the entire royal household plunged into mourning black and the queen, still largely isolated and often querulous, complaining of "the agony of Wehmuth [melancholy], the bitterness of the blank" which "did not get better with time."[9] Her half sister Feodore, warm hearted and sympathetic, had come to stay, and doubtless she and Victoria reminisced together. Yet Victoria remained weak and very nervous, depressed by memories of her mother's "love and interest and solicitude." When a military band played a march the duchess had written many years earlier, Victoria could not stand to hear it and broke down.

Vicky sent her two-year-old son Willy to stay with his grandparents for the summer, and the presence of the lively child helped to distract the ailing Albert from his pains and burdens. Albert adored the "sweet, darling, promising" little boy, and wanted so much to protect him from becoming a "conceited Prussian." Like Bertie, Willy would one day be a king, succeeding his father Fritz; Albert could not bear to think that the lovable, winning child would be molded into a rigid, narrow military man like most of Fritz's male relations.[10]

Boys, as Victoria remarked to Vicky, always cause much more suffering than girls, and the Prince of Wales was a prime example of this maxim. At nineteen, overweight and barely educated, possessed of an uncontrolled temper and childish eccentricities, Bertie was anything but prepared to perform his public duties as heir to the throne. His parents hoped that marriage to a levelheaded princess would settle him down and in time bring on maturity, and to that end they invited the Danish princess Alexandra to visit England in the fall, hoping that an engagement could be announced soon thereafter.

Bertie was spending the summer in Ireland, in a military training camp near Dublin. He had shown an interest in army life—from a distance—and now he was being given a heavy dose of it. Only, as usual, it was too heavy; Albert invariably overburdened his son and this summer's regimen was no exception. Bertie was expected to do in a few months what it took most men years to accomplish. He was to learn, from the ground up, what it was to serve in every rank, from ensign to general. And while he accomplished this immense task, he was to be kept away from all subversive influences, especially other young officers.

Predictably, Bertie failed to meet his instructors' expectations, and his training stalled. Reports of his unsatisfactory progress reached Osborne, and Victoria and Albert agreed that they needed to bring the weight of their presence to bear on the worsening situation. In August Victoria roused herself from her isolation and the royal couple traveled to Ireland, despite Albert's feverishness and severe muscular pains. He was miserable, and growing thinner, yet as he wrote his brother Ernest, "I go on working at my treadmill, as life seems to me."[11] He was determined to make Bertie understand that he too must get on his treadmill, and learn to like it.

But Bertie was incorrigible. He returned his parents' appraising gaze with a "sallow, dull, blasé"' look (so unlike the bright, lively expression of Alice's fiancé, Victoria noted), and continued to turn in a mediocre performance for his instructors. He was feeling trapped, and rebellious. As he told Vicky two months later, he felt that his parents were forcing him prematurely into marriage with a girl who was not to his taste. Alexandra was only sixteen, virginal, innocent and pretty to be sure, but not pretty enough to suit Bertie. He wanted an earthy, experienced, full-bodied woman—the sort of woman many of his comrades-in-arms kept as a mistress.[12] He was a healthy young male, fun-loving and sensual. Why must his perfectly natural desire for sexual satisfaction be martyred on the altar of duty?

Victoria and Albert returned to England, and Bertie pursued his studies with his customary half-hearted apathy. But unknown to his parents, he had broken free of the restrictions they had placed on him. He had secretly socialized with the other young officers of the Grenadier Guards. They toasted him, they took pity on him—and they arranged an assignation for him with a voluptuous young actress named Nellie Clifden, who was spirited into one of the officer's huts, no doubt amid much champagne-enhanced giggling. Bertie met Nellie there on a number of occasions, and when at the end of the summer he left the camp, he arranged to see more of Nellie in England.

The liaison was not secret for long. Bertie had been indiscreet, even taking the daring step of bringing Nellie to Windsor Castle early in November where he slept with her under his parents' noses. Nellie was calling herself Princess of Wales and bragging that she had seduced the heir to the throne. It was all deliciously scandalous, especially to the gossips who knew how straitlaced Albert was and how tight a rein the queen had always tried to keep on her wayward eldest son. The story flew from club to club, court to court. Soon all Europe knew of it. The aging Stockmar heard the story in Coburg, and hastened to write what he was hearing to Albert before more damage could be done.

The news, coming as it did just after Albert had learned, to his great grief, that his favorite cousin Pedro, King of Portugal, had died of typhoid, struck the Prince Consort with the force of a mortal blow. He investigated the matter and discovered, as he told Bertie, "a course of deception and profligacy" in his son that filled his heart with shame. More heartbroken than angry, he sat down at his desk and composed a letter to his son.

"I write to you with a heavy heart on a subject which has caused me the deepest pain I have yet felt in this life," he began, "having to address my son, in whom we had during twenty years fondly hoped to rear a Prince, and an ornament to a great and powerful and religious nation, as one who has sunk into vice and debauchery."[13]

He had always known, Albert went on, that Bertie was thoughtless and weak, ignorant and easily led. But he had not believed him to be "depraved." Now he knew the truth. The letter implied, though it did not explicitly say, that Albert saw rising in his son the ugly spirit of Hanoverian debauchery and dissipation, that family curse that had made George IV and his more scandal-ridden brothers so odious to decent English men and women.

But it was not merely that Bertie seemed to Albert destined for a life of corruption; he seemed bound to drag the monarchy down with him. All that Victoria and Albert had worked so hard to achieve would be permanently, irretrievably tarnished by the consequences of Bertie's vile lust. Didn't Bertie realize, Albert wrote, that his mistress would probably make certain she became pregnant and then trumpet to the world that Bertie was the father? Couldn't Bertie see that if he denied being the father, Nellie would take him to court, where she would "give before a greedy multitude disgusting details of your profligacy"? It would be worse than the worst days of the 1820s, when George IV had put his adulterous wife Queen Caroline on trial for immorality and had been "hooted and yelled at by a lawless mob." Nothing but shame, dishonor, and the ruin of all Albert's own years of effort could result.

The ruin of all he had undertaken—this was Albert's fevered vision as, shaken as never before by the prospect of a family shattered by vice and deceit, he tried to go on with his work in the waning days of November. He couldn't sleep, his old shoulder pain tormented him, and with winter coming on he felt himself beginning to succumb to a deeper malaise.

Victoria watched him, as she always did, and attributed his decline to the rapid changes of temperature accompanying the change of season, and the ever-frigid corridors of Windsor. But he had caught a chill while visiting Sandhurst on a very wet day, and lay in his bed, shivering, unable to sleep or eat. Sir William Jenner, who had become Albert's doctor earlier in the year, examined him and assured the queen that he would be well again in two or three days, though Albert himself, "depressed and low," sensed that Jenner was overly optimistic.

On into the first week of December the royal patient continued to suffer what Victoria called "this hasty, feverish sort of influenza and deranged stomach."[14] He slept badly or not at all, could eat almost nothing and stayed in his room, wearing his dressing gown, rousing himself from his depression only long enough to make morbid comments. ("He kept saying," Victoria wrote in her journal, "it was very well he had no fever, as he should not recover!—which we all told him was too foolish and he must never speak of it."[15]) Palmerston thought another doctor should be consulted but this only made Victoria angry. She too was suffering from loss of sleep and an edgy anxiety that grew with each passing day.

"I went to my room and cried dreadfully and felt oh! as if my heart must break," she wrote distractedly on December 7. "Oh! such agony as exceeded all my grief this year. Oh, God! Help and protect him!" On the following night Albert slept—his first night of sleep in weeks—and Victoria, who had been sleeping in a makeshift bed in his dressing room, was able to rest longer than usual. But by now Albert was alarmingly thin, and the skin of his face, stretched taut across his cheekbones, was very pale. His mind wandered. At times he became cross and impatient, slapping Victoria's hand when she tried to talk to Dr. Jenner, and at times he was tender—though unsmiling—calling her his "good little wife" and clinging to her hand.

Hoping and praying for his recovery, Victoria managed to get through the difficult days, keeping a copious daily record of everything that happened in the sickroom, writing to Vicky, meeting with her ministers. Alice worked quietly and efficiently to make her father as comfortable as possible, and to calm her mother, whose nerve and courage were being tested as never before. Alice and Victoria took turns reading to Albert from the memoirs of Varnhagen von Ense, a soldier and diplomat, and from Walter Scott. Alice played his favorite hymn, "A Mighty Fortress Is Our God," with its stirring affirmative harmonies.

By December 10 Albert was eating once again, and continuing to sleep at night, though he was shockingly thin and too often delirious. "Gastric fever" was now the diagnosis, and though he had been ill for three weeks, the doctors insisted that it might be four weeks before his fever broke and he began to return to himself.[16] Victoria consoled herself with the thought that, if he was not actually recovering, at least Albert was not losing ground, and that "not losing ground is a gain, now, of every day."[17] She tried not to think of how often her husband had told her that unlike her, he "did not cling to life," and that if he fell really ill he should "make no struggle," but "give it up at once."[18]

On the afternoon of December 11 there came a subtle but unmistakable change. Whether Albert, who now slept most of the time, reached a critical point or whether Dr. Jenner, whom Victoria respected, made the true gravity of the prince's illness clear to Victoria for the first time, her attitude began to shift from hope to dread. She stopped writing in her journal, though she did still scribble hasty notes on scraps of paper. She watched the five doctors who now came and went, relying on Jenner and avoiding the specialists. She said her prayers, and held Albert's white hand, with its weakening pulse, and felt her stomach tighten. "I am very wonderfully supported," she wrote, "and, excepting on three occasions, have borne up very well."[19]

She did not have to bear up much longer. On December 13 the prince lay very still, his face ashen and his breathing labored. Lenchen, Louise and Arthur were brought in to see their father (Beatrice was thought to be too young for such a solemn scene), and later Bertie too came by train from Cambridge to stand by the bedside, his thoughts an enigma. Vicky, pregnant with her third child, had been unable to make the trip from Berlin, and Affie and Leopold were traveling abroad and could not return for several days.

The following morning, with an exceptionally brilliant sun illuminating the warm brown stones of the castle, and with a military band playing faintly in the distance, Albert's life quietly ebbed. "Never can I forget how beautiful my darling looked lying there with his face lit up by the rising sun," Victoria wrote later, "his eyes unusually bright gazing as it were on unseen objects and not taking notice of me."[20] For days Victoria had suffered paroxysms of praying and crying, already in agony over the loss that now seemed inevitable. Now, with Alice supporting her, her sorrowful tears flowed from calmer eyes.

Her final vigil lasted most of the day. Toward the end she bent her face low over Albert's and asked him for one last kiss, and between rapid breaths, his cool lips brushed her cheek. She had to leave the room for a time, overcome by sobbing, but soon returned and took up her customary position, holding his hand in hers.

A little before eleven o'clock that night he drew several long breaths, still holding Victoria's hand, and then his breathing ceased. A hush fell in the candlelit room. "I stood up, kissing his dear heavenly forehead and called out in a bitter agonizing cry: 'Oh! my dear Darling!' and then dropped on my knees in mute, distracted despair, unable to utter a word or shed a tear." Her Angel had gone to rest with the angels.

Chapter 15

———— ✤ ————

EXHAUSTED, WEEPING, HER KNEES weak and her heart pounding,
Victoria allowed herself to be carried away from Albert's bedside and into the Red Room, where an attendant heard her
murmur, "There is no one to call me Victoria now."

Her eyes moved, words came from her mouth, but the void that
now began invading her heart was fathomless. She stared at nothing,
and her words were empty forms. She called for her children, who
gathered around her, red-eyed and pale, and she ordered telegrams
sent to Affie and Leopold and Vicky. The members of the Cabinet had
to be informed, and *The Times*, and Ernest in Coburg and Uncle
Leopold in Brussels. It was nearly midnight when she went in to the
nursery where her youngest daughter, Beatrice or "Baby Bee," lay
sleeping, and kissed the small composed face.

Warm, motherly Annie Macdonald, a Scotswoman who had been
Albert's cleaner, took charge of the shaken queen and put her to bed,
but sleep would not come. The mournful tolling of the bells of St.
George's Chapel kept her awake, indeed every sound seemed magnified and bruising to her heightened sensitivity, and at last one of the

doctors had to come and sit beside her until, near dawn, she fell into a disturbed sleep.[1]

On the following day Victoria left for Osborne with her daughters. She wanted no part of the funeral. She did not want even to keep vigil beside the cold, still body on its mattress; she left that to Albert's valet Rudolf Löhlein, whose extremely close resemblance to Albert must have aroused mixed feelings in her—at once a chilling sort of comfort and a haunting reminder of what she had lost.[2] She did, however, see to it that Alice, Lenchen, Louise and Beatrice all had their hair cut off to be placed in the coffin with their father, and no doubt some of her own graying locks were added too.

Fierce cold winds whipped the Solent to a churning froth and howled through the chimneys at Osborne when Victoria and her party arrived. All the rooms were chilly, the windows banged and the gardens—gardens Albert had designed and laid out with great care—were full of leafless branches and frostbitten shrubs. The bleakness of the landscape echoed the queen's inner emptiness, yet Osborne was her only refuge—Balmoral would have been far colder and too inaccessible in the coming political season. So it was to Osborne that the mounds of consolatory telegrams were sent, and there the relatives forgathered.

Eight-year-old Leopold came from Cannes, where, ironically, an outbreak of typhoid had threatened him and killed one of his companions. Feodore came also, and offered much sisterly warmth and comfort. ("She often held me in her arms and pressed me to her heart when I was in such despair!" Victoria told a correspondent later. "Never shall I forget her goodness and love at that time."[3]) Albert's brother Ernest crossed the Solent in a gale to join his sister-in-law. The widow and son of Victoria's half brother Charles of Leiningen also made the long journey to England, as did the aging, crippled Uncle Leopold, the sight of whose sad decline must have added another layer of melancholy to Victoria's grief.

Osborne was full of visitors, indeed the house had never been more crowded, yet Victoria was very much alone. Everywhere she looked she saw reminders of Albert: in the house itself, in the life-size statue on the stairwell, in the mementos on his desk—his inkstand of Balmoral granite, his marble paperweight, the amber ball that had belonged to his grandfather—in the music on the pianoforte and the notes and memoranda in his handwriting. A marble bust of Albert (one of many) sat on a pedestal beside the mantel, and his portrait, kept wreathed with fresh, sweet-smelling white immortelles, hung over his pillow on their bed.[4]

It was customary in wealthy German households to preserve the room in which the head of the house died as a "death-room," its contents kept exactly as they were on the day the occupant died. Victoria thought this custom morbid, and preferred to create a room in which Albert, as it were, still lived. His room was kept as what she called a "living beautiful monument," with servants coming and going as if to provide for his needs, the curtains opened and closed as they were during his life, and his clothes and even his shaving brush brought out each day for the absent owner's use.[5] In truth, though she knew that he was gone, Victoria continued to feel Albert's presence, and one of the worst torments of her mourning was that she could not help expecting to see him any moment, even though her common sense told her she would never see him again.[6]

Victoria had loved her husband with the full strength of what she called her "warm passionate loving nature." Her ardor now had no outlet, and, as she confessed to Vicky, "the never quenched flame . . . burns within me and wears me out!" Her desire lived on, even in her grief, and most of all she missed the times "when in those blessed arms clasped and held tight in the sacred hours at night, when the world seemed only to be ourselves," she and Albert had consummated their love. "The night (above all the night) is too sad and weary," she told her daughter, adding that it had been her hope to have a tenth child. "I had so wished for one other," she wrote, "and had thought it very likely that Alice and I would have followed each other very closely!"[7]

Alice was to be married on July 1, 1862, more than six months after Albert's death, yet as the day approached, Victoria's grief did not diminish. And indeed the ceremony was more like a funeral than a wedding, with all the female guests in lilac and gray out of deference to Albert, and the bride herself with an all-black trousseau, though her bridal gown itself was white. Grave and serious, Alice repeated her vows with some trepidation, for she dreaded having children and was fearful about her wedding night. In addition, she had discovered only recently that her husband had a vulgar streak and that her in-laws were cold and unpleasant toward her. Victoria was not able to offer Alice much motherly comfort, preoccupied as she was with her own racing pulse and taut nerves. She could hardly bear to see or converse with anyone. When she received her ministers—always with a bust of Albert on a table at her side—she became "excited and flushed and very feverish," and had to keep the interviews brief.[8]

The business of the government and the royal household weighed heavily on the grieving queen. For so many years Albert had managed everything, in effect predigesting all the important papers and letters that came to Victoria and reducing their contents to pithy memoranda, arranging them for her to sign, and adding his suggestions to guide her decisions. Now she had to read them all herself, which took three times as long, and in addition, Albert's meticulous method of arranging papers once they had been dealt with was abandoned, so that masses of unsorted documents began to accumulate and nothing could be found easily.

It took Victoria months to accustom herself to her new routine and increased workload, and there were other painful adjustments as well. When Albert died, his parliamentary allowance was naturally cut off, and the budget of the royal household suffered. Victoria had to provide for all his servants out of her own income—just as she had had to begin providing for her late mother's servants in the previous year— and by the end of January she had to inform the Lord Chamberlain that she was out of money. So many demands were made of her, not only financial but personal. Lodgings and furnishings had to be found for ill and aging servants; the royal organist, who was overly fond of drink, had to be discreetly removed from his duties; the invalid daughter of William IV's favorite old page was suffering from a spinal complaint and needed help.

It was the year of Victoria's Silver Jubilee, the twenty-fifth anniversary of her accession, but no official notice was taken of the fact. In her sketchbook Victoria wrote "1862—First Year of my misery." "My life is over," she wrote melodramatically in her journal, and indeed she did her best to mortify her life, ordering her dresser Marianne Skerrett to give away her dozens of satin gowns and feathered mantles, her bonnets and soft gloves and drawers full of ribbons and trimmings. Victoria had loved beautiful clothes, but from now on, for Albert's sake, she would deny herself the pleasure of wearing them. She would put on black for the rest of her life, though its harshness made her look older. And she would not permit herself the softening effect of face powder or rouge, though many respectable women had begun to wear both. No, she would show her true face to the world—the ashen, careworn face of sorrow.

The heavy, empty days dragged by. The queen struggled doggedly to do all that was expected of her, inwardly lacerated and "torn alive to pieces" by her violent grief.

"My misery—my despair increase daily, hourly," she told Vicky. "I have no rest, no real rest or peace by day or by night; I sleep—but in such a way as to be more tired of a morning than at night and waken constantly with a dreamy, dreadful confusion of something having happened and crushed me! Oh! It is too awful, too dreadful! And a sickness and icy coldness bordering on the wildest despair comes over me—which is more than a human being can bear!"[9]

At times Victoria feared for her sanity. At times she thought of doing away with herself, so all-encompassing was the darkness that seemed to surround her. At such times she went into Albert's room, and knelt beside his chair, and poured out her heart. "How fervently do I implore his aid, and how I wring my hands towards heaven and cry aloud: 'Oh God have pity, let me go soon! Albert, Albert, where art thou?'"[10]

Victoria's weakness for self-dramatization was given full rein, but the despair that prompted it was genuine, and deepgoing. She was passing through the greatest crisis of her life. And yet, even when that crisis was at its worst, she reached out to others. Only a month after Albert's death the queen received word of a tragic accident in the Northumbrian coal fields, in which over two hundred men lost their lives. She immediately sent a message of condolence to the widows, "in the midst of her own overwhelming grief." Later, on the first anniversary of her widowhood, many of those widows contributed to buying her a beautiful Bible.

Victoria's grief was cankered by a stubborn wrath against her son and heir. She could not help but hate Bertie, and blame him for bringing on Albert's fatal illness. His deceit, his selfish lust had robbed her of all she cared about, and she despised him for it. Everything about him repelled her: his loud, often disputatious voice, his "sallow, dull, blasé look, his "enormous features," especially his "true Coburg nose" that hung down and made him ugly in her eyes. The thought of his propensity toward what she called "sin and degradation" made her shudder with distaste, but even more distasteful was Victoria's realization that her dreadful son was becoming more like her with each passing year. She too was weak, and sexually ardent, violently temperamental and imperious. Her own exophthalmic eyes were often dull, her own features, in middle age, were far from attractive, and she bore the "Coburg nose." The worst of herself, and not the best of Albert, would inherit the throne, and whenever that unpalatable thought struck her, she was plunged into gloom.

Nor was Bertie the only child to disappoint her. In the fall of 1862 she learned that her second son, who was barely eighteen, and with whom she had always been so pleased, had gotten himself into trouble with a woman while at Malta. Exactly what sort of trouble she did not commit to writing, but it was clearly sexual and sordid and his conduct was, in her phrase, "both heartless and dishonorable." "Affie's terrible business" reminded her only too sharply of Bertie's relationship with Nellie Clifden—which in turn reminded her of her constant sorrow. The episode, she told Vicky, "dealt a heavy blow to my weak and shattered frame."[11] It caused her "bitter anguish," especially as Affie had not been coaxed into debauchery, as Bertie was, by others, but had embraced it of his own volition.

Rigid with anger, the queen at first refused to see her repentant son, but later relented. She admitted him to her presence, and noted how pale and thin and subdued he was, and how exceedingly anxious to please. She wanted to think the best of him, yet she knew that the world was bound to snatch him into "sin and degradation" as it did most highborn men and that she would be powerless to save him from that fate. Looking at him, she was aware that, if anything happened to Bertie, Affie would become king. Indeed a throne had already been offered to him, the throne of Greece, though she refused the offer. Affie would inherit his Uncle Ernest's title and estates, as Albert had intended. But to prevent further temptations from destroying his character, she would have to find Affie a wife. "If Affie is not to fall again and again into similar sins," she told Vicky, "he must marry early."[12]

Early marriage, Victoria believed, would be Bertie's salvation too. To her great relief, he had proposed to Princess Alexandra of Denmark and had been accepted. Alexandra, with her wide blue eyes, peach-pink skin, long elegant neck and slender figure, her amiable disposition and sweetly seductive smile, was captivating. Beyond these physical charms, she had a gentle and honest nature, with none of the false airs of the spoiled aristocratic heiress. Despite her high birth she had been raised to be frugal; she and her sister sewed their own clothes and made their own bonnets, and to spare expense she had her maid darn her stockings. She was also pious, and eager, as she told Victoria, "to improve herself in every way to be of use" to her future husband. Touchingly affectionate, Alexandra was moved by Victoria's grief; she put her head on the queen's shoulder and cried, saying it was her prayer to help and comfort Victoria as much as she could.[13]

On Bertie and Alexandra's wedding day, March 10, 1863, Victoria was at the center of the preparations, making sure Louise wore the pearls Albert had meant to give her (pearls that had belonged to his mother), letting Alice wear on her train the Duchess of Kent's miniver, approving Alexandra's ermine-trimmed white satin gown and admiring the lovely trembling bride. Victoria had now been a widow nearly fifteen months, and although it seemed as if her "constant anxiety, responsibility and interruptions" had increased, in fact her capacity to cope with more and more work was also increasing. She was paying a price, however; hardly a day passed without her suffering a headache and complaining of nervous pains. On the wedding day itself she worried that the heavily pregnant Alice, whose baby was due in only a few weeks, might go into labor during the ceremony.

Unable to face the crowds in St. George's Chapel at Windsor, and feeling "strange and bewildered," Victoria watched the wedding from Catherine of Aragon's closet, a dark little alcove above and to the left of the altar, from which she could see all while being shielded from inspection herself. Full of emotion at the best of times, she did not trust herself to endure the heartrending sonorities of choir, trumpet and organ without breaking down completely. She knew that she would miss Albert acutely, and that, missing him, she might weep uncontrollably. She did not want any of her courtiers to witness that, nor did she want to make herself vulnerable to being stifled by their impotent solicitude.

Hardly was Windsor emptied of wedding guests than Alice took to her bed to await her delivery. Victoria was determined that this grandchild should be born at Windsor, in the same bed in which her own nine children had been born, and she gave Alice the same shift to wear that she had worn—her lucky shift, nearly a quarter of a century old—confident that it would bring Alice safely through her labor. The queen felt her customary surge of indignation toward Alice's husband Louis (she wanted to give him "a good ducking and all sorts of things") for putting Alice in such an uncomfortable state, and when poor Alice began her eight-hour ordeal Victoria's indignation turned to outright anger. She had never attended a birth before, and she sat up with Alice all night, "dreadfully shaken and agitated," deciding, before the long vigil was over, that watching a birth was more dreadful than watching a death.

"I had far rather have gone through it myself!" the queen wrote to Vicky afterward. "It is far more dreadful to be born into this world than into the next!"[14]

Birth and death seemed to preoccupy Victoria in this second year of her widowhood. She kept a close eye on her new daughter-in-law Alexandra, called "Alix," hoping to observe the telltale signs of pregnancy, and began to despair when after three months Alix showed no indication that a baby was on the way. She sat by the bedside of her elderly page Whiting, a shriveled old man, full of sores and no longer able to speak, and wept to see the pleasure in his eyes at the sight of her; he died soon afterward. She fussed over Leopold, who had suddenly collapsed from internal bleeding after going riding; she worried and prayed that he would be spared, though the doctors cautioned her that he might die at any time. And she was greatly distressed to hear that one of the housemaids at Windsor, "a very good person," became despondent and jumped to her death from the roof of the palace. "It was temporary insanity!" the queen exclaimed. "But what a mercy we were not there."[15]

The royal household was in fact at Osborne that summer, and Victoria's friend and in-law Augusta, Queen of Prussia had come for a visit. Augusta, with her quick mind, her restless energy and iron constitution, was just the tonic Victoria needed, though her presence was a reminder that there was currently much strife, both political and personal, between Prussia and England.

Great changes were taking place in Prussia, where Augusta's husband William now ruled, with Vicky's husband Fritz as crown prince. William's Prime Minister, the large and truculent Count Otto von Bismarck, was thundering and roaring his way to dominance, not only in Prussia but on the larger stage of Europe. Under Bismarck's leadership, Prussia was beginning to shoulder its way toward preeminence in the German Confederacy—a position long held by Austria. The status quo was being threatened, and the result seemed ominous to Victoria, who foresaw that Prussia and England were bound to clash—and that her liberal daughter was bound to become more and more isolated at an increasingly conservative court.

Vicky was holding her own, but Bismarck complained bitterly about her, and Augusta made unreasonable demands on her, which made her situation very trying. Fortunately her marriage was happy, and she delighted in her children. A second son, Henry, had been born the previous year, giving Victoria and Augusta a third grandchild in common.

The two grandmothers consoled one another at Osborne for several weeks, amid the lilacs and laburnum on the terrace. Despite her restlessness and irritability, Augusta, who was some years Victoria's senior, had a tender side, and was able to offer comfort and strength to Victoria, who was exceptionally shaky and in need of a kind friend.

Victoria looked and felt frail. She had lost a good deal of weight, and her face was careworn. Her small person looked even more diminutive wrapped in yards of stiff black stuff, and the white widow's cap perched on her head, its streamers trailing down her back, lent her a pathetic, doll-like appearance. Her health had been poor all year, and her doctors did nothing to increase either her well-being or her confidence. In mid-June Clark and Jenner informed the queen that, if she were to faint (and she felt as though she might faint at any minute), she might never wake up.[16]

With her friend Augusta as with very few others, the queen was able to open her heart and share her fears, her sorrows and her sense of childlike bewilderment. She felt, she told Uncle Leopold, "like a poor hunted hare, like a child that has lost its mother, and so lost, so frightened and helpless."[17] She both feared and welcomed the doctors' threatening edict: feared it, because if she did die, Bertie would take over in her stead, and just at this time Bertie was at his most frivolous and pleasure-loving, diving headlong into the social season and losing himself in all-night revelry; and welcomed it, for if she died she would rejoin Albert in a happier place, as in her saddest hours she longed to do.

When at Windsor she visited Albert every evening, before going to bed, in his recently completed mausoleum at Frogmore. There in his "dear, holy chamber" she gave vent to her most acute feelings, and prayed for her Angel to guide her in all that she did. On those evenings it was hard for her to tear herself away, so peaceful was the lovely candlelit vault, so vivid were her memories of the man whose "earthly robe" rested there. Part of her, the sensible part, knew that presently she would have to make her way back to the castle and seek what rest she could. But another, and at times a stronger, part of her yearned to lie down on the cold tiles beside her beloved's remains and rest there, as close to his dear flesh as possible, until she yielded up her spirit and left all earthly cares behind.

Chapter 16

TOWARD THE END OF the year 1863 events on the Continent threatened once again to draw Britain into war. At issue were the two duchies of Schleswig and Holstein, the former largely German in population, the latter entirely so. Although the King of Denmark had long ruled over both territories, the German Confederation, with a bellicose Prussia in the forefront, began to agitate for their independence. In December, forces from Saxony and Hanover crossed the frontier and occupied Holstein, and Prussian and Austrian troops massed in readiness to occupy Schleswig.

The ever choleric, ever intemperate Palmerston, bent with age and crippled by gout but as alert and sharp-tongued as he had been a decade earlier, leapt to the defense of Denmark and warned the German states, especially Prussia, that Britain was only too eager to back the Danes with arms. The British public was roused to sympathy for Denmark, home of their Princess of Wales, and the newspapers were full of provocative stories against Prussia.

It was just the sort of situation in which, in past years, Albert had been at his best, helping to cool the debate, settling the agitated queen down, finding his way through the labyrinth of competing interests toward a rational solution. But Albert was no longer available—though Victoria insisted that from beyond the grave, he continued to guide her and to "work on for us all."[1]

Victoria braved the crisis as best she could, angry that no one heeded her opinion and galled by Palmerston, who was "extremely impertinent" in his sketchy communications with her and exasperatingly brazen in making bold pronouncements without her concurrence. She was bombarded by opinions, especially from Fritz and Vicky, who were visiting her ("Fritz is very violent"), and from Feodore ("very anxious and at times violent"), until she became "almost frantic" in her helplessness, and found her relatives "very painful and trying." Her motto became "I must bear it, till the Lord pleases to take me"—the words of an old woman she had been visiting who was dying of cancer.[2]

In the midst of the ongoing crisis, in the first week of January, 1864, Alix went into labor prematurely and gave birth to a tiny, feeble son, who was given the names Albert Victor. The baby was born at Frogmore, and Victoria went at once to help out the new mother, exerting herself so much that she developed bad headaches. Small and delicate as he was, the infant managed to survive, although his grandmother confided to Vicky that he seemed "backward."[3] Still, Albert Victor was destined one day to succeed his father as king, and Victoria honored his arrival by ordering an elaborate christening cup with special inscriptions and figures of angels and warriors.

When early in February German armies invaded Schleswig, the queen was beside herself with vexation, angry with Vicky, annoyed with Bertie and Alix for being more concerned about the fate of Denmark than the well-being of Britain, irritated with Palmerston and very much afraid that the British navy would be sent to oppose the Austrian navy off Copenhagen. She brought to bear what pressure she could for peace, and was gratified when in April an armistice was arranged. A wider war was avoided, but in the end, Schleswig and Holstein were permanently removed from Danish rule, and Prussia triumphed.

The widespread indignation of the British public over the Schleswig-Holstein affair reflected the growing popularity of Bertie and Alix. They had been staunchly anti-Prussian throughout the crisis, in opposition to the queen whose pro-German sympathies were only too well known. And Bertie, made daring by the strong tide of public sentiment, defied his mother that spring by attending a reception given for London's most celebrated visitor, the Italian patriot Garibaldi. Victoria was piqued. She had made, and heretofore enforced, strict rules about whom Bertie could and could not see socially, and this act of disobedience was unprecedented.

Victoria sought, in every possible way, to control her son. She received frequent reports on what went on at his London residence, Marlborough House, just as in her youth John Conroy had received detailed reports of what went on at Kensington Palace. Though she often said that she did not expect to live much longer, the queen refused to allow Bertie any experience in governing, and made certain that her ministers did not share with him any important information about foreign affairs. Victoria was determined to keep Bertie, and his raffish Society friends, from becoming the focus of an informal political opposition.

But she could not prevent his popularity, though it pained her to compare the favor shown to Bertie with the scorn and coldness so many of the English had shown toward Albert during his lifetime. Now that Albert was dead his widow was intent on raising as many monuments as possible to his memory. Paintings, busts, life-size statues proliferated. Testimonials were delivered. Buildings were christened in memory of the late Prince Consort. Women even wore a special variety of mourning brooch called an "Albert," as a gesture of commiseration with the queen.

The "Albertizing" of England, tolerated at first by Victoria's sympathetic subjects, soon began to be perceived as tedious in some quarters, and the queen's prolonged grief and protracted period of seclusion led to criticism, and even to rumors that she had died. Very gradually, however, she began appearing in public, always protesting that such appearances overtaxed her shattered nerves. She was present at the dedications of the omnipresent statues, she rode in her carriage on public view, and eventually, in response to increasing public pressure, she began attending receptions and giving a few private audiences.

Yet she longed, as she told those closest to her, to "throw everything up and retire into private life" tending the poor and sick. "My political and queenly tasks are the hardest for me," she told Augusta of Prussia. "Only a sense of duty and the knowledge that my Angel wishes it and that I must answer to him force me to carry them out."[4]

In February of 1866 the queen managed, with heroic effort, to overcome her monumental reluctance and agreed to open Parliament. On a fine, if windy, winter morning she left Windsor, feeling "terribly nervous and agitated," with a large entourage. Wearing her customary evening dress of black silk trimmed with miniver and crape, her white widow's cap with a long veil, and over the cap a diamond and sapphire coronet, she rode in her carriage through the huge London crowds, enduring the jarring noises of blaring bands and shouting well-wishers.

Though Lenchen and Louise were riding with her, she felt very much alone, and only with great difficulty restrained her tears. She confided to the Prime Minister that since Albert's death she had feared a "complete breakdown," and as she steeled herself to endure the noise and tumult outside the open carriage windows she must have wondered whether the moment for her breakdown had come.

"When I entered the House, which was very full, I felt as if I should faint," Victoria wrote in her journal. "All was silent and all eyes fixed upon me, and there I sat alone. I was greatly relieved when all was over."[5]

A turning point in her widowhood had been reached. From now on, though she would complain bitterly of the insensitivity of those who expected her to make a spectacle of her sad, shaking self, she would nonetheless submit to their pleas that she appear in public (while continuing to insist that "the Queen will not be dictated to"). Her grief had at last begun to abate. She admitted to Vicky that she had begun to feel more cheerful and to take more interest in things, and that she cried much less than before.[6] So marked was the change, in fact, that it disturbed her; she feared that to grieve less was to dishonor Albert's memory.

Others noticed the alteration in the queen. Though she still wore the black uniform of sorrow, and her jowly face had "the look of sorrow and suffering," she radiated "calm decision and high resolve and energy." Beneath the sorrow there was a renewed sense of purpose, a renewed hold on life.

For one thing, she felt needed. It was clear to her that Bertie, with his empty head and his propensity for silly pranks (he liked to slide down a flight of stairs on a tea tray, and enjoyed provoking his inebriated friends by poking them with billiard cues), was utterly unfit to become king. Alix too had severe shortcomings. She was growing deaf, and she had never been able to grasp the magnitude of her position, or to fulfill its duties to her mother-in-law's satisfaction. No, Victoria would have to remain queen for some time to come. And besides, she was discovering that she could do the work of governing, even without Albert to guide her. Moreover, she could put her years of experience to good use in bringing about positive change.

"I consider my vocation to be that of trying to do good in the world," Victoria wrote in the spring of 1866, and indeed she did try, traveling to the Continent and meeting with the German and Austrian emperors in an effort to avert war, writing letters on behalf of humanitarian causes, as well as interesting herself in the lives of her servants, her children and her growing number of grandchildren.

Doing good in the world meant setting a good example, and the queen was persuaded that, with society drifting into hedonism and vice, her own good example was much needed. She had become convinced that the upper classes were all but worthless, devoting their empty days to the frivolous pursuit of pleasure, gambling and carousing and indulging themselves sexually while selfishly ignoring their obligations to their inferiors. As in the giddy, gilded final years before the French Revolution, the aristocrats rushed headlong after luxury and amusement, heedless of anything but their own gratification. "The danger really is very great," she told Vicky, "and they ought to be warned . . . or some dreadful crash will take place."[7]

Nowhere was this danger more apparent than in the royal family itself. Victoria had hoped that marriage to Alix and fatherhood would settle Bertie down, but after three years of marriage and two children (another son, George, had been born in 1865) he remained incorrigibly light-minded and pleasure-loving. Gentle, patient Alix put up with his debauchery and infidelity without complaint, while remaining herself free of scandal.

And Affie was much worse. Though he had a naval career to occupy him, and was given his first important command, of the *Galatea*, in 1866, Affie was at home in London society and had become distant from his disapproving mother. To her he was a "slippery youth," reserved and touchy, willful and untrustworthy. She was "not at all pleased or happy" about him.[8] He had threatened her carefully crafted family arrangements by falling in love with Alix, then shortly afterward by having an indiscreet affair with a much older married woman, Constance Grosvenor, who was the daughter of Victoria's former Wardrobe Mistress. He drank too much, he made a nuisance of him-

self. Worst of all, in Victoria's eyes, he was nothing like his saintly father. The monster Society had sucked him into its voracious maw, and
the queen doubted whether he would ever find his way to a decent
and orderly life.

But if she could not persuade Affie to marry and settle down, she
could at least make arrangements for Helena. From the outset of her
widowhood Victoria had been determined that at least one of her
daughters would stay with her for the rest of her life. Plump, unattractive Helena, her preferred confidante, was the natural choice. After
some searching, an adequate husband was found for Helena—Prince
Christian of Schleswig-Holstein, a hapless princeling who had lost his
estates, his military career, indeed everything but his title in the aftermath of the war with the German Confederation.

Helena and Christian made a suitably unattractive couple, for although he had the ramrod-straight posture of an ex-officer, and could
tell an amusing anecdote after dinner, Christian was prematurely bald,
addicted to cigars and notably lacking in charm. Cruel gossip spread,
fed by popular resentment of the queen's reclusiveness. Christian, it
was said, was a madman who had already fathered fifteen children;
Helena would have to look after them. Once the truth became
known, there would be no marriage. The unfounded rumors annoyed
poor Helena, and caused Victoria to wring her hands and cry "Oh!
why is the world so wicked? I can't really understand it."

Just how wicked the world could be was about to be made clear to
her. In late 1864 her favorite Highland servant, John Brown ("Johnnie"
in his youth, now plain John), had been brought to Windsor to wait on
her, at the recommendation of Dr. Jenner and others in the household
who were worried about her constant nervous state. Brown's brusque
common sense and strong masculine presence had always soothed the
queen—indeed Albert had approved of Brown and appointed him to
wait on Victoria while they stayed at Balmoral. Once he arrived at
court, Brown quickly became indispensable to Victoria, and with
every month he became more and more conspicuous, in his kilt, at her
side. He led her horse when she went riding. He sat on the box of her
carriage when she went out. He stood near her while she worked, preventing others from interrupting her. He carried her messages, pinned
on her shawl, chided her when she overworked, and in general became
maid, groom and all but mother to her.

Victoria considered Brown's presence to be deeply gratifying. "God knows how much I want to be taken care of," she told Vicky, and Brown took care of her as no one else did, except perhaps the other motherly Scot in her household, Annie Macdonald.[9] She needed sympathy, and Brown gave it to her in overflowing measure. "There is one person whose sympathy has done me—and does me—more good than almost anyone's and that is good, honest Brown," she wrote to her eldest daughter in the summer of 1866. "You . . . do not know what a heart and head, what true, simple faith and sound sense and judgment there is in him. He has, when I have been very sad and lonely—often and often—with his strong, kind, simple words—so true, and so wise and so courageous done me an immensity of good—and so he would to anyone in sorrow and distress."[10]

Victoria could not say enough about Brown's fidelity, his attentiveness, his understanding. So loyal a servant was beyond price, as Victoria well knew, for she had had difficulty finding personal servants who pleased her; a series of maids had recently come and gone in rapid succession, none of them satisfactory in the queen's eyes.[11] Brown's blunt, no-nonsense style, his guilelessness, his candor and even his rough, heavily accented speech inspired Victoria's trust—and her acceptance. That he was handsome and strong, with a manly beard and well-shaped, muscular legs did not entirely escape her notice, and may have helped her to overlook his weakness for whisky.

One of the many bonds between the queen and her Highland servant was that Brown had been a part of the Balmoral household in happier days, before Albert's death. Another was that, like Victoria, Brown had lost beloved relatives to typhoid—in his case, three of his brothers and a sister.[12] (Despite this loss, he had many siblings left, among whom one brother became Prince Leopold's valet, another head of the Windsor kennels, another a royal shepherd at Balmoral, still another keeper of the Queen's Lodge at Osborne, and still another tenant of a royal farm on the Dee.[13]) And there were other ties as well. Though rough in speech and manner, Brown was, like Victoria, a great reader, well informed about contemporary events. He was also a shrewd judge of people. Like his royal mistress, he hated obfuscation and circumlocution. He had no patience with court etiquette, or any other form of artificiality. He was a thoroughgoing democrat who ignored titles and social distinctions, and he treated the queen with the same bluff kindness as he would have treated his mother—or his wife.

And therein lay the root of the problem. Others at court thought

Brown was entirely too familiar with Victoria, and a story spread that indeed she was his wife—or at least his lover.

Like the rumor years earlier that Albert had been committed to the Tower of London as a German spy, the story that the queen had secretly married her Highland servant quickly took on a life of its own. Brown was seven years younger than Victoria, and certainly good-looking, and the queen, in the mid-1860s, was only in her late forties, still young enough, many of her subjects surmised, to want and need a man.

Malicious gossip gathered force and spread to the newspapers. In Scotland, "wicked, idle lies about poor, good Brown" appeared in the papers. The *Gazette de Lausanne* printed a story that Victoria and Brown were secretly married, and that she was pregnant, which accounted for her unwillingness to appear in public. Other accounts said that the two were not married, but that the queen was Brown's mistress, and likely to become pregnant soon. Cartoons in the British press hinted wickedly at impropriety, though they stopped short of outright accusation. And in the gentlemen's clubs, those hotbeds of hedonism and vice of which the queen was so critical, Victoria was referred to laughingly as "Mrs. Brown."

"Lees, all lees," Brown thundered in his broadly accented English when he learned what was being said about himself and Victoria. His outrage, like everything else about him, was unfeigned. The queen too was outraged—and at the same time genuinely bewildered. Honest, straightforward person that she was, lacking in pretense and guile, she simply could not understand malice in others, nor could she fathom being so grotesquely misunderstood. How, when she had held forth so plangently and so long on the subject of her deep grief, could anyone possibly think that she had profaned the sacred memory of her beloved Albert by taking Brown as her lover? Even if (unthinkably) she had wanted a lover, how could anyone imagine that she would choose a man so far below her own station? Furthermore, how could anyone who knew her, and knew her to be honest to a fault, believe that she was capable of so wicked a deception?

Victoria's more worldly courtiers could have told her that people will believe what they choose to believe, that malice is rampant in human affairs, and that genuine understanding is as rare as genuine kindness. But then, it was difficult to tell the queen anything she did not want to hear, and nearly impossible to talk to her about Brown. Her advisers, including those who had summoned Brown from Balmoral in the first place, now tried to persuade her to send Brown away, but she refused. She would not be bullied or coerced. "The Queen will not be dictated to." Brown stayed, and was given a raise in salary. In time, the titillating stories about the queen and her Highland servant lost their newness and ceased to be repeated.

If her subjects did not understand her, Victoria reasoned, then why not give them a glimpse into her mind and heart by publishing her jottings on her life in Scotland?

In 1865 she had circulated a privately printed edition of her Highland journals from the 1850s, with the title *Leaves from the Journal of My life in the Highlands*. It was a very modest, quite undistinguished little book, pedestrian in style and, on the whole, rather dull in content. Not a travel book, though it contained a great many place names and itineraries, nor a work of description, nor a study of Scotland or her people, *Leaves* was a simple record of experience, told in clear, unpretentious prose. And in its simplicity lay its charm, for Victoria, in writing down all that she saw and felt, revealed herself as ingenuous, good-hearted and pure-minded, deeply sentimental about her husband and family, affectionate and rich in feeling.

The response to the book from her children and others in her immediate circle was disappointing—they thought that Victoria had revealed too much of herself, making herself vulnerable to ridicule, and they were clever enough to be aware that the queen's amateurish jottings were hardly literature. But when early in 1868 the book, carefully edited and purged of all references that might embarrass the family, was made available to the public, it created a sensation. Eighty thousand copies were sold in the first four months, and the public clamored for more. Under Victoria's supervision another work appeared in the same year, a two-volume illustrated study of the Highlanders.

The Romantic Highlands were taken up as fashionable, and the queen's books were on every bedside table. "From all and every side, high and low, the feeling is the same, the letters flow in, saying how much more than ever I shall be loved, now that I am known and understood," Victoria told Vicky—whose response to the initial appearance of *Leaves* had been underwhelming. "It is very gratifying to see how people appreciate what is simple and right."[14] The queen's book helped to put her relationship with John Brown in perspective, for Brown appeared often in its pages, along with Albert. It was clear that

Brown was a valued servant, deserving of devotion, while Albert was the sole object of Victoria's romantic love. More important, it was hard to reconcile the unimaginative, stolid, fond author of *Leaves* with the scandalous image of Victoria as a sensualist secretly married to her handsome servant.

When the poet Tennyson met Victoria a few years before the publication of her book, he was struck by her self-possession, her sad, sweet voice, and another quality unique to her. She had, he wrote, "a stately innocence about her, different from other women." More than a little of Victoria's stately innocence came through in her Highland journal, and it touched many hearts. In an age of increasing complexity and galloping impropriety, what was simple and right about the queen made compelling reading.

Chapter 17

———— ⚭ ————

VICTORIA OFTEN SAT BEFORE her spinning wheel at Balmoral, letting the thick strands of grayish-white wool run through her plump, nimble fingers. Sometimes her favorite Scottish clergyman, Norman Macleod, sat beside her in the cold, dimly lit room, reading to her from a book of poetry. At other times her gillie John Grant supervised her work, telling her, "ye spin as well as any old woman in the country," and assuring her that his wife concurred.[1] More often she sat alone, or with the taciturn Brown in attendance, letting her thoughts wander as she twisted the rough wool, listening to the silence of the thickly draped, thickly carpeted castle and remembering happier times.

By the late 1860s Victoria had become "very large, ruddy and fat," with several chins and bulging cheeks. The creases on her brow and the set of her small mouth bespoke determination, even stubbornness, and her faded blue eyes, when not pain-filled or fearful, held a look of steady resolve. The pronounced redness of the queen's complexion worried Dr. Jenner, who saw in it "a species of madness," but he was less concerned about her increasing girth, which was easily explained.

She indulged in too much rich food, stuffing herself at meals and, between meals, stuffing herself further, with pralines and fondant cookies and chocolate sponge cake. No one was bold enough to tell her to eat less, and she would not have heeded the advice had she heard it. By and large, she did what she liked, now that Albert was no longer there to impede her, and what she liked was to have her own way.

"I have now been thirty years in harness," she announced, "and therefore ought to know what should be." An entire generation had come of age knowing no sovereign but Victoria. The last of the old guard had died out: Palmerston had collapsed at his desk, in the midst of writing a letter, a half-opened cabinet box in front of him, and Uncle Leopold had succumbed in the same year, 1865, in the same ominous mid-December season that had claimed Albert. If Victoria professed still to be "terribly shy and nervous," she was also aware that, because of her long years of experience, she had achieved a certain status; she was, as she put it, "the doyenne of the sovereigns," and there was no prominent man in British political life who could match her for sheer endurance.

Endure she had, but as she approached her fiftieth birthday, Victoria had undergone a metamorphosis. Much of the brightness and charm had been leached out of her. What her secretary General Grey called "the long unchecked habit of self-indulgence" reigned in her, making it "impossible for her, without some degree of nervous agitation to give up, even for ten minutes, the gratification of a single inclination, or even whim."[2] Her view of the world, and of the men and women in it, had darkened, and if her view of herself was equally severe—it was at this time that she destroyed many of the letters and journal entries she had made in the earliest years of her reign, disgusted by her own frivolity and vacuity—it was nonetheless pitiless. She often gave in to a cranky irritability that revealed itself in acts of petty spite. She kept invited but unwelcome guests waiting for hours or even days before she would see them; she crumpled her brow and pursed her lips peevishly when an unappetizing dish was served at dinner; she snapped at servants and household officials who broke the glum silence around her with an ill-judged laugh. Turned in on herself, she moodily declared that she took no pleasure or enjoyment in anything any more, and burdened those around her with the nearly impossible task of amusing her and drawing her out of her melancholy.

At least one of those closest to her had reached a point where she was reluctant to take on the queen's sullen humors. Feodore, now six-tyish and in uncertain health, declined Victoria's invitation to come to Osborne for a visit, and admitted that it was her half sister's apathy and world-weariness that deterred her.

To be sure, Victoria was never at a loss for company. John Brown was always within arm's reach, Helena and Christian were close by, Annie Macdonald and Emilie Dittweiler, her German dresser, hovered near, and there were ladies-in-waiting to go out riding with the queen, or to read to her, or to sketch with her. But these official companions could not entirely take the place of family, and most of the royal children were either grown or gone. Even the three youngest were not children any more, although Victoria tried to keep Beatrice a child for as long as possible.

For the most part Victoria lived in quiet, settled isolation, spending most of her time either at Osborne or at Balmoral. When she was at Windsor, she gravitated to her private sitting room, now working at her desk, now sitting on her overstuffed sofa with its print of large daisies, surrounded by the cluttered remains of her past. A huge portrait of Albert dominated one wall, along with paintings of Vicky and the late Princess Charlotte, Uncle Leopold's first wife, scenes of Balmoral, and a large picture of Victoria and Albert with their young children playing at their feet.

When at Balmoral, she sought solitude in Glassalt Shiel, the new fifteen-room house she built following Albert's death, at a site "quite in amongst the hills" that had been Albert's favorite wild spot. A waterfall cascaded from the high hillside far above the house, and below it a swiftly running stream ran into Loch Muick. It was more difficult for "inquisitive reporters" to harass her at Glassalt Shiel, and in general the interruptions of the world seemed more remote there. The peace of the wild country, the sound of the rushing water, the mists that often enshrouded the house were a balm to Victoria's nerves, and when she settled in there on a chilly evening, with a fire burning in the stone hearth and one of her ladies reading to her from one of Mrs. Oliphant's novels, a plate of sugary confections near at hand and a glass of neat whisky beside it, she reached a pinnacle of contentment.

The queen's taste in literature ran to the pedestrian. She preferred the banal, innocuous vaporings of Mrs. Oliphant to the clever, mordant Trollope, whose novels were then in fashion, admiring in the former her abundance of "good and right feeling and observations of

feelings which one has so often experienced and yet never seen written down."[3] Victoria disliked controversy, particularly where "right
feelings" was concerned, yet she was broad-minded in her opinions on
the religious debates of the day. She agreed with the much criticized
Bishop Colenso who argued that the Pentateuch was not to be taken
as a literal record of events, but was to be looked on as a reconstruc-
tion composed by men living many centuries later. Where worship
was concerned, the queen called herself "very nearly a Dissenter—or
rather more a Presbyterian" and was alarmed at how ritualistic the
Church of England had become. "The state of the church is very serious," she told Vicky, "and I am sure there will have to be a new Reformation."[4]

Reformation or not, Victoria was grateful for kind, sympathetic
ministers like Norman Macleod, whose own faith was so strong and
his warmth and humanity so expansive that it spilled over to enrich
her impoverished emotional life. She trusted Macleod, and confided in
him, and allowed his sincere belief to undergird her own. "How I
loved to talk to him, to ask his advice, to speak to him of my sorrows,
my anxieties!" she wrote, looking back on the first decade of her widowhood. "No one ever felt so convinced, and so anxious as he to con-
vince others, that God was a loving Father."[5] At a time when many of
her subjects were tormented by doubts, and others were turning their
backs on organized religion, Victoria clung to a simple but deeply held
religious belief.

By the end of the 1860s a subtle yet unmistakable shift in the
queen's view of herself and of her late husband had become apparent.
While she continued to regard Albert as very nearly a saint, and to give
as gifts bound copies of *The Principal Speeches and Addresses of H.R.H.
the Prince Consort*, she had come to look on him as "too perfect for this
world." His own goodness had made it impossible for him to live in
the wicked world without grief and torment; he had not been able to
muster the "pluck" to fight against that wickedness, and so, in the end,
he had given in. His life had been admirable, indeed almost Christ-
like.[6] And yet, something had been missing in him—something she
herself possessed. It was, simply put, the courage to endure. Unlike Albert, Victoria could face, and survive, the wickedness she saw around
her. She could name it, confront it, and do her best to oppose it. She
had pluck. She did not give in. She had to acknowledge that, in the
end, she was stronger than her beloved husband, the man to whom

she had deferred, whose superior intelligence and wisdom she had extolled, had ever been. In her strength, she was superior to him.

The portrait of Albert she carried in her heart had changed. She now saw him as a gifted, remarkable man—but a man with fatal flaws. Whereas she, far less gifted, far more ordinary in every way, was able to do what the world asked of her, and to go on doing it year after year, coping with crises, never giving in to the temptation to run from her responsibilities, doing her best and achieving (sometimes after much internal anxiety) a measure of peace and tranquillity no matter what challenges she faced. Victoria had found, in her widowhood, a fairly large measure of self-satisfaction.

A major political realignment was under way, and Victoria, by now a seasoned veteran of such shifts, rode it out with aplomb. Once again, as in the early 1830s, demands for reform were loud and strident. Demonstrations, public meetings, marches and threats of crowd violence made the Conservative government of Lord Derby, who had succeeded Palmerston, uneasy in the extreme. The queen acquiesced in the widespread view that the franchise ought to be greatly extended, to include most working men (after all, as she wrote to Vicky, "we are before God all alike"), but many members of Derby's party were adamantly opposed to any further democratization of British government, and it was only the adroitness of his Chancellor of the Exchequer, Benjamin Disraeli, that achieved passage of the Second Reform Bill in 1867.

Early in 1868 Derby stepped aside, a victim of painful gout, and Disraeli became Prime Minister. Disraeli's advent was welcomed by Victoria, who after her initial meeting with him wrote in her journal that "he was amiable and clever, but is a strange man."[7] She had known for a long time that he was strange; in fact he was celebrated for his unconventionality—and for his novels, thought-provoking if fanciful works of social criticism that sold well and stimulated much dining room conversation.

Born in 1804, Disraeli was fifteen years older than Victoria and remembered vividly hearing the news of her birth. He belonged—just barely—to the generation that took Byron as its hero, and as a young man he delighted in Byronic escapades, swaggering through the streets of Malta dressed as a Greek pirate in a red cap and shirt with silver buttons, touring Turkey in a turban, smoking a six-foot hookah, indulging in sexual adventures (which resulted in his having to take a "mercury cure" for venereal disease), and generally making his mark as a wealthy young poseur.

He was distinctive also in that he was Jewish, and although baptized as a Christian, young Benjamin looked and acted like an outsider to upper-class British society. Anti-Semitism stigmatized him, and would continue to do so all his life. Partly to flaunt, partly to counteract this, Disraeli created a bizarre, romantic persona that underscored his exotic looks and Middle Eastern heritage. He wore his black hair in foppish long ringlets. He dressed flamboyantly and theatrically in velvet coats and lace cuffs, gold chains and many flashing rings. Disraeli was not a handsome man, there was a simian cast to his features and his physique was far from Adonis-like. (His future wife wrote of him, "His eyes they are as black as Sloes/But oh! so beautiful his nose."[8]) But he had an unctuous, insinuating charm and he adored women, and they responded to his adoration in varying degrees.

The one woman who responded most warmly was Mary Anne Wyndham Lewis, a garrulous, aging coquette given to making foolish remarks that betrayed her inadequate education. She was a dozen years older than Disraeli, and there was an element of mother-son attachment in their romance, but his love for her was sincere and his gratitude immense, for if she had no fortune of her own, she at least had the use of her late husband's money during her lifetime, and Disraeli was deeply in debt. The queen was more astounded than charmed by Mrs. Disraeli, whose social blunders and eccentricities in dress—she was a sort of elderly Bo-Peep—were truly alarming. Yet Victoria recognized the deep affection that bound the couple, and, remembering her own happy marriage (in retrospect it was totally happy, never clouded by conflict), she graciously accepted the odd Mary Anne.

It did not take Victoria long to realize that she liked Disraeli more than she had liked any of her Prime Ministers since Melbourne. He was always concerned for her comfort, and sensitive to her moods and her nervous states. He seemed instinctively to know how to handle her, perhaps because of his inordinate fondness for women in general, perhaps because he too had been a victim of nerves at one point in his life, having suffered a breakdown whose aftereffects lasted for several years. When Victoria told Disraeli that she was feeling the weight of her years, and that "she really had neither inclination nor energy sufficient to educate boys for such offices as war and admiralty," he did not remonstrate with her; he merely yielded to her disinclination, and found another way to train the "boys."9

Of his dealings with the stubborn, often irritable queen, the Prime Minister avowed, "I never contradict; I never deny; but I sometimes forget." He improvised, he invented, he avoided distasteful subjects, or when he could not avoid them, he buffered them with more palatable topics. He had, Victoria said, a "wonderful, happy disposition," and was always ready to float off into a romantic reverie, or to bring up a diverting subject such as what nightingales ate, or how beautiful the roses at Osborne were.

Disraeli wooed Victoria, and his wooing helped her to forget the harshness of life and of her own unenviable position. He called her "the Faery." It was a reference to her diminutive stature, but it was also more than that, for the elderly Disraeli well remembered the young Victoria of the 1830s and early 1840s, slim and ardent and glowing with life, and with his ability to idealize, he saw her that way still. Beneath her layers of fat, her lined face and heavy round cheeks, he glimpsed the shadow of the happy young woman she had been, and he paid tribute to that part of her; she in turn, basking in his idealizing vision, brought forth her best self in his presence.

It was, and at the same time it was not, a romance. And it was brief, for Disraeli and the Conservatives were decisively defeated in the elections of November, 1868—elections in which, for the first time, the broadened franchise he had helped to usher in participated—and Disraeli resigned. Victoria summoned William Ewart Gladstone to lead the new Liberal government.

Tall, erect, the picture of uprightness and Victorian manliness, Gladstone was ten years Victoria's senior and her better in every respect but birth—or so many people believed. When he spoke—as he often did for four or five hours straight in the House of Commons—he sent chills through his listeners; he inspired awe. Like the preachers who drew huge crowds at Exeter Hall, Gladstone was mesmerizingly righteous. He seemed to trail clouds of glory. His eyes flashed like those (one imagined) of an Old Testament prophet. His moral suasion was frightening, and frighteningly effective.

As far from the insinuating, seductive, oblique Disraeli as it was possible to be, Gladstone radiated blunt honesty and straightforwardness—qualities that Victoria had always admired above all others. In an age marked by furious energy, diligent effort and prodigious productivity, Gladstone was even more energetic, industrious and productive than he had any right to be. He was a great walker. Visiting Balmoral in 1863, when he was fifty-four years old, he thought nothing of walking twenty-five miles in a day, then rounding out his recreation by dancing for hours at a Gillies' Ball. He climbed mountains, he went on long expeditions, taking bogs in stride, he felled huge trees and kept pace in most other outdoor activities with men half his age. At the same time, he wrote dozens of letters daily, read voluminously, and spent a good deal of time scrutinizing his conscience and kneeling at the side of his bed in prayer.

Victoria might have been expected to get along well with Gladstone—but she did not. He was too loud, too excitable, too uncompromising. He leaned too much to the view that the sovereign reigned at the sufferance of Parliament. He even had the temerity to lecture the queen on her duties—one of which, in his view, was to appear more often in public. He did not understand that when coerced, Victoria immediately dug in her heels, and as a result, they were soon at odds.

"I cannot find him very agreeable," Victoria wrote of her new Prime Minister, "and he talks so very much." He seemed to her unbalanced, overly ardent in defense of ill-advised policies and given to following Palmerston's bad example in sending out official documents without first receiving the royal assent. She missed Disraeli, with his cool, amusing manner and his flattering affability. She missed his epigrams. ("A little sincerity is a dangerous thing, and a great deal of it is absolutely fatal," Disraeli quipped, and the barb would have been aptly applied to Gladstone.[10]) Still, the Liberals were the dominant party, and no matter how "overbearingly obstinate and imperious" Gladstone was, she had to endure him.

He became particularly insufferable when war broke out between France and Prussia in July of 1870. Victoria was at Osborne, trying in vain to find relief from a heat wave, when telegrams began to pour in from the Continent. The government of Napoleon III, it appeared, had become impossibly arrogant and demanding in its quarrel with Prussia over who should assume the vacant throne of Spain. France had seized the initiative and declared war. (In actuality, Bismarck had worked behind the scenes to orchestrate a diplomatic and military collision between the two rival powers, but at the time, the Germans seemed to be blameless victims of French aggression.) Dreading war, and foreseeing only misery, suffering and death, Victoria lamented the situation.

"This frightful bloodshed is really too horrible in Europe in the nineteenth century," she wrote solemnly to her friend Augusta of Prussia, who had taken refuge in Switzerland from the fighting. And as the fierce, pitiless bloodletting continued into August, with the grossly inferior French forces repeatedly mowed down by the well-trained, well-equipped Prussian armies, Victoria's ill-concealed pride in the German victories was exceeded only by her concern over dissension in the family.

Vicky's husband Fritz, Alice's husband Louis and Victoria's brother-in-law Ernest were all in command of troops, and in the thick of the fighting. Vicky had just given birth to her third daughter and seventh child, Sophie, yet she threw all her energy into organizing a military hospital, building new wards at her own expense, and recruiting nurses trained by Florence Nightingale. Alice was reluctant to leave Darmstadt, and worried about Louis's safety and the safety of her children. Feodore, full of "violent and bitter" feeling against England, was angry with Victoria for not coming to the aid of her Coburg homeland, and many of the other relatives concurred. England had declared neutrality, yet as King William pointed out in a friendly, temperate letter to Victoria, England's "neutrality" did not prevent her from shipping horses, coals, even millions of cartridges to France.

"These divided interests in royal families are quite unbearable," Victoria declared. All her sympathies were with the German armies and the German people, but she agreed with Gladstone that Britain could not risk being drawn into the war—a "war of exasperation," in Gladstone's view. She wished that her sister, her children and her in-laws would try to understand, to see things from her point of view as Britain's ruler. Personally she had done all she could to promote peace. Certainly she deplored the chaos and waste of life, and prayed earnestly for the war to end. She crocheted a comforter for Fritz, and sent Vicky as much old linen as she could spare to make bandages for the Prussian wounded. But more, as sovereign, she could not do.

Then on September 2, 1870, a bare seven weeks after France declared war, the conflict took a sudden turn. The French under Marshal MacMahon were forced to capitulate. Over a hundred thousand French officers and men were taken prisoner. Napoleon III too was in German hands, no longer an emperor but a prisoner of war. The Second Empire had collapsed, and a triumphant Germany, united under Prussian leadership, was poised to become the leading power in Europe.

With dizzying swiftness the dazzling, glittering regime of Napoleon and Eugenie had been swept from the stage, its boasts of preeminence revealed as mere sham and hollow pretense. "Such a complete tumbling to pieces of their empire and its far famed army has really never been seen!" Victoria wrote to Vicky. "It does seem like a judgment from heaven!"[11]

The former Empress Eugenie had barely escaped arrest, fleeing from the Tuileries with her young son and making her way to Deauville, where an Englishman, John Burgoyne, took her aboard his yacht. She arrived in England seasick, thin and pale, with none of her belongings and nowhere to go. Victoria came to her aid, and went to visit her.

It must have been a sentimental yet sorrowful meeting between the heavy, aging English queen in her widow's weeds and the dispirited, still beautiful former empress, shorn of her finery and plainly dressed in black as a sign of mourning for her defeated country.[12] "Oh! If only we could have peace!" Eugenie exclaimed, shaking her head over all that had happened in the intervening years since the two women had last met on that brilliantly sunny spring day in Paris fifteen years earlier. Eugenie asked tactfully after the health of Vicky and Alice, and brought out her son, the former Prince Imperial, to meet the English queen. ("A nice little boy, but rather short and stumpy," Victoria thought.) Little was said about the war, or the new government in Paris, or the future fate of the former emperor.

The visit was a brief one, and soon Victoria was on her way back to Windsor. It was a dark, cold afternoon with a raw wind, toward the end of a grim year, full of tensions and tragedy. The queen had much to ponder as she prepared to write in her journal on the last day of 1870.

"The bloody, sad, eventful year '70 has sunk in dark clouds," she wrote, "and '71 rises as sad and gloomy, but God, we pray in His mercy, may soon grant us peace." As the new decade opened, nothing was certain but that Victoria, stolid and courageous against the wickedness of the world, would soldier on.

Chapter 18

CRINOLINES WERE OUT, BUSTLES were in. The Romantic look, with women's nether parts hidden under yards of frothy petticoats and stiff whalebone frames, their girlish faces wreathed in curls, gave way to the bolder, more frankly seductive look of the early 1870s. Bustles emphasized the posterior, and slim women wore "bustle pads" to make themselves look more ample from the rear. Clothes clung to the figure, necklines plunged, making "bust improvers" a necessity and creating new fads—bathing in strawberries or sage tea, rubbing small breasts with a mixture of tincture of myrrh, musk and elder-flower water to make them larger, wearing the round, hard artificial devices called "lemon bosoms" to give them definition.

Even in elegant drawing rooms, and even in the presence of the sovereign, women abandoned all modesty and wore light-colored, revealing gowns, "without a particle of shawl or scarf," the queen noted disapprovingly, and did not retreat discreetly to the shadows of the ballroom when they were pregnant. Victoria complained to Vicky that she had seen women dancing "within a fortnight of their confinement," and waltzing in their eighth month! "Where is delicacy of feeling going to?" she asked rhetorically, and her outcry was echoed by many of her contemporaries.

"In evening costume," the *Saturday Review* trumpeted, "our women have reached the minimum of dress and the maximum of brass. The female bosom is less the subject of a revelation than the feature of an exposition."[1] It was not only the low-necked dresses, but the daring glances of the wearers that the older generation found so disquieting. The "Fast Girl" of the 1850s now seemed downright coy in comparison with her bolder daughters of the 1870s, and one particularly vehement social critic, Mrs. Eliza Lynn Linton, spoke for many when she attacked "the girl of the period" for her brazen face-painting, hair-dying, tasteless dressing, slang-flinging, and provocative flirtation with worthless males.[2]

As the new decade opened, English society faced a genuine and little-understood problem: there were too many women. The phrase "redundant women" came into general use to describe those women who had not managed to find husbands—not because of any personal failings, but because of the demographic imbalance. Even the royal family reflected this imbalance; there were five girls and only four boys, one of whom suffered from a very serious illness and was not expected to survive for the length of a normal life span. The queen's daughter Louise, that "peculiar" child born in the year of revolutions, 1848, would probably not have married had she not been a princess; a husband was found for her, Lord Lorne, but the marriage was rocky.

When the redundant women tried to enter the universities, the male students held mass rallies in protest. And when—heaven for-fend!—the movement for female equality began, and writers such as J. S. Mill advanced the outrageous view that women were in no way inferior to men and ought not to be subordinated to them by law or custom, the response was furious.

Victoria hastened to align herself against the movement for women's rights—a subject that she said made her so angry she "could not contain herself." She was, she declared "most anxious to enlist every one who can speak or write to join in checking this mad, wicked folly of 'Women's Rights,' with all its attendant horrors, on which her poor feeble sex is bent, forgetting every sense of womanly feeling and propriety." Feminists, she insisted, "ought to get a good whipping." Were women to "unsex" themselves by claiming equality with men, they would become "the most hateful, heathen and disgusting of be-ings," and would surely perish without male protection.[3]

The queen's antifeminist campaign did little to stem the demand for change, which gathered force and became a hallmark of the era, along with bowler hats and checked trousers and the heavy, clumsy "boneshakers"—ancestors of the bicycle—which began to appear in the crowded streets.

The capital continued to expand outwards, and to be convulsed with massive new construction projects. Critics called it "the New Babylon," and shunned it as morally repulsive and physically mon-strous. Yet the charms of the antique City were intact, the street mar-kets were colorful and flocks of sheep still mingled with the picnickers in Regent's Park. Full of the noise and disruption of growth as London was, it emanated vitality; one had only to stroll along the newly built Thames Embankment, that thick concrete wall that buttressed the north shore of the river, and observe the dozens of steamers sailing pur-posefully upriver and down to feel the vibrant pulse of London life.

Near London Bridge factories spewed smoke and the City of Lon-don Brewery Company operated day and night churning out barrels of beer to supply the thirsty capital. Trains rattled into the huge Cannon Street shed, omnibuses rolled over the cobblestones and, beneath the street, the London Underground roared through a labyrinth of tun-nels. To the east, where the vast stretch of St. Katherine's Docks, India Docks, and Victoria Docks spread themselves along the riverbank, acres of masts swayed gently in the flux of the tide. Thousands of tons of goods were unloaded and stored in vast warehouses, and sailors and clerks and customs officials swarmed through the crowds of heavily laden dock laborers and porters, passengers and shipbuilders, intent on tracking the flow of incoming and outgoing vessels.

Amid the hubbub, London still offered pockets of quiet. Old for-gotten churchyards, their tombstones askew, abandoned cottages not yet condemned to the wrecker's ball, odd corners of park and waste remained to remind visitors of the Georgian city, and late at night, when the street traffic died down and the music halls were closed, homeless families huddled on the bridges and the Little Sisters of the Poor drove their green carts along the alleys, searching out the old and the dying, to take them in.

Peaceful to the point of tedium and beyond, the long, dreary Sundays marked the mournful beginning of the week. The majority of people sat through two- or even three-hour services, listening to sermons brimming with biblical learning, responding through endless litanies. Hard seats and kneeling-boards tortured knees and backs, and gave concrete meaning to the biblical word longsuffering. When at last afternoon came, and with it blessed release from church, there was little or nothing to do; to indulge in entertainment or recreation on Sunday was not allowed in pious households, and only prayer, and the reading of uplifting books, were permitted. Evening brought another long service, followed by personal devotions and bed.

Most English men and women were deeply serious about their faith, it undergirded their lives to an extent unimaginable to nonchurchgoers in our own time. Sin and redemption, godliness and ungodliness were defining concepts that framed experience. Thus in London's bleak, comfortless prisons, where men and boys were put to work on the treadmill (then called the "treadwheel") for many hours each day, the call to lay aside the work of the devil and take up the path of the Lord was ever-present. On the walls were signs reading "BE SURE YOUR SINS WILL FIND YOU OUT!" and "CHOOSE YOU THIS DAY WHOM YOU SHALL SERVE." In schools, shelters, even places of work the symbols of Christianity and its messages were prominently displayed. Poor men recited psalms on street corners for pennies. Poor women embroidered Bible covers. Middle-class girls stitched samplers with the words of Christ. Biblical Christianity was thickly intertwined in the fabric of Victorian life, even though doubt had begun to erode its preeminence.

But by 1870 secular institutions were beginning to take over humanitarian work once done by religious organizations. Social improvement began to be uncoupled from moral improvement, and the Evangelicals were displaced by government officials as agents of progress. At the same time, a small but growing group within the population embraced agnosticism (the term was coined by T. H. Huxley in 1870), discarding the idea that each individual must either accept or reject religion; the agnostics boldly asserted that nonbelief (rather than disbelief) was a valid human norm, and in time might become the prevailing one.[4]

Steadfast amid the swirling tides of change stood the fifty-one-year-old Queen, to many of her subjects a shadowy figure, much less distinct than her balding, bearded, twenty-nine-year-old son. Bertie, who was much in the public eye, had always been popular, and his popularity did not wane substantially when, in 1870, he was called into court to testify in a sordid divorce case.

It was a paradox of the age that the same subjects who denied themselves amusements on Sundays and kept themselves in a state of heightened awareness of sin had always been so ready to overlook the flagrant sinning of their future monarch. Bertie's love affairs with his wealthy friends' wives were widely known, and widely discussed. Yet until the winter of 1870, he had avoided open scandal. Now, however, his letters to Lady Mordaunt, wife of his sometime friend Sir Charles Mordaunt, seemed to implicate him in adultery, and when Sir Charles sued his wife for divorce the Prince of Wales had to take the stand.

In a courtroom crowded to bursting with spectators avid to hear explicit details of a royal liaison, the future king took his place and swore to tell the truth. He held himself with regal dignity, and when asked whether he had ever engaged in "improper familiarity" with Lady Mordaunt he shouted out a resounding "No, never!"[5] Apparently it was the truth; by an odd quirk of fate, the unbalanced Lady Mordaunt—who, at the time of the trial, had been committed to a mental institution—had been one of the few women of the prince's acquaintance who had not occasioned his lust. He had, however, written her "foolish and imprudent" letters, and the existence of these letters, plus the disgrace of the trial, tarnished the prince's reputation somewhat and hurt his patient wife and his disparaging mother very much.

Victoria despaired of her pleasure-loving, feckless son, yet as she grew older she was coming to terms with his limitations. She knew that she could not entrust any of the serious business of governing to him, but she was beginning to force herself to enhance his formal position nonetheless. She deputed him to make speeches for her at official ceremonies. She gave him the place of honor beside her. She treated him, in public, with the respect the heir to the throne deserved.

Privately she still tried to control him, but her attempts had less and less effect. Bertie and Alix were celebrities, quasi-independent of the court—indeed with a court of their own, albeit a somewhat vulgar, morally tainted one, at Marlborough House. The queen dared not overcontrol her son, lest she make an enemy of him—an enemy who could easily be exploited by the political opposition. So she temporized, reminding herself that Bertie was as warmhearted as he was wayward, and being thankful that his worst traits—his meanness, his violent bad temper and spiteful pranks—had mellowed.

In late November of 1871, shortly after his thirtieth birthday, Bertie fell ill. It was typhoid, contracted at a house party at Scarborough; nearly all the guests had come down with the disease. When Victoria learned that her son was ill she immediately became anxious, especially after hearing that others in the house party had died, and that Bertie was delirious. Like Albert in the early stages of his typhoid attack, Bertie was feverish, had difficulty breathing and wandered restlessly from room to room. She became even more alarmed when Dr. Jenner announced that Bertie's attack was far more violent than Albert's had been, and on November 29 she went to Sandringham.

The queen was none too well herself. For the past several months she had had severe gout in her foot—so severe that at times she couldn't walk—and rheumatic pains in her shoulder and hands. Hardly had she recovered from one complaint than another assaulted her, confining her to bed and lowering her spirits terribly. "My utter helplessness is a bitter trial," she wrote sadly, "not even being able to feed myself." She couldn't write, and had to dictate her journal to Beatrice. Not until late November did she begin to return to normal, only to be called immediately to Bertie's bedside.

The scene that met Victoria's eyes at Sandringham was enough to send her into a relapse. In the darkened sickroom, with only a single lamp burning beside his bed, Bertie lay in a stupor, attended by Jenner, two nurses and the distraught Alix, "the picture of sorrow." Alix had hardly left her husband's bedside since his symptoms began, and she was exhausted. Her own physical state was none too strong; earlier in the year she had given birth to her last child, a tiny girl who died the following day.

Clearly Bertie was far more ill than Albert had been, and Victoria began to realize that he might not recover. "How all reminded me so vividly and sadly of my dearest Albert's illness!" she wrote in her journal. Everything was the same: the same fearful symptoms, the same time of the year—late November—the same doctor, the same pervasive sense of gloom. Only now it was the heir to the throne who struggled for life, and if he died, all Britain's hopes for the future would come to rest on his eldest son, Albert Victor, called "Eddie."

None of Bertie and Alix's five children was robust. Victoria referred to them as "poor, frail little fairies," and confided to Vicky that, had he lived, Albert would have been in despair over how "miserable and puny" they were.[6] Slight, delicate Eddie, now seven years old, was the strongest, but he was very unpromising. Dull-witted, lethargic, scarcely able to read and with neither charm nor good looks, Eddie seemed to lack both the strength and the rudimentary intelligence to be king one day. Yet if his father died, the nation would look to Eddie—and it would be up to Victoria to undertake the monumental task of making the fragile child into a future king.

After a few days Victoria returned to Windsor, though she received frequent bulletins from Sandringham. At Windsor a minor tragedy awaited her; her faithful dog Dacko died. "The dear old dog was so attached to me and had such funny amusing ways," she wrote in her journal, memorializing Dacko, "with large melancholy expressive eyes, and was quite part of my daily life, always in my room, and I and all will miss him much."[7]

Hardly had she laid Dacko to rest when a frightening telegram arrived from Sandringham, early on the morning of December 8. Bertie was much worse. His fever had risen to 104 degrees, and his breathing was rapid, as Albert's had been just before he died. Dr. Jenner and his colleague Dr. Gull declared themselves to be "very anxious."

Victoria and Louise started for Sandringham that afternoon, Affie arrived at midnight and the other children the following morning. The weather had turned savagely cold. Snowdrifts muffled the sound of the arriving carriages, and the windows of the mansion were lined with thick frost. The doctors permitted family members to enter the sickroom one by one, and restricted them to standing behind a screen. Bertie was "very bad," Dr. Jenner said. The danger was great. The fever, the panting, were signs that the end was near.[8] The illness had reached its crisis, and each spasm could be the patient's last.

Another agonizing day passed, and then, on December 11, Victoria was awakened at five-thirty in the morning by her maid with a message from Jenner saying that Bertie had had two very severe spasms and was not expected to endure another. She had hardly gotten out of bed when Jenner came into her room and urged her to come at once. Her heart pounding, she flung on her dressing gown and went in.

"It seemed," Victoria wrote later, "that his precious life was about to end." In the candlelit room Alix and Alice kept vigil, along with two nurses. Victoria sat behind the screen and was soon joined by her three other sons and Louise. No doubt they clung to each other as, in the flickering candlelight, they listened to Bertie's fearfully labored breathing. He choked, gasped, and seemed to drown; at the last moment he caught breath again and revived, only to begin choking and gasping once more. After what seemed an eternity his breathing eased, and Victoria left the room long enough to dress and eat, assured by Jenner that she would be called back the moment there was any change.

Meanwhile throughout Britain, and in many parts of the world, there was deep distress at the news that the queen's eldest son lay near death. From India, Canada, America, Australia, the telegrams poured in. Government receptions, political gatherings, meetings of all kinds were suspended while Britons and British subjects held their breaths in anticipation of news from Sandringham. The streets in front of the newspaper and telegraph offices, police stations, and at Marlborough House were crowded with people at all hours of the day and night, despite the piercing cold, and when a positive bulletin was received, cheers went up. Dull, troubled faces betokened grim news. In every church prayers were offered for the prince's life, and for Victoria and Alix "in this day of their great trouble." In Catholic churches, synagogues, and, in India, in temples and mosques special prayers were intoned for Bertie, and Gladstone, eloquent in his piety, wrote the queen a beautiful letter of consolation.

"[Mr. Gladstone] knows not how either to touch, or to leave untouched, the painful subject, which in the very street seems to absorb the mind of every passer-by," the Prime Minister wrote, using the third person, "and which is now pressing with such fearful weight on Your Majesty. . . . Mr. Gladstone will not mock the sorrow of this moment by assurances which, even when sincere, must seem so poor and hollow; but he earnestly commends the sufferer and all the afflicted round him, most of all the Mother and the Wife, to Him who alone is able either to heal or to console, and who turns into mercies the darkest of all His dispensations."[9] For once Victoria did not regret Gladstone's long-windedness.

Coughing, choking, at times scarcely clinging to life, Bertie lay in his twilight world, not recognizing anyone, clutching at the blankets in agony, unable to eat, and so deathly pale that family members admitted tearfully to one another that there could be no hope. Discreet preparations were begun for a royal funeral. After all, the anniversary of Albert's death, December 14, was approaching, and there would be a macabre symmetry—and no small irony, in Victoria's mind—in Bertie's dying on or near his father's deathday.

Then, on the raw, damp morning of the fourteenth, the unexpected happened. The doctors reported that Bertie was showing signs of improvement. His fever went down slightly, he slept peacefully and was even able to take a little food. When in the following days no relapse occurred, the family wept happy tears and dispersed, Victoria returning to Windsor where she planned to spend a very happy Christmas. By Christmas Day Bertie was able to issue a message to his household servants, though he continued to convalesce in bed.

The telegrams continued to pour in to Sandringham from all over the world, but now they contained messages of congratulation, and in every London theater "God bless the Prince of Wales" was enthusiastically sung.

Two months later a formal service of thanksgiving for Bertie's restoration to health was held in St. Paul's, and Victoria and Bertie rode in an open landau amidst densely packed, wildly cheering crowds from Buckingham Palace to the cathedral. The extraordinary celebrating went on for hours after the ceremony ended. Victoria and Bertie were called out onto the balcony of the palace late in the afternoon to receive still more plaudits and demonstrations of affection, and thousands of people danced and sang in the London streets long into the night.

Worn out by all the emotion, and feeling the weight of her years, Victoria lay on a sofa, reflecting on all that had happened and on the good fortune that, for the moment, seemed to rest on her family and her realm. She was gratified to note that Bertie, though still delicate and pale, seemed to have been changed by his illness. He was gentler and kinder, she told Vicky in a letter, he spent more time with Alix and he appeared to take a special pleasure in ordinary things, as befitted one who had come close to losing them all. [10]

She was gratified, yet the realist in her remained wary. Clearly Bertie had been given a second chance at life, but he might, given his prodigal temperament, squander the opportunity. "We all feel," the queen told Vicky, "that if God has spared his life it is to enable him to lead a new life—and if this great warning is not taken, and the wonderful sympathy and devotion of the whole nation does not make a great change in him, it will be worse than before and his utter ruin."

Chapter 19

ARLY IN APRIL OF 1873 Queen Victoria entered her state carriage and set off toward the slums of east London. She rarely, if ever, entered the poorest and dirtiest neighborhoods of her capital, but on this occasion she had been invited to open Victoria Park in Hackney, and she readily consented.

The dark, narrow streets of Islington, Bethnal Green and Shoreditch had been purged of the worst of their grime in honor of the queen's visit, the open sewers flushed clear and the piles of refuse that normally clogged the streets carted away. Yet no hurried cleansing could remove the stench that clung to these overcrowded, disease-infested alleyways, and as the royal carriage slowed to a trot, then to a walking pace as it made its way toward the park, the queen must have discreetly held a scented handkerchief to her nose.

She knew that she was taking a risk in leaving the relative safety of the prosperous West End. Discontent and agitation against the government and the monarchy thrived in the poor quarters of the city, and only a year earlier Victoria had been terrified when a young man pointed a pistol at her as she was getting out of an open landau.

(Brown, ever nearby, grabbed the young Fenian and disarmed him.[1])
Still, on this April morning the ill-dressed crowds that greeted their
sovereign with cries of "God bless you," and "Come again," seemed
touchingly loyal, and Victoria noted in her journal afterward that
"nothing could have been more hearty or cordial than my reception by
those poorest of the poor."[2] It warmed her heart to receive the plaudits of her people, however low their station, and she did her best to
overlook the raggedness of their clothes and the unsightliness of their
houses for the duration of her tour.

Compassionate as she often was toward individuals who suffered
misfortunes, Victoria was capable of astonishing blindness when it
came to the aggregate of her people. In 1873, with the economy suffering a disastrous downturn and unemployment on the rise, with
some two-thirds of English men and women badly off and many tens
of thousands destitute, it would never have occurred to the queen to
throw the weight of her prestige and influence behind a campaign to
alleviate human misery.

To be sure, when a giant procession of poor matchmakers
marched on Parliament to protest the imposition of a match tax,
Victoria told Gladstone that she regretted the imposition of the tax,
as it would affect "a vast number of the very poorest people and little children, especially in London."[3] And in fact the match tax was
abandoned. Yet although she must have known—for she read the
newspapers and kept herself well informed—that by one estimate
there were thirty thousand homeless young children sleeping on the
London streets, winter and summer, that workers in the white lead
factories and steel mills and ironworks were grossly underpaid and
largely unprotected from industrial hazards, that all employment
was insecure and life expectancy low, these evils never roused her to
indignation as did, say, the evils of vivisection or the difficulty of getting perfumed violets or the rise of ritualism and what she referred
to as "the imminent fall of the Church of England."

Victoria took it as an article of faith, as did a great many of her contemporaries, that poverty, disease, and suffering were unfortunate but
unavoidable, and that given time, and the inevitable workings of
progress, they would diminish, if not disappear entirely. Beyond this
she did not examine the issue. That Conservatives, led by Disraeli, and
Liberals, led by Gladstone, were having to come to grips with social issues and were in fact realigning their social philosophies was some-

thing she observed but did not truly understand; to judge from her letters and journal, the powerful tides of social change came only fleet-
ingly within her notice.

To Victoria's deep satisfaction, the elections of February 1874 returned a substantial Conservative majority and Gladstone, who the
queen believed had "contrived to alienate and frighten the country,"
resigned. Disraeli now became Prime Minister again, and promptly
launched an extensive campaign of legislation aimed at improving
working-class lives. Within a relatively short time the new Conservative government had achieved passage of acts to protect women and
children working in factories, to safeguard public health, to regulate
the sale of food and drugs—both of which were often sold in adulter-
ated form, especially in poorer neighborhoods—and to build better
housing for the working poor.

But important as these achievements were, it was in the field of
foreign affairs that Disraeli gave his sovereign most satisfaction.

Unlike Gladstone's Liberals, who took a narrowly pragmatic view
of international affairs and declined to interfere in European quarrels,
Disraeli envisioned, and promoted, the enhancement of Britain's role
abroad. Disraeli's grand aim was timely, for by the early 1870s Britain
was losing ground economically, and losing prestige militarily. Both the
newly federated Germany and the United States threatened to over-
take Britain not only in the production of coal and steel and manufactured goods but in the more problematic arena of military supremacy.
(A decade earlier, during the American Civil War, Palmerston had
warned Victoria that, once the war ended, the United States might
well use her immense army to attack England.) Germany had given
ample demonstrations of her formidable military strength, and Victoria was horrified by Bismarck's aggression and by his callous declaration that territorial gain was well worth the expenditure of thousands
of lives.

Though she commanded a vast empire, Britain did not habitually
defend it aggressively or expand it enthusiastically. When Disraeli
came to power in 1874, India and Africa were largely neglected, despite the recent building of the Suez Canal, which made the former
much more readily accessible, and when new territories (such as Fiji
and other islands in the Pacific) came into the possession of the
crown, they came as gifts, or as the unlooked-for benefits of treaty
making. But Britain's manufacturers, if not her politicians, were well

aware that, with prices dropping and exports declining, the expansion of the empire represented a potential for expanded trade. And the public at large, excited by the empire and proud of Britain's might, were eager for expansion and even world domination.

A new mood prevailed after 1874, a mood of fervent interest in exotic lands accompanied by a restless, prowling expansionism, even belligerence, fed by the press and stimulated by government policies abroad.

"I contend," declared Cecil Rhodes, avid to expand British rule over all southern Africa, "that we are the first race in the world, and that the more of the world we inhabit, the better it is for the human race."[4] Most of Victoria's subjects agreed with this breathtaking pronouncement, convinced as they were that the benefits of Christianity, improved hygiene and British-made goods were self-evident to all right-minded people.

Only a few years before Rhodes made his ringing declaration they had followed with attentive curiosity the long trek of Henry Morton Stanley across Africa in his search for the "lost" missionary David Livingstone, experiencing at second hand the heat, the rains, the fevers and the encounters with exotic tribes. They had rejoiced when at last, against all odds, Stanley found the aged missionary, so debilitated he was little more than a "ruckle of bones," and spoke the famous words, "Dr. Livingstone, I presume." Stanley's seven-hundred-page account of his discovery of Livingstone was eagerly bought and eagerly read by the same public that had enjoyed the queen's Highlands book, and that would soon buy up everything they could find on the Ashanti War and its hero, Sir Garnet Wolseley.[5]

Sir Garnet, at forty the youngest general in the British army, subdued the Ashanti with his army of regulars from the Black Watch and Rifle Brigade, undaunted by the accoutrements of tropical warfare—cholera belts, veils to keep off the savage mosquitoes, respirators to prevent faintness from the heat. So well did he complete his assignment that the queen herself reviewed his army in Windsor Great Park, and pinned on his breast the decoration of Grand Commander of the Order of St. Michael and St. George. The phrase "all Sir Garnet!" passed at once into popular use, a synonym for anything put into ideal shape with dispatch and aplomb.

It was but a short step from rejoicing over a British victory to envisaging many British victories all over the globe, and the glory that they would bring. Zealous for conquest, ardent to back British arms, Victoria's subjects began to welcome, nay to invite, shows of force. It was as if, in their newfound access of swaggering confidence, they had forgotten entirely the wretchedness and misery of war, and set aside all humanitarian concerns in the pursuit of preeminence.

Thus when in 1875 Disraeli managed to purchase from the debt-ridden Khedive of Egypt slightly less than half the outstanding shares in the Suez Canal, the public cheered and the queen lauded the Prime Minister's financial coup (achieved with the aid of the Baron Lionel de Rothschild) as "an immense thing." And when, in the following year, a somewhat reluctant Parliament conferred on Victoria the title Empress of India, the public lauded the change as only natural and the queen took delight in signing herself "V.R.I."—Victoria Regina et Imperatrix—whenever possible.

Victoria was captivated by India, that mysterious, unfathomable place where fabulously wealthy maharajas ruled, tigers stalked, cobras swayed and alien customs such as suttee—the burning alive of high-born wives when their husbands died—provoked a not altogether unpleasurable frisson of horror. After some hesitation, she allowed Bertie to make a State visit to the subcontinent in late 1875 and early 1876, where he charmed potentates and attended children's fetes, hunted quantities of game and (for his brush with death had not, alas, reformed him) enjoyed the company of a variety of women.

The multiple fascinations of India were exploited by the popular press, which recounted in great detail the ceremony at Delhi during which the queen-empress was proclaimed. Under vast spreading tents, and with the Indian army marshaled in full array, the Indian princes, glittering with jewels, came to pay homage to the absent Victoria. At the end of the long ceremony, the crowd acclaimed their empress as "Shah-in-Shah Padshah"—the Monarch of Monarchs. The press invariably reported splendid ceremonials, but did not neglect the full story of Indian life, which was often a chain of catastrophes. Only a few months after the proclamation of the empress, the Great Madras Famine captured popular attention. A terrible drought had destroyed the crops throughout large areas of southeast India, and half a million people were left to starve. Vivid pictures of near-naked, skeletal bodies, of dying children and dead animals, filled the *Illustrated London News*, a stark reminder of the burdens that went along with the benefits of empire.

The Monarch of Monarchs celebrated her newfound imperial status at a banquet at Windsor on January 1, 1877, her usual black gown buried under winking diamonds and huge uncut emeralds, enormous pearls and the shining Star of India. Her elevation was one of the few welcome events in a season of increasing worries. The nation was caught up in controversy.

Ever since the previous summer, when word had reached England of savage attacks by Turkish troops against Christian subjects of the Porte in Bulgaria, political opinion had been divided between those who favored supporting the sprawling, feeble Turkish Empire, corrupt as it was, and those who preferred to let it disintegrate—even though that would inevitably lead to Russian expansion westward. For Russia was swift to take advantage of any fissure in Turkish power, and when the victimized Bulgarian Christians appealed to St. Petersburg for aid, Alexander II was only too pleased to offer it.

The division of opinion was made particularly bitter by the personal feud between Disraeli and Gladstone, and by the queen's near loathing for the fanatically upright Liberal leader. Gladstone had in fact gone into retirement, but emerged once again into the limelight when the Turkish crisis arose, fulminating eloquently against the demonic forces of the sultan.

To Gladstone and others in opposition, the issue was simple: Turkey represented cruelty, inhumanity and moral evil, and must be swept from power. To subtler minds, such as Disraeli's, the tumult in Eastern Europe was an elaborate chess game in which, through careful use of diplomatic pressure and the threat represented by British military might, Russian ambition could be checked without recourse to war. To the queen, ever the soldier's daughter, Russia was a menacing bully, Britain the stalwart champion of right and honor; honor demanded that a duel to the death be fought, and without delay.

Thus when Russia declared war against Turkey in April of 1877 Gladstone was pleased, Disraeli thoughtful, and Victoria bellicose. When her Prime Minister seemed slow to respond, the queen bombarded him with messages encouraging him to act boldly against "these horrible, deceitful, cruel Russians" before they destroyed the Turkish army and seized Constantinople. Not since the days of the Crimean War had Victoria mounted such an urgent campaign to sway the prevailing government to adopt her views. Shaking off her nervous tremors and other physical complaints, she roused herself to compose memoranda—as Albert had once done—and sent them to Disraeli, along with twenty-page letters and frequent telegrams. Throughout the summer and autumn of 1877, as Russian armies overpowered the forces of the Porte, Victoria besieged her Prime Minister, and subjected the pacific Colonial Secretary Lord Carnarvon to impassioned harangues.

"I pitched into him," she told Vicky of one overheated conversation with Carnarvon, "with a vehemence and indignation—which was at any rate inspired by the British Lion—and he remained shrinking but still craven-hearted! . . . I own I never spoke with such vehemence as I did last night."[6]

Carnarvon shrank visibly under the queen's withering tirades, and Disraeli, who had been suffering for months from severe gout, asthma, and bronchitis, and was in fact considering resigning because of his continual ill health, had to struggle to retain his good humor and his customary gallantry when the queen blew upon him her wintry blasts. She gained an exiguous victory when Disraeli wrung from his Cabinet a grudging agreement that should Russia succeed in taking Constantinople, Britain would declare war. But by the end of the year she was beside herself with frustration. She fulminated. She hectored. More than once she threatened to abdicate. Lady Salisbury, wife of the Indian Secretary, wrote in December of 1877 that the queen "had lost control of herself," so agitated was she in badgering her ministers and exhorting them to go to war. She was almost ready to enter the fray herself. "Oh, if the Queen were a man," Victoria burst out, "she would like to go and give those horrid Russians . . . such a beating!"[7]

Gladstone declared that his sovereign's constant harassment of her ministers was an affront to the constitution, and he ridiculed her recently assumed title of Empress as "theatrical bombast and folly." He accused her of being wrongheaded—but she accused him of worse. He was fanatical, dictatorial, a "half-mad firebrand"—and a victim of depraved impulses besides. Word had reached Victoria, quite possibly from Disraeli, that Gladstone had an unsavory inclination to seek out and redeem prostitutes—or at least, to invite them to redemption, and to a less unhealthy, dangerous and self-destructive way of life. Clearly there was something unwholesome about such a desire, laudable though its goal might be; normal men did not accost prostitutes in the streets unless they wanted to patronize them. Victoria's instincts told her that something was disturbingly wrong, and her instincts were sound. Though she was unaware of it, in fact Gladstone was a masochist who entered into "strange and humbling acts" with the prostitutes he encountered and, afterward, flagellated himself. [8]

A break seemed to come in the war tensions when Russia agreed to a truce at the end of January, 1878, but the agreement did not hold; it would be six months before a fully satisfactory peace could be made. By then, all parties involved in the conflict were weary and Disraeli, who went to Berlin to negotiate at an international conference on Britain's behalf, was not only weary but very ill. Still, he dominated the peace conference, and on his triumphant return to England Victoria offered him the Order of the Garter and a dukedom. (He had been created Earl of Beaconsfield two years earlier.) At last, Russia had been brought to heel, and the aged Prime Minister had been the one to accomplish it. The queen was elated. Disraeli was gratified. Gladstone was furious.

During the Russo-Turkish War an incident had occurred that embittered Victoria toward her ever troublesome second son. Affie was in command of a British warship, and went with the fleet to lie off Constantinople as a deterrent to Russian aggression. His personal sympathies were divided, however, for four years earlier he had married the only daughter of Emperor Alexander II. Thus while at his post he invited the aide-de-camp of the Russian Commander-in-Chief to dine aboard his vessel—a gesture of conciliation, even perhaps of solidarity, with the Russian enemy.

Red-faced with anger when she heard of this outrageous breach of loyalty, Victoria demanded that her son receive an official reprimand. He in turn threatened to insist that a court of inquiry be convened to judge him. Victoria saw Affie's attitude as defiance, and grew stony toward him. In the end, it fell to Disraeli to mollify her—indeed, he and Brown were the only ones who could—and lead her gently to take a less harsh stand against her son. Affie had shown questionable judgment, but had not broken any law or betrayed any secrets; although the queen complained that he was "cold and remote," and generally disliked, she had to do her best to accept the fact that at thirty-four, and with three children of his own, he was his own master.

Affie's intractability confirmed Victoria's frequently stated belief that children generally grow up to do precisely the opposite of what their parents want them to do, and that because of this "as a rule children are a bitter disappointment."[9] Her own children, the oldest of them now middle-aged, the youngest in their twenties, continued to present her with challenges. Vicky was an admirable woman in many ways, but the dynastic tie between the British and German ruling families had become thorny with Bismarck's rise to power. Bertie, bald and paunchy, was and would always be a third-rate heir to the throne. (Victoria confided to Vicky that she often prayed that Bertie would not live to survive her.[10]) He and Alix were not raising their children with proper care or attention, and this added to the queen's many burdensome concerns.

Alice, complex, introspective and self-sacrificing, caused her mother difficulties by being openly jealous of Lenchen because the latter's husband Christian had a large state income while she and Louis were relatively poor; Alice had also been known to give offense to the servants during her stays at Windsor with her large family. (She also gave offense to her mother by breast-feeding her children; such "disgusting details" of nursery life ought to be left to a wet nurse who was "more like an animal" than highborn women were, Victoria thought.)

Lenchen, at times touchy and easily insulted, and spoiled by her husband, had prolonged periods of ill health that worried Victoria, and was at times quite difficult to live with. Victoria had expected that Lenchen, living nearby first at Frogmore and later at Cumberland Lodge, would be constantly available as a companion; instead she and Christian kept to themselves, a reminder to the queen that loneliness was the inevitable accompaniment of advancing age.

Louise, now thirty years old, had in Victoria's words "a very marked character," and it was becoming more marked all the time. Artistically gifted but unhappy and acidulated, Louise stirred up trouble wherever she was, offending her in-laws, making spiteful remarks, failing to develop warm relations with anyone. Others saw her as ill-natured and dangerously manipulative, and even Victoria, who praised her beauty and talent, shied away from confiding in her.

Arthur, always Victoria's favorite child and the least troublesome, was contentedly and successfully pursuing a military career, yet even Arthur was not a model son in every respect. While he avoided the evils of womanizing, he annoyed Victoria by becoming engaged to a less than satisfactory princess. Louise Margaret, daughter of Fritz's loud, blustering cousin Prince Fritz Carl of Prussia, was a plain young woman with coarse features and broken teeth. Her parents were unpleasant and lived apart from each other, a situation that verged on scandal, and Victoria wanted to avoid associating her family with scandal at all costs. It pained her to see her most promising son throw himself away on an inferior match, and probably she was a bit jealous of Louise.

Leopold, Victoria's child of anxiety, had given her more worry than all the other children put together. That he had survived into adulthood was a miracle, for he had been on the point of death a dozen times and had attacks of internal bleeding every two or three months. For long periods of time he was a complete invalid, lying on a bed or couch with painful swelling in his joints and occasional hemorrhages.

Understandably, Leopold was both spoiled and frustrated; his agile mind raced, he longed to live life to the full and chafed under the physical restrictions his illness imposed on him. Everyone agreed that, of the boys in the family, Leopold most resembled his father in his mental gifts, and he took a keen interest in politics. He studied at Oxford, though his formal education was often interrupted by prolonged convalescences, and at the age of twenty-five Victoria made him her secretary. Yet his state of health and his often obstreperous temperament nagged at her.

"Leopold really is a cause of sorrow and indignation," she told her friend Augusta of Prussia. He refused to do what his doctor and attendant told him to do, and would not take proper care to avoid injury. If told to sit quietly, he ran and jumped and became overexcited; if told to remain immobile, he tried to go for a walk. The queen, watching the constant tension between her unruly son and his guardians, lived in constant dread that he would injure himself once more, and that this time the injury might be fatal. "I am very indignant, I confess," she confided to Augusta, "and feel deeply the great ingratitude of this child of anxiety. One really cannot pity him. Forgive me for writing to you like this, but we are very cross with him! With only a little prudence he could lead quite a useful and happy life.[11]

In contrast to Leopold, Beatrice, at twenty-one, was her mother's delight and solace. She was, Victoria said, "like a sunbeam in the house," "a dove, an angel of peace who brings it wherever she goes and who is my greatest comfort."[12] Capable, sensitive, attractive and amiable, Beatrice seemed to disprove Victoria's often-stated contention that children inevitably disappoint their parents. When the queen sat down at the piano to play duets with her talented youngest daughter, or glanced admiringly at her across the dinner table, she felt pleased and relieved that at least one of her children was, for the time being, a source of unalloyed satisfaction.

It irked Victoria that no one seemed to realize what a time-consuming encumbrance it was to her to be both head of a large and growing family and reigning sovereign. "The very large family with their increasing families and interests is an immense difficulty," she told Vicky, "and I must add burden for me."[13] Her children seemed to be multiplying "like the rabbits in Windsor Park." By 1878 she had twenty-seven surviving grandchildren, and a great-grandchild, the daughter of Vicky's daughter Charlotte, was on the way. (Victoria's first great-grandchild would be born in May of 1879 and called Feodora, after Victoria's late half sister.)

There were so many births, so many childbed emergencies to worry over, so many small garments to knit and quilts to sew—it was no wonder Victoria stayed up late and complained of never getting enough rest. Each grandson had to have the name Albert as one of his Christian names, each granddaughter had to bear the name Victoria along with her other names. ("I lay great stress on this," Victoria told her children.) Once past the hazards attendant upon birth and infancy, each grandchild had to be properly raised and educated, properly groomed for his or her station in life, suitably married, and eventually guided through the perils of parenthood. To the best of her ability, the queen attempted to oversee the development of each of her grandchildren, giving freely of her advice and criticism. But this immense task wearied her, and often led to discouragement, for her grandchildren were far from perfect.

In Victoria's view, Bertie's sons were puny and his daughters plain. Vicky's son Henry was "ugly," her daughter Victoria shy; her son Waldemar frightened his royal grandma by bringing a pet crocodile into the palace and her oldest son Willy, with his withered arm, crooked neck, weak legs and wandering left eye, was constantly having to receive bizarre and worrisome medical treatments.[14] When Vicky's beloved two-year-old son Sigismund died suddenly of meningitis, Victoria mourned with her daughter, and when Alice lost her son Frederick to the dread "bleeding disease" at the age of six, the queen was deeply distressed.

But if there were burdens associated with being a grandparent, there were also blessings. Windsor, Osborne and Balmoral were at times crowded with grandchildren, they swarmed around their short, stout grandma with fearless affection, and she called them "dear little things" and hugged them to her. She liked them to be comfortable with her, she made jokes with them and fed them fondant cookies and chocolate sponge cake and laughed what one of them remembered later as her "wonderful laugh." And if at times a wistful look came into her fading blue eyes, and a shadow seemed to fall across her face, the moment passed quickly, and the children did not notice. She wished—how she wished!—that Albert had lived to see their grandchildren grow up, and the next generation begin. But she was reconciled to her widowhood, and what had once been an acute pain was now a dull, nostalgic ache and a cluster of cherished memories.

Every December, as the anniversary of Albert's death approached, Victoria prepared herself to honor his memory, and to give thanks for Bertie's recovery from typhoid. In December of 1878, however, she was again anxious, for telegrams from Hesse informed her that Alice, having lost her baby daughter May to diphtheria, was severely ill with the disease herself. "Nervous and shaken," Victoria waited for more news, superstitious about the approach of the significant day December 14, recalling how it had been Alice, seventeen years earlier, who had watched untiringly by Albert's bedside in his last illness and helped to lay him to rest.

On December 13 more telegrams arrived from Darmstadt. Alice was having great difficulty breathing. Victoria, terribly upset, and feeling helpless with her beloved daughter so far away, clung to Beatrice, then walked with her to the Mausoleum to say her prayers beside Albert's tomb. The remainder of the day was an agony. No matter how hard she tried, Victoria couldn't concentrate on anything. Lenchen and Beatrice remained with her, the three of them dreading the imminent arrival of the worst news of all.

Somehow Victoria got to sleep that night, but woke often, "constantly seeing darling Alice before me," as she wrote in her journal later. When morning came, she awoke to face the "terrible day," filled with dread, and at midmorning the fateful news arrived. Alice had died at seven-thirty that morning.

"It was too awful! I had so hoped against hope." Victoria wept for her "dear, talented, distinguished, tender-hearted, noble-minded sweet child," and embraced her weeping daughters, and steeled herself for the sad task of telling Bertie that his favorite sister was no more.

When Disraeli had an audience with the queen a few days later, he found her saddened, but far from incapacitated by her grief. She was calm and pleasant, and even amusing at times. She did not try to avoid talking about Alice's death, but "treated it naturally" discussing the details without breaking down. She seemed to embrace the macabre coincidence that Alice and Albert should have died on the same day as a mystery beyond human explanation, and told the Prime Minister that "if she had been able to choose a day for anything so sad, she would have preferred that it should have been on the anniversary of her greatest sorrow."[15]

Victoria's capacity for endurance had deepened. She was no longer crushed by sorrow, she bore it with dignity, though as she reached the end of her fifties she admitted that she had lost some of her "elasticity." Alice's death brought new responsibilities, for her five surviving children would now, to a degree, look to their grandmother to take their mother's place.

Less than a month after their mother's death the Hesse children, ranging in age from fifteen to six, arrived at Windsor, for a stay of two months. Victoria comforted them and spent time with each one, satisfying herself that their educational progress was acceptable and their manners polite. She conferred with their English governess, and arranged for detailed reports to be sent to her from time to time once the children returned to Hesse. For the time being, Lenchen would become their surrogate mother, but Victoria considered marrying Beatrice to Alice's widower Louis—until she remembered that, under British law, such a marriage was prohibited.[16]

In the spring of 1879, a tall granite cross was erected "to the dear memory of Alice, Grand Duchess of Hesse, Princess of Great Britain and Ireland . . . by her sorrowing mother Queen Victoria." It was a spare memorial, lacking the Gothic flourishes and Italianate ornamentation characteristic of the age, but it seemed appropriate to mark Alice's thirty-five years. Victoria, who had been so proud of having nine children, now had only eight. And she would forever couple Alice with Albert in her memory, imagining them together in "another better world," as she put it, where they awaited her.

Chapter 20

VICTORIA LOVED TO TRAVEL. Few things delighted her more than to drive along the roads of Switzerland or Italy in her carriage, with Beatrice and one of her ladies-in-waiting beside her, taking careful note of the picturesque vistas, the quaint villages they passed through, the animals and oddly dressed people—all the things that made the place different from England. Often she stopped to sketch what she saw, with Brown and several members of the local police to keep away the gawkers who turned out to stare at her.

They knew who she was, of course; she traveled incognito but with such an immense suite of servants and an immense number of bags—and her bed, which went with her everywhere—that her true identity was obvious. Even if her entourage had not given her away, her small, stout body, black gown and world-famous profile would have, for by the 1880s Queen Victoria's image was on mustard jars and tea packets, billboards and postage stamps, not to mention newspapers, magazines and annuals all over her far-flung empire. She was the "Mother of Europe," who had been on the throne for the better part of five decades; everyone knew her, or knew of her.

In fact it pleased Victoria that when she drove through the Italian countryside the children ran alongside her carriage, pointing at her and shouting "La Regina d'Inghilterra!" even though Brown barked at them and tried to shoo them away. Brown in his kilt, sporran and knee socks made the children laugh, despite his frowns. He disliked foreigners, and foreign places, but where the queen went, he dutifully followed, quenching his disgruntlement with whisky.

Italy, Switzerland, later on southern France, even Spain beckoned to Victoria in her later years. She went abroad every year in the spring for six weeks, then to Balmoral from late April until June or July, avoiding the London Season. When abroad, she would rent an entire hotel, or arrange for a local villa to be refurbished to accommodate her traveling party. Special trains transported her from one destination to another on the Continent; within Britain the North-Western Railway assigned her a train with her own private railway car. Wood-paneled and with gilt brass metalwork, the royal railway car had chairs, desk and other furnishings of yellow satinwood with blue silk upholstery, a bedroom with two small brass beds and—luxury of luxuries—a blue and gold water closet.[1]

When she traveled, Victoria was shielded, as much as possible, from inconveniences and discomforts, and she liked to have familiar people and familiar objects around her. At Windsor, Osborne and Balmoral too she preferred well-known faces and things: her coachman Bourner who had been with her from 1845, her dresser Emilie Dittweiler whose service to her was in its third decade, the many pages and grooms, gardeners and maids with whom she had been comfortable for years.

The queen liked an unvarying routine. After breakfast, she worked for several hours, then after luncheon, she went for a drive, returning to more work before a late supper at nine-fifteen in the evening. As Victoria was a hasty eater (even as a girl she had "gobbled her food"), supper was timed to last exactly half an hour, with servants in knee breeches bringing soup, fish, cold sirloin of beef, sweet and dessert courses in rapid succession. Any dinner guest who had not finished his or her course had the plate swept away, and slow eaters such as Gladstone found dining with the queen an extremely vexing procedure. After dinner the guests were expected to play whist, that relic of Georgian times, and as no one under the age of sixty remembered how to play, the wagering was less than spirited.[2]

There was a staleness at Victoria's court that her younger servants and officials found oppressive. To step across the threshold of Windsor or Osborne was to step back a generation, into a musty world of doddering retainers and antique furnishings that could never be moved by order of the queen. A stuffy obsolescence reigned, and Victoria did her best to perpetuate it by rejecting the by-products of technological change. She preferred candlelight to electric light, handwritten documents to typewritten ones, though Remington typewriters were available from 1876; Edison's phonograph was not to be found among the palace furnishings, and when Alexander Graham Bell came to Osborne to demonstrate his telephone, she held the instrument to her ear and declared that the sound was "rather faint." Telephones were never to become welcome fixtures of Victoria's life, though she did eventually have two phones installed at Buckingham Palace for her guests to use in ordering their carriages.

It was not that these symptoms of modernity were abhorrent, they were merely unnecessary. The old ways worked perfectly well, and were comforting besides. The queen was content with them, and saw no reason to change.

One change she could not prevent, however. While she herself strode resolutely on into her seventh decade, others around her were less hardy. Disraeli, who left office in the spring of 1880, died a year later, worn out and too weak to recover from an attack of severe bronchitis. At the end he was too weary, even, to receive the favor of a royal visit, though his wit never deserted him. ("Better not," he remarked when he learned the queen wanted to pay her respects in person. "She would only ask me to take a message to Albert.") He did request, however, that a photograph of Victoria be buried with him.

Victoria's next loss was much more painful. John Brown caught cold and quickly sank into his fatal illness, dying late in March of 1883. Victoria, who was recuperating from a bad fall and was unable to walk, was "utterly crushed" by the terrible news. She likened the trauma of Brown's death to the shock she had received when Albert died—a comparison her advisers thought unfortunate, considering the old scandal that her relationship with her Highland servant was more than platonic. Victoria had always assumed that Brown would outlive her, and indeed she had taken comfort from imagining that, when she was on her deathbed, Brown would watch over her and, after her death, he would lift her lifeless body into its coffin.[3] That he should predecease her added confusion to her grief. "Every link has been shaken and torn," she told her secretary Ponsonby. To Vicky she confided that "the shock—the blow, the blank, the constant missing at every turn of the one strong, powerful reliable arm and head almost stunned me and I am truly overwhelmed."[4]

The loss of Brown overshadowed Victoria's life for many months. She sought seclusion, in order to do battle with the nervous attacks that invariably followed a major loss. She worked at her new manuscript, another account of her life in the Highlands in the years since Albert's death. She worked at putting together yet another volume, a memoir of Brown, and commissioned memorial busts, commemorative tie-pins with Brown's portrait encircled in diamonds, and a bronze statue of the handsome Highlander to be placed at Balmoral. She fought to conquer the "anguish that overcame her like a wave," whenever she remembered that her friend and protector was gone forever, but her fight was arduous. Physically, her recovery was very slow; her leg injury hung on and on, forcing her to use a wheeled chair. Emotionally, she fought depression.

"Every thing upsets me now," the queen wrote to her granddaughter Victoria, the oldest of Alice's children. "A heavy cloud overhangs every thing." Even if Victoria's spirits had been buoyant she might well have had occasion to worry, for in 1883 the government seemed at times as unsteady as the queen's shaky legs. Irish terrorists, aggrieved by Parliament's unwillingness to grant Home Rule, blew up the Local Government Office in London sending shards of stone and splinters of glass everywhere. The shock waves made the walls of Buckingham Palace tremble. An explosive device was found at the offices of The Times as well, but it failed to detonate, and shortly afterward an entire "factory" manufacturing nitroglycerin was unearthed by the police.

"We are engaged," one government official announced, "in a moral struggle with an army of assassins."[5] In Ireland, "assassination societies" flourished. Plots and rumors of plots were rampant, and though in time some of the plotters were caught and convicted, there always seemed to be more to take their place. Victoria was the victim of yet another assassination attempt in 1882, when a would-be murderer attacked her in her carriage. (Once again, she was spared harm; two Eton boys rushed forward to beat the assailant into submission with their umbrellas.)

Wars and skirmishes in various parts of the empire caused concern and grief, and invariably pitted the queen against Gladstone, who had become Prime Minister once again in 1880.

With his overbearing manner, his wrongheaded opinions—as the queen believed them to be—and his disregard for her views and authority, Gladstone was Victoria's nemesis. Too deaf to hear any voices raised against him, and too full of conviction to care, the aged Prime Minister was the bane of Victoria's existence. In later years Victoria would recall that Gladstone caused her "more pain, anxiety and trouble" than any of her previous Prime Ministers put together.[6]

The queen was convinced that Gladstone was not a patriot but a party man. He did not "have the honor and power of his country strongly at heart." He had wild-eyed republicans in his government, people such as Joseph Chamberlain and Charles Dilke who openly advocated abolition of the monarchy and attacked the aristocracy as sybaritic parasites (an opinion with which the queen rather agreed) and called for an end to the House of Lords. He stormed and raved like a madman—indeed Victoria privately believed him to be mad— and habitually ignored her authority, failing to ask her advice or take counsel with her before making important decisions.

Gladstone, for his part, was equally vexed with his sovereign, and not only because they differed politically. He found her infuriatingly manipulative. He heard via palace gossip that she hated him. He knew that she, like many others, was repelled by his midnight expeditions to London's disreputable districts. Most of all, he was frustrated by her personality, that unique mix of little-girl stubbornness, toughness and petulance combined with shrewd common sense born of long experience in governing.

Now imperious, now with an edge of spite, now surprisingly insightful, Victoria was a baffling enigma to her Prime Minister. Like most men of his time, Gladstone expected women to be enigmatic— and, on the whole, inconsequential except when it came to matters of the heart and womb—but he could not afford to dismiss Victoria, nor could he find a way to deal comfortably with her.

As Earl Granville, Gladstone's Foreign Secretary, wrote in 1882, "it was impossible to treat the Queen as a great statesman because she was such a child, but it was equally impossible to treat her as a child because she had the aperçus of a great statesman in some things." (Victoria, for her part, considered Granville "a very weak reed to lean upon."[7])

They battled on, queen and Prime Minister, like two great warships destined for collision. Their ultimate conflict was to come in the struggle over Egypt and the Sudan.

As Britain's empire grew larger, so did the potential for hostilities around the globe. In 1882 a revolt in Egypt against the authority of the ruling khedive—a puppet of the British and French—led to the dispatching of Sir Garnet Wolseley to the scene; in what the London papers called "a great and decisive battle" at Tell el-Kebir Sir Garnet led fifteen thousand troops against a much larger Egyptian rebel force and went on to capture Cairo.

All England rejoiced, and no one more than the queen, whose favorite son Arthur was in Sir Garnet's army and, on his return from Egypt, brought his mother a carpet taken from the tent of the defeated enemy. She proudly stood on it as she pinned medals on the valiant veterans of the brief but glorious campaign.

The following year, however, the khedive's tottering authority was again threatened, this time in the Sudan, where a charismatic religious leader calling himself the "Expected One," or Mahdi, defied both the Egyptian ruler and the foreign troops that were propping him up. Late in 1883 Britishers were horrified to read of the massacre of ten thousand Egyptian troops loyal to the khedive under the command of General Hicks, who died along with his men. The Mahdi's hordes, having overrun Hicks and his army, were poised to overrun Egypt.

Victoria demanded that Gladstone send a rescue force to protect British interests in the Sudan, but the Prime Minister and his Cabinet had other ideas. Only the garrisons would be protected, he announced—in particular the garrison at Khartoum. In the new year 1884 the newspapers brought word of another terrible military disaster, the slaughter of still another loyal army attempting to relieve the garrison of Tokar. Stories of brutality inflamed the public—of panicked Egyptian soldiers throwing away their rifles, flinging themselves on the ground and screaming for mercy, of the Mahdi's fierce spearmen executing every loyal soldier they saw, of "wild Arabs, their long hair streaming behind them," darting here and there, hacking and thrusting with their spears, reducing all to gory confusion.

It was too much for British pride to bear. Victoria wrote and telegraphed again and again to Gladstone and his colleagues, demanding that help be sent—and soon. Finally, late in January, the Cabinet decided to send General Charles George Gordon, a veteran of colonial warfare with a penchant for self-aggrandizement and a mystical bent, to the Sudan to observe the situation there in preparation for evacuating all the British troops. It was a popular move, if an ill-calculated one; Gordon was cheered lustily by happy crowds as he boarded his ship. He was expected to be another Sir Garnet, who would wave his wand, subdue the wild Arabs and restore appropriate British preeminence.

By mid-March Gordon had managed to reach Khartoum, but instead of beginning preparations to lead the British troops safely out of the turbulent region, Gordon—"that unrivalled master of Oriental diplomacy," as the press called him—decided to stay on. Almost immediately the enemy cut the telegraph wires, making it impossible for any message to reach Gordon. His safety, and the safety of all the colonial soldiers, was now presumed to be in peril.

While her worries about Gordon increased, Victoria was distracted by the reception of her second book, *More Leaves From the Journal of a Life in the Highlands*. This new book, less skillfully edited than the queen's first collection of journal entries, and overburdened with references to the late Prince Consort, did not reach as large or as enthusiastic an audience as its predecessor. To the queen's younger subjects, the book's charms seemed stale, and to her children, especially Bertie and Vicky, it was an embarrassment. To her critics, on the other hand, it was a godsend; nothing was easier to lampoon than the queen's style, with its artless candor, and her many blithe, innocent references to John Brown scattered throughout the book provided fodder for lampoons. One such lampoon, *John Brown's Legs, or Leaves from a Journal in the Lowlands*, caused endless chagrin.

It was characteristic of Victoria that she was oblivious to the opportunity her book offered for mockery, and to the damage such mockery could cause. Guileless honesty was her watchword; until harshly reminded otherwise, she made the assumption that the world would take her honesty at face value, and respect it.

But those around her knew otherwise. When Victoria circulated her memoir of Brown, a memoir that contained, according to Henry Ponsonby, a record of her "innermost and most sacred feelings," her advisers saw disaster looming.[8] It was clear to them that Victoria must be prevented from publishing—even privately, and for a limited circulation—her all-too-candid outpourings of sentiment for Brown. What she saw as a record of a deep and affectionate friendship would, to others, seem mawkish and ill judged at best and at worst, pitiably obsessional, and possibly immoral. No objective person, they believed, could read the queen's memoir of Brown without experiencing a shudder of distaste.

It was a delicate situation, but Ponsonby, the queen's friend Dr. Lees of Edinburgh and others persuaded her, with great tact, to defer publication of her memoir of Brown, until eventually it became clear to her that what they really meant was that she should never publish it at all. She was angry and offended, but her common sense prevailed. The memoir never saw publication.

While the queen was still grieving for Brown, and mourning the loss of his constant companionship, another emotional blow left her reeling. Her son Leopold died suddenly, the victim of a brain hemorrhage. He was not quite thirty-one.

"I am profoundly shattered and crushed," Victoria wrote to her aging friend Augusta of Prussia. She had always known that Leopold could die at any time, yet his loss was a grievous one, occurring as it did on the anniversary of Brown's death. Moreover, Leopold left behind a pregnant widow and a daughter—more relatives for the queen to feel protective of.

More than ever before, Victoria was feeling her age. "I am a poor desolate old woman," she confided to her journal, "and my cup of sorrow overflows! Oh! God, in his mercy, spare my other dear children!"[9] She told Dr. Lees, with her customary overstatement, that all happiness was at an end for her and that her life was henceforth to be one of sorrow. The most she could hope for was to occasionally give pleasure to others.

But in fact neither her physical infirmities nor her darkened mental outlook kept her from playing a skillful role in resolving the next crisis faced by the government. Gladstone's Liberals had passed a Reform Bill in the Commons that extended the franchise to include most farm laborers and virtually all property-owning city-dwellers. But the Bill failed to pass in the House of Lords, and the result was that the more radical wing of Gladstone's party began to agitate to restrict the power of the Lords or abolish it altogether. Riots, wild speeches, popular clamor against the Lords were the inevitable result, and the queen, convinced that the Lords, with its Conservative majority, was a necessary counterweight to excesses on the left, threw her energies into bringing about a compromise.

That she still had influence with Disraeli's party, and with its current leader Robert Cecil, Marquess of Salisbury, was soon shown. It took her months of patient effort, but in the end, by the fall of 1884, she was able to persuade the more moderate Conservatives in the Lords to accept a somewhat modified version of the Reform Bill.

She did not have long to savor this triumph, however. The situation in the Sudan, where General Gordon had been besieged for months in Khartoum by the forces of the Mahdi, reached a fearful crisis early in 1885. Gordon sent an urgent plea for military assistance, unaware that Sir Garnet Wolseley was already on his way up the Nile with a rescue force of ten thousand men. Wolseley's progress was aggravatingly slow, however, and he did not reach Khartoum until the end of January—by which time the enemy had swarmed into the town and overwhelmed the half-starved garrison, massacring every British soldier, including Gordon.

Horrified, Victoria blamed Gladstone and his government for shedding Gordon's "innocent, noble, heroic blood."[10] She sent the Prime Minister a caustic telegram criticizing him sharply for his callous neglect of Gordon, and complained that the Liberals were ruining Britain's reputation. Thanks to their shameful conduct of the Sudan affair, it looked to the rest of the world as though Britain had been "foiled by savages."[11] "We are becoming the laughing-stock of the world!" the queen exclaimed, privately lamenting the loss of Disraeli and wishing that he and the Conservatives were still in power.

Her sorrow over the death of Gordon, and her anger at Gladstone made Victoria ill. She felt the pain of recent events "dreadfully," she told Ponsonby. She sat in her armchair, "feeling very weak and wretched," with a high temperature, chills and a bad cough, while Beatrice read to her from a book of prayers.[12] It was all too much to bear, the sorrows, old and recent, the political turmoil, the deaths of loved ones, the constant threats from the hostile world. (Only a few days before news of Gordon's death reached the palace, two terrorist bombs had exploded in Whitehall, and it was feared that more bombs had been planted.[13])

Victoria would soon be sixty-six, and even though she still had bursts of physical activity—she had recently surprised and pleased herself by riding a tricycle around the grounds at Osborne, elated at the exercise—she was losing ground physically. Her teeth hurt, it was harder and harder for her to read documents and her hand had grown so shaky it was difficult for her to sketch or to hold a paintbrush. She walked with a cane, but preferred to be pushed in a wheeled chair, and the consequent loss of exercise increased her already prodigious girth. An Englishman who glimpsed her in 1884 remarked that she was "almost as broad as she was long."

Age had been unkind to her plain face. Her eyebrows now permanently slanted downward, giving her a cross look, her nose was larger and redder, the nostrils prominent and unattractive. In repose, her downturned mouth conveyed sadness and resignation, while her eyes, puffy and heavy-lidded, held hauteur, dissatisfaction, and loss. Bravely she looked at herself in the mirror and pronounced herself ugly.

Yet there was a rare beauty in her imperious, self-willed face—not the beauty of unlined youth, or of radiant innocence, or the more mature beauty born of knowing confidence, but a different order of loveliness altogether. It was the beauty of restrained power, disciplined passion, of a governed self. It was, in the words of Tennyson, the stark and awesome beauty of one who stood "so alone on that terrible height," ruler of half the world, yet always, ultimately, on her own.

Chapter 21

B EFORE THE FIRST PINK flush of dawn on the morning of June 21, 1887, troops were assembling on the grounds of Buckingham Palace and in the adjacent streets, the clopping of cavalry horses and the scraping of carriage wheels creating a ceaseless din. By six o'clock, bands were playing and soldiers taking their positions for the great parade that would mark the Queen's Jubilee, the fiftieth anniversary of her accession.

Half a million people had come to London to witness the events of this day, and many of them had spent the entire previous night in the street, in order to be in position to have a good view of the queen's carriage as it made its way from the palace to Westminster Abbey later that morning.

All along the parade route police scrutinized the crowds, watchful for foreign-looking faces, sullen expressions, any evidence of dark intent; the queen had escaped harm at the hands of assassins many times, but on this day she would ride in an open landau, with no protection but her mounted military escort, and there must be no violent incidents.

Fortunately the morning dawned bright and fair, and the sun was warm on the spectators, heightening their already jubilant mood. Her little Majesty would soon be riding past them, the quaint old lady who had ruled for half a century, whose authority reverberated around the globe, who had been their beloved sovereign since before most of them could remember. They began cheering long before the procession got under way, and in the palace, in the Chinese Room, where the queen was having breakfast with Beatrice and Arthur, Victoria heard their cheers and smiled.

She remembered only too well the June 21 of 1837, the day she had had to dress up and be escorted to St. James's Palace for her formal proclamation, a girl of eighteen then and full of nervousness and fears. Then, Melbourne had calmed and encouraged her. Now, Melbourne was long dead and she knew as much about governance as he had, or more.

Gifts and flowers had been arriving at the palace all morning, so many she could not possibly acknowledge them, along with numberless telegrams from all over the world. From the queen of Hawaii came an exotic feather lei. From other sovereigns came artworks, messages of congratulation, tokens of esteem. Victoria's household servants presented her with a magnificent vase, for which she thanked them—"As a work of art it is most beautiful both in design and workmanship," she told them, "and I cannot sufficiently thank you all for it; but I value it quite as much as a mark of devotion and attachment to my person, which is very precious to me."[1]

After breakfast the queen spent a few minutes with three of her youngest grandchildren, then went to dress. Though all the women at her court wore gowns made in the prevailing fashion, with tightly fitted bodices and skirts drawn up at the back with a bustle, Victoria still clung to the voluminous skirts and flounces of the 1860s, which made her look like an antique doll or, as one diplomat thought, "an old angel." Her black silk gown marked her endless mourning for Albert, but her white lace bonnet sparkled with diamond ornaments, there were pearls around her thick neck, and all her orders glittered on her chest. Among them was a portrait of Albert set in blue enamel ringed with pearls, which hung from a gold chain around her neck.

At eleven-thirty the spectators got their first glimpse of the royals. Bertie, wearing the scarlet tunic and tall plumed helmet of a Field Marshal, rode with Affie and Arthur at the head of the family, followed by Victoria's five sons-in-law, nine grandsons and many grand-sons-in-law. All were in uniform, and splendidly mounted.[2] Behind them, as escort to the queen's landau, rode twelve magnificently ac-coutred Indian officers, so handsome they put nearly all the other rid-ers to shame. Then came the queen, a tiny figure, except for her girth almost as small as a child, riding with Vicky and Alix in her open car-riage, smiling and nodding to the crowd, clearly delighted with the thunderous cheering that greeted her.

"There was such an extraordinary outburst of enthusiasm as I had hardly ever seen in London before," Victoria wrote in her journal later, "all the people seemed to be in such good humor." A sea of waving hands, a roaring of acclamation, a panorama of banners, bunting, flags and ribbons, and the warm sun shining down on everything: it was an epiphany, and Victoria savored every moment of it. In those emotion-ally charged moments, it seemed to the queen that "fifty years' hard work, anxiety, and care" were at last appreciated, and that her empa-thy with all her subjects, even the "sorrowing, suffering and humble" was being acknowledged.[3]

The clergy were waiting to receive the queen at the door of West-minster Abbey, dressed in the gold-trimmed velvet robes their prede-cessors had worn fifty years earlier, and escorted her the length of the Abbey's central aisle while solemn music played and a reverent hush fell over the immense crowd. All the Members of Parliament were present, together with the principal members of the government, the royal household, representatives of foreign states and dignitaries.

"I sat alone (oh! without my beloved husband, for whom this would have been such a proud day!) where I sat forty-nine years ago and received the homage of the Princes and Peers," Victoria recorded in her journal. She sat in the chair in which she had been crowned, the Coronation Chair of Edward III, her robes "beautifully draped on the chair," throughout the service, and at its conclusion each of her chil-dren and grandchildren came forward to bow or curtsy and kiss her hand. "It was a very moving moment," she noted, "and tears were in some of their eyes."

They wept out of affection for her, and admiration for all that she had been and done, and for all that she represented. They wept, too, to see how she had aged, and no doubt many of them reflected sadly that the sweetly regal old lady in the Coronation Chair would not reign over them too much longer.

The afternoon had become very hot by the time the procession made its way back to the palace via Piccadilly, and Victoria, with no protection from the sun, was uncomfortable in her heavy black silk and welcomed the occasional gust of wind that swept up from the river. Many of the women spectators fainted—dozens of them lay in a pathetic row in Trafalgar Square, where journalists took note of them for the illustrated weeklies—and in the terrible crush of people, inevitably there were accidents, a few of them serious. On the whole, however, the crowds were orderly and confined their excitement to shouting enthusiastically for the queen.

When Victoria finally arrived at the palace it was nearly three o'-clock, and, tired though she was, she took the time to present special Jubilee brooches and pins to her numerous relatives before sitting at the head of the table for a long feast. After more present-giving and a brief military review, the queen, "quite exhausted and ready to faint," lay down to rest—though even then she occupied herself opening telegrams. When evening came, she had to retire early, but her rest was interrupted by singing outside the palace windows; hundreds of people formed themselves into impromptu choirs and milled in the street just outside the courtyard, singing "God Save the Queen" and "Rule Britannia" until the early hours of the morning.

The celebrating went on for weeks, with banquets, garden parties, reviews and receptions, all of them gratifying to the guest of honor but tiring nonetheless. Finally, toward the end of the summer, she retreated to the peace of Balmoral. Even here, however, she was not out of reach of the telegraph, and it soon brought the troubles of the world to her door.

Vicky's husband Fritz was gravely ill. He had a growth in his throat, which affected his speech and was feared to be malignant. Though the queen had known of Fritz's condition for months, she had allowed herself to be optimistic because of the reassuring reports of his Scottish physician, Dr. Mackenzie. Fritz's German doctors took a darker view, and recommended an immediate operation to remove the growth. It was a drastic solution, for such an operation could easily prove to be fatal and Fritz was heir to the imperial throne. His father the emperor, ninety years old and in failing health, could not endure much longer, and if both Fritz and his father should die, the throne would pass to Vicky and Fritz's son Willy, the obstreperous, ungovernable boy who had grown into a strutting, self-important man.

Now it appeared that Fritz would not live much longer, and Victoria, who had always been fond of her senior son-in-law, wept for him and for Vicky, who was the object of increasing hatred and calumny at the Prussian court. The following spring, the aged emperor died, and Fritz became Emperor Frederick III. He was too ill to attend his father's funeral, however, and Bertie, who went to Berlin as his mother's representative, wrote home that Fritz was terribly thin and had a "hunted, anxious expression."[4] Because Fritz was hardly able to breathe due to the swelling in his throat, the doctors had inserted a steel tube in his windpipe. Hearing this, and knowing that Fritz's imminent death and Willy's accession would have a far-reaching impact on European affairs, Victoria decided to visit Berlin herself on her spring trip to the Continent.

After spending several weeks in Italy the sixty-nine-year-old queen arrived in Berlin in April of 1888, where she went at once to Fritz's bedside. Clearly he had not long to live, and while very sensible of his tragedy, the tragedy of a man dying while in his prime, having just gained imperial power, Victoria was even more sympathetic to the sad fate of her unfortunate daughter. Not only was Vicky anguished over Fritz, but she was menaced by her many political enemies at court and treated badly by her son, who was estranged from her and in whose hands her fate would soon lie. Vicky was trapped, and Victoria, predicting that Vicky's sufferings would only worsen after Fritz died, was full of concern for her.

To see a bad situation clearly, and not be able to do anything about it, wrung Victoria's heart, yet she did what she could, giving comfort to Fritz, spending time with the weeping Vicky, attempting to persuade Willy, who could already taste power and was making preparations to take over, to treat his mother with tenderness and consideration. Victoria had a long interview with Bismarck, the fiery Chancellor who for decades had incarnated German aggression and autocracy. Both white-haired, both elderly, Victoria and Bismarck could look back together over a long political span. She was surprised at his mellowness and gentleness, he at her shrewdness and impressive grasp of affairs. ("What a woman!" Bismarck exclaimed afterward. "One could do business with her!"[5])

The frail Empress Augusta, Victoria's close friend for well over thirty years, hovered in the background of the royal visits, a shriveled figure in a black dress and long black veil, seated in a chair, "quite crumpled up and deathly pale, really rather a ghastly sight."[6] The loss of her husband and the imminent loss of her son combined with her own advanced age to bring Augusta to death's door herself. One hand was paralyzed, the other palsied. She could barely speak above a whisper. The sight of Augusta, once so forceful and vital, a veritable termagant, now reduced to a quivering nonentity saddened Victoria, and must have made her thankful that at sixty-nine, she was still able to travel, enjoy her growing family and reign effectively over her empire.

Back in England, her visit at an end, Victoria was full of all that she had seen and done. Without forgetting the plights of Fritz and Vicky, she was effusive and enthusiastic about her trip. "She talked and laughed incessantly," wrote her lady-in-waiting Marie Mallet, whose book of reminiscences offers a valuable portrait of the queen in her old age, "and was full of all the interesting people she had seen."[7] Mallet and others noticed a buoyancy about the queen, a newfound flow of high spirits and pleasure, that were to mark the remaining years of her life.

It was as if, on the threshold of her seventies, Victoria entered a sort of charmed second childhood, a span of gilded years in which she was the adored object of everyone's attention, fondly indulged the way she herself indulged her grandchildren, with (for the most part) grating personalities and stressful, demanding situations kept at bay. Her happiness overflowed; long gone were the days when she prayed to rejoin Albert, and announced that life held no more gratification for her; now she prayed for a longer life ("May He preserve me yet for some years!") and entered with a renewed verve into the maelstrom of the late 1880s and early 1890s.

It was a turbulent age, unsettled and fruitlessly obsessed with self-definition. Faith in the inevitability of progress in human affairs had given way to a pervasive mood of skepticism. Many sophisticated people believed that God had retreated from the world, to be replaced, not by the faith in science that had made them doubt God, but by the doubt itself. And doubt, everyone acknowledged, was a poor foundation for social order—indeed it was profoundly destructive of social order. The once rigid backbone of Victorian society had given way to a spineless degeneracy, journalists wrote; evidences were all around, in the excesses of the rich and the effronteries of the poor, in the horrors of the Oscar Wilde scandal, in the brittle wit that had taken the place of humor and the stylized, narcissistic aestheticism that had supplanted art. The six-day workweek was gone. Now those who could afford to relaxed on "weekends," the welcome two days of rest taking the place of the one day of reverence that had given shape to the week a generation earlier.

Periodicals announced universal decline—the Decline of Genius, the Decline of Education, the Decline of Marriage (the marriage rate, temporarily at least, appeared to be dropping), even the Decline of Cricket. The Decline of Manners that, in Victoria's view at least, had been under way for decades appeared to be reaching a new low. Standards of decorum were falling. Politeness could no longer be taken for granted in civilized society, indeed, some observers thought, people were cross to one another more often than they were civil.

With a new century looming not far off, much was made of newness. Critics wrote of the New Drama, moralists of the New Paganism, Cassandras of the New Woman, that bicycle-riding, rights-demanding, lipstick-wearing young woman of the nineties who was both annoyingly self-reliant and disturbingly provocative. Pessimists thought they could discern other disturbing new trends—a downturn in prosperity, a general cultural deterioration, and the onset of an imperial twilight marking the ebbing of British influence in the world.

Victoria read of all these things in newspapers and periodicals—or rather, she heard them read aloud to her, for her sight was too poor to permit her to read very much—and responded with opinionated bluntness. Certain causes attracted her. She was against cruelty to "her poor dear friends the dogs," and opposed to the shooting of strays. She strenuously argued for improving the conditions under which animals bound for slaughter were kept. "Nothing brutalizes human beings more than cruelty to poor dumb animals," she insisted, "whose plaintive looks for help ought to melt the hardest heart."[8]

She sided with those who argued that women should not ride astride like men because their legs were too short. She debated with Vicky, by letter, the merits of her favorite author Marie Corelli, insisting that Corelli "would rank as one of the greatest writers of the time," while Vicky dismissed her as shallow and inconsequential—as representative of the Decline of Genius, in fact.

When a series of gruesome murders occurred in the East End of London the queen wrote at once to Lord Salisbury urging the "absolute necessity for some very decided action," and recommending better lighting in the overcrowded slums, improved detection and

"sufficient surveillance" in the worst and most crime-ridden neighborhoods. "You promised, when the first murder took place, to consult
with your colleagues about it," she reminded Salisbury with asperity.[9]

Though cross and acrimonious when occasion demanded it, Victoria
appeared, to those who met her in her seventies, to be a kindly, ap-
proachable old lady whose inherent warmth counteracted the intimi-
dating effect of her high station. A visitor to Balmoral, the composer
Ethel Smyth, meeting the old queen for the first time, was charmed by
her "wonderful, blue, childlike eyes" and thought that she had "the
sweetest most entrancing smile" she had ever seen. At odd moments "a
silvery, really amused little laugh" would escape her lips, "a sweet, crys-
talline peal of laughter" that enchanted everyone around her.[10]

At seventy, Victoria was paradoxically girlish. She giggled, she
blushed, she covered her face with her fan like a young girl when
something improper was mentioned. There was a charming shyness
about her, a shyness that deserted her, to be sure, when something
struck her as enormously funny. One evening at dinner, when a mildly
risqué story was told, the queen "put down her knife and fork, hid her
face in her handkerchief and shook and heaved with laughter till the
tears rolled down her face."[11]

Though she could be glum at dinner, more often the queen was
cheery, even effervescent. She could even be witty. At her "Ladies'
Dinners," with only the most intimate and trusted of her women present, she was often "in excellent spirits," Marie Mallet wrote, "making
jokes about her age and saying she felt quite young." She reminisced
about her childhood, not about Conroy and his repression, or her es-
trangement from her mother, but about light, amusing incidents such
as the time she mistook her fork for her fan at a ball supper and
walked into the ballroom with it, or the time her mother absentmind-
edly put the candle snuffers into her pocket instead of her handkerchief, and went out for a walk with the heavy brass snuffers in her
pocket.[12]

After many years of denying herself the pleasures of large-scale entertainments as part of her strict mourning, Victoria decided to relax
her self-imposed restraints. She went to the opera, she invited famous
singers and actors to perform at Windsor and Balmoral, she went to
see Buffalo Bill's Wild West Show and was pleased with it ("a very extraordinary and interesting sight"). She invited Hengler's Circus to

perform at the Riding School at Windsor, ostensibly as a birthday present for Leopold's three-year-old daughter Alice but in actuality for her own amusement as well. Later she did the same thing at Balmoral, paying Pindar's Circus to give a performance for all the tenants and servants on the estate.

Small everyday things gave her great pleasure—the Neapolitan violets floating in the finger glasses at a dinner party, Bertie's little green parrot in the hall at Sandringham that chirped "Three cheers for the queen," a mantelpiece crowded with photographs of grandchildren and great-grandchildren, the Gloire de Dijon and Madame Falcot and Maréchal Niel roses in the greenhouse at Balmoral. She looked forward inordinately to her meals, still avid for pralines and chocolate sponge cake although she now had to be more careful of her digestion and had to eat Francatelli's Marrow Toast at every meal to prevent upsets and constipation. A single perfect Ledbury apple was a great treat for Victoria, who ate it, Marie Mallet noted, "with evident relish" and could not stop saying how large and beautiful and flavorful it was.

Astonishingly, at seventy Victoria was still attending to dispatches many hours a day, signing documents in her large, firm hand, insisting on correcting the court circular herself with great attention to detail. Four huge bags, "as big as large armchairs" of material arrived at the palace every day for her perusal. But more and more often now it was Beatrice or Fritz Ponsonby who perused the mountains of paper. Her secretaries wrote out long memoranda about important issues, but Beatrice, diligent but somewhat undisciplined, was often lax in reading them to her mother.[13] Besides, Beatrice was married now—she had married Prince Henry of Battenberg in July of 1885—and was starting a family of her own.

Discreetly, Bertie was brought forward, not as co-ruler, but as ruler-in-training. He was kept informed of every significant issue facing the government, and even given his own key to the Foreign Office dispatch boxes—something the queen had never been willing to permit before. At last, having reached his fifties, Bertie was allowed to begin his political education as England's next king.

Very slowly and gradually, and with some reluctance, Victoria was letting the reins of power go slack in her hands. She still protested, urged and complained, particularly when her nemesis Gladstone returned to office for several trying years, but more often she acquiesced, quietly and without fuss, in decisions made by others. On the whole she was content to let the rising generations take on the yoke of power.

But here fate intervened. In January of 1892 Victoria was surprised and troubled to receive a telegram from Bertie saying that Eddy, second in line to the throne, had developed pneumonia. His condition grew steadily worse, and within days he was dead, his death occurring on the dreaded fourteenth of the month, a day that always made Victoria shudder.

"Words are far too poor to express one's feelings of grief, horror, and distress!" the elderly queen wrote in her journal. "Poor me, in my old age, to see this young promising life cut short! I, who loved him so dearly, and to whom he was so devoted! God help us!"[14]

Never mind the unpalatable truth that dull-witted, lethargic Eddy had been dissolute and shallow.[15] To Victoria he would always be "dear kind Eddy," her beloved grandchild, "so good and gentle," who had gone to be with Albert and Alice and Leopold and Fritz in a better world. "I truly did love and understand the darling boy and how I shall miss him!" Victoria wrote, hardly able to see the words her shaking hand wrote on the page. Eddy's loss was one more challenge to surmount, one more pain to carry in her heart, one more reminder that the swift years were passing and that, endure as she might, she too was bending beneath their wearying weight.

Chapter 22

WHEN THE OLD QUEEN breakfasted at Windsor, everything on the table before her was of solid gold. There were gold plates, gold knives and forks, a gleaming gold teapot, even a gold eggcup to hold the royal egg, with a gold spoon with which to eat it. Standing motionless behind the queen were two gold-turbaned Indian waiters, dark-skinned and bearded, ornaments as essential to the gilded tableau as the gold toast tongs or the gold chafing dish. Victoria was becoming increasingly infatuated with her Indian empire, and human reminders of that empire were never far out of reach.

Sheikh Ghulam Mustafa and Sheikh Chidda were the queen's personal servants in the year of her Jubilee. Then two more servants arrived at court, two young men who came into the royal presence, bowed low, and kissed the queen's shoes. One, Mahomet Baksh, was dark and smiling and forgettable; the other, Abdul Karim, was "much lighter, tall and with a fine, serious countenance."[1] Abdul Karim interested Victoria. He was only twenty-four, handsome and intelligent, altogether exceptional in every way. Though he began as a table servant and general factotum, she soon realized that to confine him to menial duties was to demean Karim; with his proud bearing and evident air of self-regard, he was made for more important things.

Victoria decided that she wanted Karim to teach her Hindustani, and to instruct her in Indian social customs. Painstakingly, because of her dimming sight, she learned to draw Hindustani characters, and to converse haltingly in a tongue she had never before heard spoken. The learning, the romantic images the language evoked, and the handsome Abdul himself charmed the aging queen, and filled her mind with Oriental fantasies. The India she imagined was of course very far from the real thing; it was a fairy-tale India, full of smiling turbaned men and sari-clad women, in a landscape of temples and palaces and elephants wearing bells around their ankles.

Real or not, India began to dominate Victoria's thoughts. She nurtured a private dream of visiting the subcontinent. She collected Indian furnishings and paintings and *objets d'art*, and ordered a vast new wing built at Osborne to house them. Here one walked down the long Indian Corridor, past paintings of India, into the huge ornate Durbar Room, its white and gold walls embellished with flamboyant plasterwork. Patterns of scrollwork, flowers, leaves, even peacocks cascaded from the ceiling, the effect quite as overwhelming as if one were entering a maharaja's palace. Here Victoria held banquets on important occasions, heaped with jewels like a maharani, pleased to be surrounded by so many rich symbols of her imperial eminence.

The most important symbol, though, was Abdul Karim, who quickly eclipsed Mahomet Baksh and rose to become Personal Indian Clerk to the Queen, with a large staff of Indian underclerks under his supervision. Karim was now known as the Munshi Hafiz Abdul Karim, or "the Munshi," the queen's teacher. He occupied an anomalous position in her household, well above the lower servants yet not quite on a level with her senior staff. He was exceedingly conscious of his rights and perquisites, and complained forcefully to his mistress when he was not given a fine enough carriage to ride in or an honored enough place at the dining table.

Yet it seemed to the other servants and officials that the Munshi had been exalted far more than was appropriate, given his qualifications and talents. They resented him, and they made their resentment known. Why, they asked one another, should the Munshi have constant personal access to the queen, when nearly everyone else had to approach her in writing, using the formula, "so and so presents his humble duty to Your Majesty," and waiting tediously for a reply that might never come? Why had Victoria given the Munshi not one but three houses of his own, Frogmore Cottage, Arthur Cottage and Karim Cottage at Balmoral? Why did she come to his sickbed, and all but nurse him herself when he was ill?

The rapid advancement and personal arrogance of the Munshi would inevitably have led to his unpopularity, but the fact of his race made all emotions run hotter against him. Racialism was a scourge of the age; it went hand in hand with belief in the appropriateness of Britain's global dominion. For a dark-skinned Indian to be put very nearly on a level with the queen's white servants was all but intolerable, for him to eat at the same table with them, to share in their daily lives was viewed as an outrage.

Yet the queen was determined to impose harmony on her household. Race hatred was intolerable to her, and the "dear good Munshi" was deserving of nothing but respect. She gave each of her servants a Hindustani phrase book to facilitate conversation, and promote understanding, between them and Karim. She refused, adamantly, to hear criticisms of her teacher, and wrote indignant notes when she learned of dissension among the staff. Meanwhile the Munshi, ever more secure in Victoria's esteem, got older, fatter, and grander year by year, taking more and more advantage of his position—so it seemed to his enemies—and preening himself like a sleek cat that swallowed the royal mouse.

Each spring when the queen made her annual visit to the Continent she took along many Indian servants—along with a number of Highlanders. Everywhere she went the crowds that gathered to welcome her became accustomed to the sight of her small figure, flanked by a sturdy, gray-bearded Highlander on one side and a gold-turbaned Indian on the other, being lifted from her wheeled chair into her carriage. She still tried to walk, on occasion; in Florence in 1893 she managed to make her way with the help of her cane through the Uffizi, though she often had to stop and rest and eventually called for her wheeled chair.

Though she invariably worked when abroad, Victoria was somewhat at loose ends. Relentless sightseeing wearied her, then made her rheumatism flare up, until her legs were so stiff and painful that she couldn't walk at all. Still she had herself driven out in her pony cart, or arranged for an entertainment to be presented to the court, or visited with relatives or friends.

Not all the visits were equally welcome. Albert's elderly brother Ernest came to visit Victoria at Grasse in the spring of 1891, a decayed, ugly old man who for years had been writing "anonymous" pamphlets attacking his sister-in-law and Vicky.[2] Victoria had turned against him decades earlier, disgusted by his immorality. She liked him no better in his seventies, but was polite to him for Albert's sake. It must have been unnerving for her to see him, and to recall the charming, handsome young man he had once been, and even more unnerving to listen to him talk, for his voice had always been very like Albert's.

Albert was never far from the queen's thoughts. Sometimes, when she went driving, Victoria worried her companions by reaching for the miniature picture of her late husband that she wore around her neck and holding it up, so that Albert could "see" some particularly arresting view.

In a woman with less astuteness and general grasp of affairs such eccentric behavior would have made others shake their heads and dismiss her as peculiar. As it was, the queen's children worried about their mother's sanity and stability, given her excessive infatuation with things Indian, and with the Munshi. And in her seventies, Victoria was developing other quirks. She took with her wherever she went a "birthday book" with a page for every day of the year. Everyone she met had to write his or her name in the birthday book; she seemed so attached to the book, and fussed over it so excessively, that casual onlookers assumed it was the Bible.

Somewhat more freakish was Victoria's enthusiasm for funerals, an enthusiasm that seemed to surface most prominently when she was abroad. "The Queen takes the keenest interest in death and all its horrors," Marie Mallet wrote. She liked nothing better than to talk of "coffins and winding sheets," and whenever she heard of a death she made minute inquiries about the corpse and went to see the funeral procession.[3] Once while she was staying at Grasse, one of the housemaids died. At once Victoria ordered a private funeral to be held in the dining room of the hotel where she was staying. A coffin was found, the body was prepared for burial. The entire household—well over a hundred people—dressed in their evening finery and filed past the macabre display in the dining room, the servants in tears.

"The Queen was very grieved and placed a wreath on the coffin rather tremblingly," Marie Mallet recalled. But the entire macabre event was deeply unnerving to Marie and to others. It was stagy, it reeked of the dramatic and the artificial. Victoria's solicitude for the dead housemaid was, Marie Mallet thought, overdone, and "very trying for the Household."

Much more trying for the household was the smiling, sly, almost sinister presence of the Munshi, who by the mid-1890s was assuming a larger and larger role in the circle of servants around the queen. He tended to loom unexpectedly at family gatherings, like the skeleton at the feast whose appearance left everyone speechless. He obtained more and more special favors and special treatment from Victoria, while bringing more and more of his relatives and friends from India to drink at the trough of the royal largesse. No one dared criticize him to the queen's face, but when her back was turned, tempers flared and there were frequent clashes.

Affie refused to allow the Munshi to attend his daughter Victoria Melita's wedding (she married her cousin, Alice's son Ernest), and since the wedding was to take place in Coburg, where Affie now reigned as duke, having succeeded the loathsome Ernest, Victoria was unwilling to peremptorily override Affie's commands.[4] Through intermediaries, Victoria repeatedly made known her desire to have the Munshi present at the ceremony, and Affie repeatedly denied him permission to enter the chapel.

After much wearisome negotiation, the Munshi was permitted to watch the ceremony from the gallery—and was promised that he would not be demeaned by having to share the gallery with other servants. But this pledge was broken; Karim saw, to his horror, several other servants in the gallery. He left at once, and wrote, in halting English, a letter of protest to Victoria. Once the ceremony was over, the letter was handed to her. She was mortified. She wept, no doubt she cursed her son inwardly, and she saw to it that for the rest of her stay in Coburg, the Munshi was invited to every social function and shown the greatest respect.

Battles of will such as this one between Victoria and Affie threw into relief the undeniable fact that, by the mid-1890s, Victoria was slowly giving ground to her sons. The three of them, Bertie, Affie and Arthur, now burly middle-aged patriarchs, were older than Albert had been when he died; all of her daughters were now older than Victoria had been when she was widowed. There were twenty-nine surviving grandchildren—so many that, despite the prompt to memory represented by her birthday book, Victoria could no longer send each of them a gift for his or her birthday. A card from "Gangan" sufficed. As for the great-grandchildren, their name would soon be legion, their exact number did not bear thinking about.

And still the old queen hung on, looking well, her spirits high, her passions ever close to the surface on matters close to her heart. By the fall of 1896 she had reached a milestone.

"Today is the day on which I have reigned longer, by a day, than any English sovereign," she noted in her journal on September 23, "and the people wished to make all sorts of demonstrations, which I asked them not to do until I had completed the sixty years next June." Still, people bombarded the court with telegrams, not certain that Victoria would live until the following June—or merely impatient for an occasion to congratulate their beloved sovereign. She accepted their kind good wishes graciously, but took no credit for either her longevity or her success as queen. It had all been God's doing. Through fifty-nine years, she wrote, "God has guided me in the midst of terrible trials, sorrows, and anxieties, and has wonderfully protected me."[5]

And just as God had protected the queen, so he had provided for the continuity of the dynasty. When Bertie's son Eddy died, his brother George took his place as next in line of succession after Bertie. Now George had a son, Prince Edward, called David, who would follow his father as king.[6] Victoria had lived long enough to see the next three generations of monarchs, and all of them pleased her. She thought little David was "a most attractive little boy, and so forward and clever." She even liked the way he barked out orders to the Indian servants in his small voice—though never daring to give commands to the Munshi, of course.

Secure in her heirs, and secure also in her subjects' affection, with the Munshi close at hand and a staff of Indians to serve her, Victoria entered her late seventies. Nothing changed around her. There were "the same chairs in the same places, the same plum cake, even the number of biscuits on the plate and their variety, absolutely identical."[7] Conversation varied little, the queen's schedule hardly at all. Inevitably, some of the ancient retainers died or were pensioned off, and new collies, Pomeranians and pugs now followed Victoria's pony cart. Finally there came a day when whist was no longer played at court after dinner, replaced by parlor games and dancing among the servants, and the drinking of a rather "potent punch" after the queen retired to bed.[8]

There were still occasional tedious evenings when the queen's family and staff presented "tableaux vivant"—living pictures from the past. In these stiff, awkward presentations, costumed characters appeared in statuesque poses, as if frozen at climactic moments of their lives. Beatrice appeared as Queen Elizabeth, in wide ruff and pearls, Louise represented Mary Queen of Scots ("her expression beautiful and sad beyond measure," one observer thought), the Munshi took the stage dressed as a Bedouin and even Victoria's doctor and confidant, James Reid, put on armor and portrayed a French noble.[9] Often the tableaux vivant lasted for two or three hours, with the Marine string band playing during the long intermissions between the scenes.

Victoria was as enthralled by these amateurish entertainments as she had once been enthralled by much more professional performances. She laughed, she clapped her hands with delight like a child. Occasionally she nodded off, but soon roused herself, unwilling to miss even a moment of the badly lit, poorly executed tableaux.

The sight of her children and servants in their places on the makeshift stage was comforting—as comforting as the keepsakes the queen kept near her: the miniature of Albert hanging from its neck chain, the quilt made by Feodore, the ruby-studded dagger that had once been Disraeli's, which she kept on her desk, the cross, cut from a single magnificent emerald, given her by Eugenie.

She was acquiring new keepsakes every day. Her apartments were littered with toys belonging to Beatrice's four young children, Alexander, Ena, Leopold and Maurice. One of their favorites, a large furry horse on wheels, was often to be found in the Grand Corridor at Windsor. Other reminders of these youngest of Victoria's grandchildren were to be found out-of-doors, or in the palace outbuildings: their poultry pens, their ponies, their favorite Jack Russell terriers and Blenheim spaniels, their gardening smocks and hats, tennis racquets and butterfly nets.

Victoria was surrounded by comforts, loving relatives, well wishers without number. But with great reluctance, she was being forced to admit that the man she had placed at the center of her household, and on whom she had lavished, wisely or unwisely, the majority or her affection and concern, was turning out to be other than what he seemed. In championing the Munshi, Victoria was nurturing a viper at her bosom.

It came to her as a painful realization, one she reached after much complexity of thought and much venting of emotion. Abdul Karim had represented to Victoria all the hopes she held for her Indian empire. He had grace, intelligence, physical beauty, knowledge and ability; she prized these qualities in him, and made allowances for his darker qualities of vanity, arrogance, greed and unrestrained ambition. Believing as strongly as she did in social and racial equality, she could not help but try to use the Munshi as the thin end of the wedge to break down social snobbery and race prejudice among her servants. Then too, the Munshi represented something far simpler and in a way, far stronger: Victoria's yearning for the Indian paradise that was the private dream of her old age.

But by 1897 the queen's dream, like her cataract-ridden eyes, had clouded over. She had finally begun to allow herself to listen to what trusted members of her household were telling her about the Munshi—that he and his friends had stolen things from her, that he had lied about his family background and about the jobs he had held in India, that he had gonorrhea (the queen and James Reid had "an interesting talk" on that subject), that he was "complicit in Muslim Patriotic League affairs," and might even have dangerous political connections.

She didn't want to hear any of it, and at times she became so enraged that she shouted and pounded her fist and swore. When her entire household rebelled at the prospect of having to share quarters with the Munshi while the queen was taking her spring holiday at Cimiez in 1897, she became so angry that she swept her arm across her writing desk, sending papers, pens, inkwell and Disraeli's jeweled dagger crashing to the floor. Old age had not cured her tantrums.

But in the end, she came to see that she had allowed herself to be drawn into a toxic situation with Abdul Karim. The more she gave him, the more he wanted. When she refused his demands, he shouted at her. There was no real warmth between them, only aggrieved petitioning on his part and thankless, placatory generosity on hers. The Munshi was not John Brown come back to life, nor was he India incarnate. He was nothing more than a venal intriguer exploiting a wealthy old woman's dreams.

Still, she did not send him away. Karim receded into the background of Victoria's life—after Reid threatened to disclose to the queen more details of his hypocrisy and dishonesty unless he stopped trying to advance himself. He remained at court, but in a less prominent role, still ever-present should the queen require his services, but no less ornamental, in his golden turban, than her gold eggcup and small golden spoon.

The contretemps over the Munshi, while it lasted, had raised again old doubts about Victoria's sanity. The madness question had hovered at the edges of the queen's life from childhood on—the inevitable legacy of a granddaughter of George III and a niece of the murderous Duke of Cumberland and the aberrantly fanciful George IV. Stockmar had questioned her sanity. Albert too had worried over whether she might go mad. Dr. Jenner had whispered that the queen's ruddy complexion betokened a disordered mind. Gladstone, meeting Victoria at Nice in that quarrelsome spring of 1897, noticed that her mind wandered, and passed his observations on to others. Red-faced and choleric, the old queen impressed those who came into casual contact with her as certainly eccentric, and very likely insane.

When James Reid counseled Victoria, he told her bluntly that unless she came to her senses where the Munshi was concerned, it would be generally believed that her mind had foundered.[10] To protect her reputation, he, Reid, as her doctor, would have to concur. She would be declared mentally incompetent, a regency would be established by Parliament, with Bertie as regent.

This sobered her. When talking with Reid, she broke down, then grew excited and angry, then lapsed into melancholy resignation. Of course he was right, she knew it. She had been "dreadfully nervous" about the Munshi herself for some time.[11] She was not, after all, in the grip of fantasy. Her mind was sound. It was only that, with a constantly aching leg and dimming sight, with her real authority ebbing and little but her strength of will to sustain her self-image as head of her household, she had made Abdul Karim more important than he was. She saw that now.

It seemed to those around her that Victoria had more trouble getting up from her chair than she had in the past, and that her hearing, which had always remained so keen, was becoming slightly impaired. She moved slowly, and was prone to accidents. Her handwriting was nearly impossible to read. Yet she still relished her food and slept well, enjoying her afternoon carriage rides and displaying "great amiability of manner" to her visitors. Nothing pleased her more, during these afternoon drives, than to come across a group of children. She ordered the driver to stop while she chatted with the little ones and patted their heads, beaming at them and distributing peppermints.

No one had expected her to live to be seventy-eight, but her "old birthday" came around again in May of 1897, and her birthday tables were heaped with presents, and the Marine band played for her and her grandchildren brought her flowers.[12] "Seventy-eight is a good age," she wrote in her journal in her erratic, broad scrawl, "but I pray yet to be spared a little longer for the sake of my country and dear ones."

Chapter 23

————— ⌀ —————

A T THE GOOD OLD age of seventy-eight, Victoria was lifted out of her wheeled chair and assisted into her open landau. The day was June 22, 1897, a morning of bright sunshine and pleasant warmth. London was celebrating the queen's sixtieth anniversary, her Diamond Jubilee, and the shouting, roaring crowds were if anything larger than those that had greeted Victoria on her Golden Jubilee ten years earlier.

As on that earlier occasion, the processional route between Buckingham Palace and St. Paul's Cathedral was dense with spectators, wedged into temporary platforms, lining rooftops, leaning down from balconies and windows. "The cheering was quite deafening," Victoria wrote in her journal later that day, "and every face seemed to be filled with real joy." She could not see the faces clearly, of course; even in the brilliant sunlight the world was dim for her, and the roaring that came from the thousands of throats was more a distant rumble than an ear-splitting chorus near at hand.

As the carriage neared St. Paul's the crowd surged forward again and again, bringing the parade to a halt, and people spontaneously began singing "God Save the Queen." Waves of raw emotion seemed to pulse through the mass of humanity, tides of affection and sentiment and pride. The frail, child-sized figure in her carriage was the focus of all eyes, the tender object of all hearts. No one in the crowd now thought of the dark years when the queen had been criticized for hiding herself away, or ridiculed for clinging to John Brown, or scoffed at as a quaint, naïve relic of the past in an increasingly sophisticated world. Instead the overwhelming feeling was a desire to cherish the precious sovereign who represented tradition, stability, worldwide authority. Victoria was the crown. Victoria was the empire. Victoria was the royal family. Victoria was Britain, her glory Britain's glory, her endurance Britain's triumphant durability in a world of change.

Nodding and smiling, acknowledging as well as she could the tumultuous accolade, Victoria clutched her black lace parasol nervously. For weeks she had felt "a good deal agitated," worried that something important might be overlooked in the preparations for the Jubilee ceremony, or that on the day itself something might go wrong. Whenever a huge crowd gathered there were sure to be accidents.[1]

The carriage approached the cathedral steps, and from within came the sound of massed choirs singing the *Te Deum*, the anthem of thanksgiving. When the spectators joined the choirs in singing a familiar hymn, the "Old Hundredth," the emotional fervor was overwhelming. Victoria broke down and wept. It had been decided that she would not get out of her carriage, but would simply extend her hand to the Archbishop of Canterbury and express her thanks. It was all she could do. The emotional exertion taxed her excessively, and by the time the procession made its long, slow way back to the palace she was quite wilted from exhaustion.

Still, in the following days she proved to be resilient as she undertook to fulfill a daunting schedule of celebratory events. At receptions, garden parties, banquets and court presentations she sat, smiling and affable, as hundreds of guests were brought to her, taking in stride the reverential attitude of many of her subjects (she would have preferred ordinary courtesy) and realizing that to them, she had become an icon.

Adulation buoyed her, and carried her on into the following year on the crest of a wave of exhilaration. She was, Marie Mallet thought, "in excellent spirits," joking about her age and saying she "felt quite young."[2] She felt like running and leaping—but her old tired legs would scarcely carry her unwieldy body a single step, and in fact her stamina was declining. She napped every day in the early afternoon, and while out on her carriage drives she rested her small head on Marie Mallet's shoulder. Talking to guests fatigued her, as did bad news and tense situations. Her eager mind was ever alert for information about the state of the world, current political wrangles, even the latest gossip or sexual scandal, but try as she might to retain her alertness, she could not discipline her concentration; she drifted, she faded in and out of awareness, and at times others thought she looked "feeble and depressed."[3]

She knew that she was slowly wearing out, and with her customary practicality and concern for privacy and control, she thought ahead to her last hours and death. After careful thought she wrote out a detailed memorandum about how she wished to be treated on her deathbed, and how her body should be handled after she died. Only familiar dressers and her doctor James Reid were to attend her. If she was conscious, Reid was to tell her the truth about how ill she was, and how much time she might have left. No one was to lie to her or try to lift her spirits by giving her false hope. She wished to look death in the face, as she might a hostile army, knowing its full strength and how long she might expect to keep it at bay.

Meanwhile, she continued to enjoy her days, though she could no longer recognize people by sight alone, and occasionally mistook one for another. The thought of surgery to remove her cataracts filled her with dread, and she could not face it. Instead, belladonna was put into her eyes, to dilate her pupils; unfortunately, the belladonna also made her drowsy. Now when she sat down to read dispatches or have them read to her the work she produced was wildly uneven in quality; while some of her judgments were remarkably astute, giving abundant evidence of her long experience and insight, at other times she made serious mistakes, and her long-suffering secretaries had to be watchful, so that what was done incorrectly could be surreptitiously changed.

Still, when Victoria considered those around her, she realized that she was far from being the only one with troubles, and she felt some measure of pride in being able to bear her troubles, not only with equanimity, but with a sense of quiet triumph. She was doing far better than Alexandra, who looked ill and was reportedly restless and anxious; she dreaded the coming day when Bertie would reign and she would be his queen. She had long been his wife in name only. Now the voluptuous, statuesque young Alice Keppel was Bertie's constant companion, and Alexandra—still remarkably fresh and youthful—was pushed into the background.

Tragedy surrounded several of Victoria's surviving children. Vicky had been diagnosed with spinal cancer. Affie too was seriously ill, and drinking himself into his grave. His only son, Prince Alfred, had recently ended his short and dissolute life by shooting himself after quarreling with his mother.

These and other family matters preoccupied Victoria, as did the state of the world. Disputes in Asia and Africa were causing concern. The Americans were at war with Spain in Cuba and the Philippines. From Berlin, Victoria's grandson Willy was working vigorously to undermine Britain's interests everywhere he could. And in the Sudan, the British general Lord Kitchener led a force to Khartoum and recaptured it, avenging the lamented General Gordon and gladdening Victoria's heart.

But the empire was so vast, its inner tensions so complex that the threat of armed conflict was ever-present. In the fall of 1899 Britain found herself once again at war.

This time the arena of conflict was southern Africa, where the Dutch settlers, or Boers, had been living under ill-defined and increasingly resented British political protection since the late 1870s. The Boers had welcomed the help of British arms against the Zulus, but after the Zulu war ended the Boers began to want their independence back. Tensions worsened when gold was discovered in the Boer republic of the Transvaal in 1886. British prospectors flooded in, some of them making fortunes and all of them eager to settle in the prosperous southern lands. The Boers bristled, and closed ranks. The British sent troops. In October of 1899, goaded by the British High Commissioner, the Boer states of Transvaal and Orange Free State declared war.

It could hardly have happened at a worse time. For the past three months Victoria had been looking much older and feebler, her forty-eight-inch waist had shrunk and her dressmakers had had to take in her black silk gowns. She coughed a good deal, and some nights she got no sleep at all because of the pain in her swollen, stiff leg.[4] Her waist-length white hair was thin and limp, her small red hands clutched anxiously at her skirts and her eyes were often tear-filled. She knew the demands that the war would make on her, and she dreaded that she might no longer be able to fulfill them.

"Keep me awake," she told Marie Mallet. "Shake me if necessary."[5]

She must stay alert to hear the war news. She had to lead her country in this anguishing time.

Outwardly the queen put on a resolute expression, and refused to hear any talk of defeat. The Boers were few, the British many; even though strengthened by German armaments and supported by German money, the enemy could not hold out long against superior British arms. She spoke stirringly to troops leaving for the Transvaal, reminding them that she was "confident that they would always do their duty," and maintain the reputations of their regiments. The sight of the stalwart little queen melted their hearts. They cheered her repeatedly, the officers too moved to do more than mumble their thanks and brief expressions of loyalty. Victoria too was moved. She confided to her journal that she felt "quite a lump in her throat" to think "how these remarkably fine men might not all return."[6] She remembered well the horrors of the Crimea, forty years earlier, where heat and filth and privation soon made a shambles of military order, and where more men collapsed and died from disease than from enemy bullets.

Each morning brought a fresh mound of telegrams, each day, it seemed, brought urgent new responsibilities. Engagements began, there were lists of casualties and Victoria did her best to contact the families of the dead and wounded. The early news was bad. The Boers acted quickly, before the British forces could be brought up to full strength, to compel the surrender of entire battalions. Kimberley, Ladysmith and Mafeking were under siege, everywhere, it seemed, British arms were in retreat. Victoria wept for the thousands of horses, sent in overcrowded, disease-ridden transports to the war scene, that had to be destroyed en route.

The errors of the Crimea, it seemed, were indeed repeating themselves. Inadequate provisioning, tactical mistakes, widespread incompetence were resulting in a lamentable waste of life. This was no ordinary colonial war; the Boers had sophisticated weapons, and their stubborn courage was—the queen herself had to admit it—even greater than the renowned stubborn courage of the British. Besides, they were fighting on home ground, terrain they knew intimately giving them a major advantage. They were a clever, resolute and ferocious enemy.

Victoria deplored the "terrible failures" of her troops and wept over the casualty lists. She collected photographs of all the slain officers and pasted them into an album, with the date of each man's death and a description of the action in which he fell. She read letters from the front, wanting to know what life was like for the men, and followed the movements of troops (movements that were too often retreats) with avid if fitful interest.

Before long it was apparent to all but the most blindly patriotic that the British war effort was a tissue of blunders. Victoria wrung her hands over the needless loss of life, and complained of the "very culpable" want of preparedness on the part of the military yet urged Lord Salisbury not to permit any official inquiry into the conduct of the war until it was at an end. Confidence in the government, not criticism, was what was needed.

In "Black Week," the week of December 10, 1899, terrible news arrived. The Boers handed the British forces three major defeats, and the lists of dead and wounded were sadly—and shamefully—long. Victoria's thinning face fell as she heard the telegrams read. To her, mid-December was always Black Week, with its commemoration of Albert's death. Now, however, she had more losses to ponder.

Still, she put on a defiant front. "Please understand that there is no one depressed in this house," she told a visitor to Windsor bravely. "We are not interested in the possibilities of defeat; they do not exist." But defeat was not only a possibility, it was an everyday fact, and the queen's elderly nerves were not bearing up well under it. She napped more during the day, and lay awake at night, sometimes because of the severe pain in her leg, more often because she was fretting over what she called "the very serious state of the war." More troops had to be sent. The militia had to be called out. The men needed better living quarters ("Could not corrugated-iron huts be used instead of tents?" she asked the Secretary for War.[7])

Now when her household dined on oyster soup, eggs with truffles and Circassian soufflé, Victoria ate only a little wheat cereal with warm milk. Indigestion stalked her. James Reid watched her for aphasia, loss of muscular control, mental confusion—signs of the stroke he believed to be imminent. But if the strain of the war was great, Victoria's urgent need to be involved was greater.

She visited military hospitals where, in her wheeled chair, she fitted in well among the amputees and paralytics. Before each visit she attempted to learn all about the most serious cases, and was especially concerned to help the men with wives and families. Her kindness was balm to the injured, who responded to her visits with outbursts of chivalrous sentiment. On one such visit she caught sight of a quilt she had worked, thrown across the bed of a soldier. It buoyed her to further efforts, and she joined her ladies-in-waiting and female staff in knitting caps and socks and waistcoats and sewing comforters, although she could no longer thread a needle and even sewing a straight seam must have been a near impossibility.

"I like to think I am doing something for my soldiers, although it is so little," Victoria told Marie Mallet, who could not help but notice that her mistress looked increasingly "anxious and careworn" and full of worry. In fact Victoria was preoccupied with the fate of Ladysmith, where the besieged British, having been reduced to eating their horses, were dying of starvation, their bodies rotting unburied in the harsh southern sun. In February of 1900 all her court, along with the rest of the country, was hoping and expecting that a British army was about to relieve Ladysmith. It would be a turning point in the course of the war, people said. Once the Ladysmith garrison was rescued, and the Boers were put to flight, victory would be at hand.

A special service of intercession was held at court early in February of 1900 and Victoria, knowing that her presence was essential, had herself wheeled in. She sat quietly through the entire service, her expression resolute, joining in the solemn prayers and heartening others by her look of calm confidence. But beneath her carapace of assurance her feelings were in turmoil. She had received a private message informing her that General Buller, sent to relieve the town, had retreated. The garrison was not to be rescued any time soon. The Boer siege held.[8]

Knowing what others could not know, and bearing the burden of this troubling knowledge alone, was wearing the queen down. She could no longer look at her photo album with its smiling portraits of dead young men; she ordered pictures of the living added, to make it less mournful. She described herself, to an officer about to leave for the Transvaal, as "a lonely old woman at Windsor," when she pressed an engraved cigar case into his hand, a memento of his royal interview.[9] Lonely she certainly was, and even when, to her immense relief, she heard the bells peal in thanksgiving for the relief of Ladysmith on March 1, she rejoiced alone. The Munshi was away, on a prolonged visit to India. Dr. Reid was professional and polite, always correct, but detached. Lenchen was often ill, and closeted in her room, Beatrice was affectionate but frequently preoccupied. Vicky, whose companionship and warm sympathy would have been welcome to the elderly queen, was dying in a remote castle in Germany.

By summer the war was slowly ebbing. Londoners had gone wild when Mafeking was liberated, their cheering and singing seemingly unquenchable. Though many Boers continued to hold out against the British, many others had surrendered, and it could only be a matter of time before the last resistance was crushed. Now, having done what was required of her during Britain's time of testing, Victoria felt that she could rest from her labors. She let herself rest.

The hot July of 1900 seemed to make the elderly Victoria cross. Behind her silver spectacles, her faded blue eyes were full of irritation, and she snapped at her attendants and frowned up at the sky as she might at a truculent servant. Despite her near-constant indigestion, she ate two huge dishes of chocolate ice cream at dinner, followed by a cup of apricots, and made her dining companions nervous by drinking so much ice water they thought she might burst.[10]

Nothing soothed her, not the soft voice of Marie Mallet reading a sentimental novel, not the presence of her youngest grandchildren Leopold and Maurice, not her favorite white Pomeranian Turi. She knew that Affie, far away at the Rosenau in Coburg, was gravely ill, and sensed that she was not being told the truth about his decline. Yet she no longer had the energy to insist that she be told, and it pained her to realize that now, even when she insisted, she was not obeyed.

Beatrice and Lenchen brought Victoria the telegram about Affie a little after eight in the morning of July 31. She was in her dressing room, where her two dressers, Miss Stewart and Miss Ticking, had just completed helping her into her black day dress. She asked her daughters if there was any news from Coburg.

"Yes, bad news, very bad news; he has slipped away!"

The blow fell, and even though she had known it would, she was not prepared. She cried, comforted by her daughters at first, and then by Marie Mallet, who stroked her small hand and listened while she reminisced about Affie as a happy little boy at Osborne. Her tears, Mallet wrote, were gentle. "She bore the blow both heroically and angelically, bowing to the will of God, as she always does and only murmuring, 'My people will feel for me.'"[11]

She confessed to her lady-in-waiting that the sorrows of the past few months, coming after the extreme strains of the war, were almost more than she could bear. It was hard, at eighty-one, to lose another beloved child; indeed she felt so "shaken and broken" that she was in a state of disbelief.

The queen's return to Balmoral in the fall failed to lift her spirits. Day after day, she struggled to rise out of an increasing torpor, and a state of depression that she seemed unable to shake off. The brisk air did nothing for her, renewing ties with the tenants on the estate left her unimproved. Everyone around her sensed that there had been a decisive change in her; her frail body, now in its eighty-second year, seemed to be worn past the point of recovery.

Doggedly, the queen wrote in her journal every day, though her entries were terse and telling: "poorly and wretched," "appetite completely gone," "had a shocking night."[12] Refreshing sleep never came now, only a wearing cycle of perpetual drowsiness and insomnia, with no relief from discomfort and pain. Drafts of whisky and chloral only made her symptoms worse. Ill nourished and haggard, Victoria looked out at the world through saddened eyes, unable to rouse herself from the depression that nagged at her.

The death of Lenchen's son Christian in Pretoria was one more in a series of losses that made Victoria curse the year, and long in vain for better times. She managed to add Christian's picture to her photo album before collapsing, "exhausted by her grief," surrounded by expressions of love and concern.[13] Now the look of sadness never left her. She sat for hours between sleep and waking, ill served by impudent footmen who smelled of whisky and neglected their duties. Sometimes, to Marie Mallet's horror, the queen's meager dinner was not served at all.[14]

Fall gave way to winter, and a melancholy Christmas at Osborne. Victoria's life had become a dispiriting series of hurdles to be surmounted: Could she manage to eat a few spoonfuls of broth? Could she get an hour or two of sleep? Could the pain in her leg be assuaged even a little? Could she get a stronger prescription for her glasses, so that the words on the papers before her did not blur into meaningless blots? She stumbled on, unwilling to consider giving up yet tripped up, constantly, by a body that simply could not go on.

The accursed year was ending, and with it the century. In a fury of high winds and weeping skies, a fierce storm broke over the Isle of Wight, wrecking ships and felling trees, sending animals scurrying for shelter and causing Victoria's maids to heap up the fire in her bedroom and bring in extra blankets for her bed. She was hardly aware, as midnight approached on December 31, that an era was ending. The Victorian century was passing into oblivion, its thrusting, questioning energies transmuted into the doubts and confusions of an age as yet unnamed. But as the wild winds shrieked through the tall Osborne chimneys, and the shutters banged against the wet stone walls, the old queen's dim thoughts were not of these monumental things, but of the rest she sought in vain, and the children she had lost, and the sad, cold world she could not hope to cling to much longer.

Chapter 24

———— ✎ ————

I T WAS THE TELLTALE sag in the left side of her face that told Dr. Reid that the queen had suffered a stroke. He had been watching her closely for months, privately certain that it would be a stroke that would in time carry her off. On the morning of January 17, 1901, he was certain that he detected a change. And there were other signs. She did not understand what he was saying to her. Her eyes were dazed, her speech slightly slurred. She was not herself.

For weeks the queen's mind had been unclear. Others had taken over for her, and when officials came to see her, they had to be told, discreetly, that she was unable to meet with them. Bertie, in his sixtieth year, prepared himself for the inevitable shock of his mother's death and for his long-delayed accession.

Everyone knew that it had to happen. The queen had to die, she had already outlived her time. But no one, except James Reid, seemed to be able to come to grips with the reality that one day soon she would be gone. For too long she had been the center of their universe, their fixed star. The court and household had revolved around her, her likes and dislikes had taken on the quality of immemorial custom. The sun rose and set by her moods; when she sneezed, the empire tottered. Or so it seemed.

Now, however, it was she who was tottering. When her granddaughter Thora, Lenchen's daughter, sat by her bedside, the old queen rambled on about illness and death, falling asleep in midsentence. She was no longer able to identify with confidence the people who came and went in her room. Sometimes she knew them, sometimes they seemed like ghostly strangers, even hostile strangers, and she tried to order them out. She ate next to nothing, and the sallow skin hung in limp folds over her cheekbones. Her puzzled eyes looked out from deep, dark sockets at Mrs. Tuck, the dresser Reid had designated to be the queen's nurse.

On the cold morning of January 17, Reid informed Bertie, at Sandringham, that his mother was seriously ill and told Lenchen and Beatrice that he wanted to bring in a specialist to examine her. She stayed in bed all day, while rain fell and Reid, Mrs. Tuck and various servants came and went. When toward evening she finally made an effort to dress, she was aware that she was having difficulty using her left hand.

"Are people worried about me?" she asked her daughters. It was unlike her not to go out; she felt certain her inactivity would be noticed and remarked on. Beatrice shrugged the question off. The weather was terrible. An excursion would have been impossible.

"But people know I always go out in the rain!" the queen insisted.

Something was wrong. She could feel it, but could not clearly identify it.

Reid had promised Victoria several years earlier that when he felt that her death was near, he would not hide the truth from her. Yet now, faced with a serious but perhaps not fatal situation, he equivocated. When the specialist, Sir Richard Douglas Powell, arrived at seven-thirty, instead of telling Victoria that he wanted the man to examine her, he said that Powell had come to visit him. She may or may not have been lucid enough to see through this lie. In any case, Powell examined her and told Reid that in his opinion the queen's condition was serious, but she might recover from her stroke.

The following day, however, she was markedly worse. Now all her facial muscles drooped and sagged, she could not swallow even a bite of the wheat cereal that had become her only food, and she lay in her bed, eyes closed, mouth open, from morning to evening. It was time, Reid thought, to send for Bertie and Arthur.

Arthur, as it happened, was in Berlin, attending celebrations of the two-hundredth anniversary of the Hohenzollern dynasty. As soon as he learned of his mother's condition he made preparations to leave. His host, his cousin the kaiser, decided to leave with him. It would of course be an unofficial visit, Willy said; he would not be coming to England as German emperor, merely as Victoria's dutiful grandson.

By Saturday, January 19, all London knew of the queen's illness and a bulletin from Osborne announced that she "had not lately been in her usual health." The strain of recent events upon her nervous system required her to "abstain for the present from transacting business," the announcement read, but its careful circumlocution did not conceal the seriousness of her situation. Journalists gathered at Cowes, awaiting further news. Telephone calls to the royal residences resulted in frustration; the operators told callers politely that they had no information. Inquisitive islanders formed little knots outside the Osborne gates, watching all who went in and out and causing annoyance to the detective on duty.

Bertie arrived, causing a flurry of excitement among the journalists, but he did not stay long. Victoria was much better. There were spots of color in her cheeks, her eyes were bright and she was able to listen to the latest news from South Africa.

"Am I better?" she asked Reid. "I have been very ill."

"Yes, Your Majesty has been very ill," the doctor told her, "but you are better now."

She understood that she had rallied, but that she could not count on maintaining her present level of awareness. She wanted to know whether Bertie was being kept informed of her state, and Reid assured her that he was. She trusted Reid to take charge.

"I should like to live a little longer," she told him, "as I still have a few things to settle. I have arranged most things, but there are still some left, and I want to live a little longer."[1]

In fact preparations were already under way for the change of reigns. Telegraph operators stood ready to send messages throughout the world the instant Victoria died. Government offices awaited word that the new king's reign had begun. Household officers charged with the sad responsibility of arranging the royal funeral quietly began their planning and assembled the needed accoutrements. Carpenters were fashioning a small satin-lined coffin, barely five feet long, to hold the shrunken body of the queen.

Reid too was mindful of all that had to be got ready. To him had been entrusted the intimate task of gathering Victoria's most treasured possessions that were to be placed in her coffin. Surreptitiously, with the help of Mrs. Tuck and another of the queen's dressers, he brought together the mementos Victoria had specified, along with her wedding veil of yellowed lace. She had worn it only once, nearly sixty-one years earlier; she had told him that she wished to wear it once again, after she died.

Willy's arrival at Osborne caused a good deal of consternation. Lenchen and Beatrice had urged him not to come, certain that the shock of seeing him would kill Victoria, but he would not be stopped. He brought with him half a dozen military aides and a physician, but not his customary large entourage. He behaved, Fritz Ponsonby thought, "in a most dignified and admirable manner," even offering to return to London if his cousins insisted. "I should like to see Grand-mama before she dies," he said, "but if that is impossible I shall quite understand."[2] Seeing how cooperative he was, Lenchen and Beatrice relented—Arthur had seen no objection, nor did Bertie pose any—and Willy stayed.

It was Willy, in fact, who gave voice to the splendor of the life Victoria appeared to be leaving behind. Her greatness, he told the others, had begun early, and remained "undimmed even now." Like his Pruss-ian grandfather William I who had lived to be ninety, Victoria had been a mighty figure in the world, and must die amid a fitting display of glory.[3] She had, after all, lived longer than any other British monarch, and reigned over far more subjects. These were measures of greatness, which Willy respected and understood.

With the permission of the family, oxygen tanks were brought in to the sickroom on Sunday January 20 and Victoria, who had again lapsed into a near-comatose state, probably the victim of another stroke, was moved from her high canopied bed to a small cot. A few times she tried to speak, but her words were too muffled to be intelli-gible. Only a miracle could restore her now. Reid called in another doctor, but did not believe that the queen would live many more hours. Archbishop Randall Davidson offered prayers, preparing the family for the final good-bye.

One by one the relatives, and the Munshi, were brought in to see the sleeping queen. They kissed her white cheek and touched her thin hand. Once, she held out her arms and said "Bertie." Another time, she asked for her little white dog and stroked him as he lay on her bed. Reid stayed by her bedside, ready to administer oxygen, denying himself sleep rather than risk having his patient die when he was not in attendance. Her breathing was rasping now, and a nurse was brought in to hold up her head so that she did not choke.

"She doesn't look like dying just now," Reid wrote in a hasty note to his wife. "I can't help admiring her determination not to give up the struggle while she can."[4] She managed to smile when she heard Reid's voice, though she could no longer see him.

At three o'clock on the afternoon of January 22, the sun was low in the wintry sky and the waters of the bay, visible through the windows of the sickroom, were calm. All the family were present in the room now, from young Maurice, who wept audibly, to Bertie, who cried silently but steadily. Alexandra held Victoria's head while Reid placed the oxygen mask over her face. Every breath was an effort now. The muscles of the queen's face were set in a grimacing rictus, and when she tried to move the result was a convulsive jerk.

Weary from the long vigil, tense with fatigue and anxiety, the family members watched the painful spectacle of death. Victoria did not go gracefully, she fought for life, sinking and rallying, sinking and rallying, as if pulling herself up again and again out of the abyss of unawareness into the arena of combat. It was as if, from deep inside her, a spark of will kept leaping back into life. She was not quite ready yet to die. There was still more to do. A few things more.

The struggle stamped itself grotesquely on her aged face. Blessedly, however, the room began to dim and the flattering light of the gas lamps softened the rictus.

Bertie excused himself to send a telegram to the Lord Mayor. "My painful duty obliges me to inform you that the life of the beloved Queen is in the greatest danger." The words of the telegram were placed in the windows of telegraph offices throughout the capital, where crowds of people waited to read them. Standing in the cold, dark streets, men took off their hats and women held handkerchiefs to their eyes. The valiant queen was passing. They murmured prayers for her soul.

Archbishop Davidson prayed aloud by her bedside, in the gathering dusk, along with the Vicar of Whippingham Church. From time to time members of the family called out their names to her, but she gave no sign that she heard anything. Dr. Reid and Willy knelt on either side of her cot, holding up her head, for more than two hours.

Then, just at six-thirty, the archbishop saw the queen's face suddenly relax, and knew that her struggle was at an end.

Grieving, Bertie nonetheless stepped smoothly into his role as king. He gave the necessary orders, met with officials, made certain that the funeral arrangements were in hand. He left it to Reid to prepare his mother's body for burial.

This Reid did, fighting exhaustion. Following Victoria's secret instructions, he laid in the bottom of the coffin a collection of her most treasured possessions, including an alabaster cast of Albert's hand, Albert's dressing gown and a robe embroidered by Alice. There were photographs, small statues, jewels, items of clothing. On top of these was placed the queen's tiny body, now feather-light, the Garter sash across her thin chest, her face covered by her long wedding veil, a bouquet of sweet-smelling flowers in her hands.

Under the flowers, hidden from view, Reid put into Victoria's left hand a small tissue-wrapped package. Inside was a lock of John Brown's hair, and his picture. Victoria's devotion for Brown went with her, even to her grave. But Bertie, now Edward VII, lost no time in erasing all evidence of that devotion. As soon as he decently could, following Victoria's funeral, he inspected all the royal residences, ordering them brightened and painted, refurbished and modernized. And whenever he came upon a statue of John Brown, he picked it up, smiling with secret satisfaction, and smashed it beyond recognition.

Notes

Chapter 1

1. Letter from Queen Victoria to her daughter Vicky, June 9, 1858.

2. Cited in Dormer Creston, *The Youthful Queen Victoria* (New York, 1952), p. 155.

3. *Ibid.*, 118.

4. The Duke of Sussex, sixth son of George III, made a morganatic marriage as a young man and had two children, Augustus and Augusta. They were barred from the succession because the duke never obtained his father's consent to marry. Had he asked for royal consent, it would undoubtedly have been denied.

5. Of Späth, Feodore wrote, "There certainly never was such devotedness as hers, to all our family, although it sometimes shows itself rather foolishly . . . " *The Letters of Queen Victoria. A Selection of Her Majesty's Correspondence between the Years 1837 and 1861*, ed. A. C. Benson and Viscount Esher, 3 vols. (London: John Murray, 1907), I, 25. Apparently she was both elderly and ill-favored; Wellington's unchivalrous remark about Späth was that no man would want to take her in to supper.

6. *The Girlhood of Queen Victoria: A Selection From Her Majesty's Diaries between the Years 1832 and 1840*, ed. Viscount Esher, 2 vols. (London: John Murray, 1912), I, 280.

Chapter 2

1. This was Wellington's well-informed view, confided to the diarist Greville. Cecil Woodham-Smith, *Queen Victoria: From Her Birth to the Death of the Prince Consort* (New York, 1972), p. 73.

2. Späth's devotion is described by Feodore in *The Letters of Queen Victoria*, ed. Benson and Esher, I, 25. Victoria's Aunt Adelaide thought that the aged baroness would surely die of grief when she was sent away. For Mrs. Brock, see *The Girlhood of Queen Victoria*, ed. Esher, I, 159. "Good Louis" is in *The Girlhood of Queen Victoria*, ed. Esher, I, 62 and *The Letters of Queen Victoria*, ed. Benson and Esher, I, 25. Amelia Carolath (Countess Blankensee) is recalled in *Dearest Child: Letters between Queen Victoria and the Princess Royal*, ed. Roger Fulford (New York, 1964), p. 82.

3. Conroy had three sons, Edward, Stephen and Henry, and two daughters, Victoire and Jane. But although Jane's company was sometimes forced on Victoria, it was Victoire who was inflicted on her frequently, and whom she detested.

4. Victoria sketched Victoire Conroy. Marina Warner, *Queen Victoria's Sketchbooks* (London, 1979), pp. 28–9.

5. Philip Ziegler, *King William IV* (London, 1971), p. 51.

6. The gallant "Mrs." Jordan, who was in fact never married and was herself illegitimate, was a star of the London stage in the 1780s and 1790s. Her sunny nature, joyful and infectious laugh, and natural gaiety made her immensely popular, and while her popularity and high income lasted, she shared the money with William, while giving him a child every year or two. She had never known an easy life. Seduced and abandoned, she went on the stage before she was twenty, lived with a well-known actor and had two children by him only to discover that he had no wish to marry her, and finally began her long liaison with the future William IV. William parted from her, chiefly for dynastic reasons, when she was fifty years old, with devastating consequences for her. She tried and failed to resume the acting career that had brought her fame decades earlier. Her health broke, and she died, a bankrupt, in 1816. Anne Somerset, *William IV* (London, 1980), p. 60, and Ziegler, *King William IV*, pp. 76ff, 109.

Mrs. Jordan's ten children by William IV, who were Victoria's cousins, were George, Henry, Sophia (William's favorite), Mary, Frederick, Elizabeth, Adolphus, Augusta, Augustus and Amelia.

7. Somerset, p. 38.

8. *The Greville Memoirs: A Journal of the Reigns of King George IV and King William IV,* ed. Henry Reeve, 2 vols. (New York, 1875), I, 357.

9. Ziegler, *King William IV,* p. 126. When Princess Sophia referred to Adelaide as "Mrs. Aquatic," she did not mean to refer to Adelaide's tearfulness, as some biographers have assumed. Rather the term derived from Sophia's code name for William, which was "Aquatic," an obvious reference to his naval career.

10. Adelaide was pregnant at least four times; besides her short-lived daughter Elizabeth she miscarried twice and gave birth to a baby who lived only a few hours.

11. Woodham-Smith, p. 88.

12. Creston, p. 37.

13. *The Letters of Queen Victoria,* ed. Benson and Esher, I, 70 and note.

14. *Ibid.* According to Victoria's own account of the incident, it was not her mother's resistance that caused the idea of a name change to be dropped, but a decision of the royal ministers.

15. Ziegler, *King William IV,* p. 193.

Chapter 3

1. *Greville Memoirs, Reigns of George IV and William IV,* I, 521. It was said that the British had used this same method of reducing the population in India. The British government had known for many months that the epidemic would soon reach London, and that when it did, its consequences would be devastating. Yet the royal council, albeit concerned, did nothing. At the last moment, when deaths were occurring in Rotherhithe and Limehouse, a Board of Health was set up, but the epidemic swept on unopposed.

2. The Duchess of Kent told a friend that though she repeatedly asked her daughter whether she was pleased or worried about the prospect of becoming Queen, Victoria would not say. Creston, p. 148.

3. Woodham-Smith, p. 78. In 1867, nearly forty years after the events she described, Lehzen recalled how the child Victoria had given her governess her hand and said "I will be good," adding other highly moralistic sentiments, after learning that she would one day rule. But Lehzen's account turns the eleven-year-old Victoria into a goody-goody, when most other surviving evidence shows her as far more emotionally volatile and opinionated, a creature of mood swings and prone to fears.

4. *Ibid.*

5. Christopher Hibbert, *Queen Victoria in Her Letters and Journals* (New York, 1985), p. 11.

6. Creston, p. 181.

7. Gervas Huxley, *Lady Elizabeth and the Grosvenors* (London and New

York, 1965), pp. 40–42 gives many details about Victoria's visit to Eaton Hall and Chester.

8. Huxley, p. 38.

9. "A horrible player she is," the diarist Creevey confided to his diary. Cited in Creston, p. 258.

10. Creston, p. 193.

11. *Gentleman's Magazine*, CLIII (1833), 633; CLIV (1833), 75.

12. *Greville Memoirs, Reigns of George IV and William IV*, II, 192, 198.

13. In Queen Adelaide's cottage was a model of the mean little castle of Meiningen that had been her home as a girl. Greville thought it "a wretched-looking dog-hole of a building," but to Adelaide it must have represented happier times. *Greville Memoirs, Reigns of George IV and William IV*, II, 274–5.

14. *Dearest Child*, ed. Fulford, p. 72.

15. Creston, p. 155.

16. A letter of Baron Stockmar's to the Duchess of Kent in summer 1834 pointed out that Victoria naturally resented Conroy's "undue control over herself," adding, "Your Royal Highness yourself has agreed with me that Sir John's personal behavior towards the Princess has been apt only too often to worsen this state of affairs." Woodham-Smith, p. 97.

17. Warner, *Sketchbooks*, p. 71.

Chapter 4

1. Emotional tension no doubt weakened the princess. Seven months later Leopold wrote, in a letter to Lehzen, of his "having had the courage, in Ramsgate, to tear apart the whole web of intrigue . . . " Clearly this was an allusion to Leopold's having intervened in Conroy's system of control over Victoria's household. Woodham-Smith, p. 125.

2. Typhoid fever was not identified in Western Europe until 1829. It would be another two generations before the microorganism that causes typhoid would be identified and the means of transmission understood. Very likely Victoria, her resistance weakened by fatigue, became infected through drinking polluted water or contaminated milk.

3. *Greville Memoirs, Reigns of George IV and William IV*, II, 344.

4. *Ibid.*, II, 241. A number of other people, including Princess Lieven and Wellington, thought that William IV had inherited his father's dementia. In actuality, of course, George III suffered from porphyria, of which his long periods of schizophrenia were a manifestation.

5. Victoria told Leopold that she was reading these memoirs "with great interest, and finding there is a great deal in them which applies to the present times, and a great deal of good advice and reasoning in them." Hibbert, *Letters and Journals*, p. 17.

6. *The Girlhood of Queen Victoria*, ed. Esher, I, 128–9, and *The Letters of Queen Victoria*, ed. Benson and Esher, I, 48–50.

7. *The Girlhood of Queen Victoria*, ed. Esher, I, 109.

8. *The Letters of Queen Victoria*, ed. Benson and Esher, I, 46–7.

9. Hibbert, *Letters and Journals*, p. 19.

10. "In 1836 I was extremely crushed and kept under and hardly dared say a word," Victoria recalled later. *The Letters of Queen Victoria*, ed. Benson and Esher, II, 49.

11. *The Girlhood of Queen Victoria*, ed. Esher, II, 127.

12. The eighteenth-century writer Lord Chesterfield distilled the generally accepted attitude toward women when he wrote that women were only "children of a larger growth." "A man of sense," he said, "only trifles with them, plays with them, humors and flatters them as he does with a sprightly forward child." Cited in Philip Mason, *The English Gentleman: The Rise and Fall of an Ideal* (London, 1982), p. 67.

13. Apart from her younger brother Leopold, the Duchess of Kent had five other surviving siblings: Sophia, who married Emanuel Count von Mensdorff-Pouilly; Antoinette, who married Alexander, Duke of Württemberg; Juliana, who married Constantine, Grand Duke of Russia; Ernest, Duke of Saxe-Coburg-Gotha who was Prince Albert's father, and Ferdinand, whose son and namesake married Maria da Gloria, Queen of Portugal.

14. Hibbert, *Letters and Journals*, p. 13.

15. *Ibid.*, 16; Woodham-Smith, p. 124.

16. Hibbert, *Letters and Journals*, p. 19.

17. *The Letters of Queen Victoria*, ed. Benson and Esher, I, 59.

18. Woodham-Smith, p. 121.

19. Hibbert, *Letters and Journals*, p. 17.

20. Woodham-Smith, pp. 118–19. When in 1841 Victoria's half-brother Charles of Leiningen wrote a memorandum recalling the events of 1836, he noted that "from this time onwards the connection between Albert and Victoria was regarded as the one aim to which all energies should be directed." And Albert added, "I was aware at the time of our visit in 1836 of the difficulties attending it."

21. Hibbert, *Letters and Journals*, pp. 17–19. Godfrey and Margaret Scheele, *The Prince Consort: Man of Many Facets* (London, 1977), p. 51.

22. Hibbert, *Letters and Journals*, p. 18.

23. Creston, pp. 186–7.

24. *Dearest Child*, ed. Fulford, p. 302. Writing to her daughter Vicky twenty-four years after the events she described, Victoria recalled the time of her own accession, when she was "a young girl only just eighteen placed in such a position without a single relative to support and sustain her . . . brouillée with my poor mother—so as to be almost at that time at enmity with her—my own brother acting against me."

25. Cited in Creston, p. 199.

26. Hibbert, *Letters and Journals*, p. 21.

Chapter 5

1. *The Girlhood of Queen Victoria*, ed. Esher, II, 296. Melbourne added, on another occasion, "I am always ready to see him, he is such a very clever man, and he don't stay long."

2. *The Letters of Queen Victoria*, ed. Benson and Esher, I, 106.

3. *The Girlhood of Queen Victoria*, ed. Esher, I, 193.

4. Hibbert, *Letters and Journals*, p. 22.

5. *Ibid.*

6. *Ibid.*, 23–4.

7. Cited in Creston, pp. 252–3.

8. Hibbert, *Letters and Journals*, p. 24.

9. *The Letters of Queen Victoria*, ed. Benson and Esher, I, 127; *The Greville Memoirs. Second Part. A Journal of the Reign of Queen Victoria from 1837 to 1852*, ed. Henry Reeve, 2 vols. (New York, 1885), I, 14. The Duchesse de Praslin noted that Victoria "could not hide anger or annoyance," and that "ministers tremble when this young being shows discontent at anything." Cited in Creston, pp. 304–5.

10. *Greville Memoirs, Second Part, Reign of Victoria*, I, 19.

11. Vera Watson, *A Queen At Home* (London, 1952), p. 88.

12. *Ibid.*, 51ff.

13. *Ibid.*, 16–17.

14. *Greville Memoirs, Second Part, Reign of Victoria*, I, 130.

15. *Ibid.*, I, 14.

16. Cited in Creston, p. 261.

17. John Ashton, *Gossip in the First Decade of Victoria's Reign* (London, 1903), p. 18.

Chapter 6

1. Ashton, *Gossip*, pp. 27–9. For London's severe winter of 1838, see *Gentleman's Magazine*, IX, New Series (January–June 1838), 309.

2. Hibbert, *Letters and Journals*, p. 39; *The Girlhood of Queen Victoria*, ed. Esher, II, 58.

3. *The Letters of Queen Victoria*, ed. Benson and Esher, I, 141–2.

4. *Greville Memoirs, Second Part, Reign of Victoria*, I, 94.

5. Hibbert, *Letters and Journals*, pp. 34–5.

6. *Ibid.*, 35.

7. Ashton, *Gossip*, pp. 53–5.

6. *The Girlhood of Queen Victoria*, ed. Esher, I, 128–9, and *The Letters of Queen Victoria*, ed. Benson and Esher, I, 48–50.

7. *The Girlhood of Queen Victoria*, ed. Esher, I, 109.

8. *The Letters of Queen Victoria*, ed. Benson and Esher, I, 46–7.

9. Hibbert, *Letters and Journals*, p. 19.

10. "In 1836 I was extremely crushed and kept under and hardly dared say a word," Victoria recalled later. *The Letters of Queen Victoria*, ed. Benson and Esher, II, 49.

11. *The Girlhood of Queen Victoria*, ed. Esher, II, 127.

12. The eighteenth-century writer Lord Chesterfield distilled the generally accepted attitude toward women when he wrote that women were only "children of a larger growth." "A man of sense," he said, "only trifles with them, plays with them, humors and flatters them as he does with a sprightly forward child." Cited in Philip Mason, *The English Gentleman: The Rise and Fall of an Ideal* (London, 1982), p. 67.

13. Apart from her younger brother Leopold, the Duchess of Kent had five other surviving siblings: Sophia, who married Emanuel Count von Mensdorff-Pouilly; Antoinette, who married Alexander, Duke of Württemberg; Juliana, who married Constantine, Grand Duke of Russia; Ernest, Duke of Saxe-Coburg-Gotha who was Prince Albert's father, and Ferdinand, whose son and namesake married Maria da Gloria, Queen of Portugal.

14. Hibbert, *Letters and Journals*, p. 13.

15. *Ibid.*, 16; Woodham-Smith, p. 124.

16. Hibbert, *Letters and Journals*, p. 19.

17. *The Letters of Queen Victoria*, ed. Benson and Esher, I, 59.

18. Woodham-Smith, p. 121.

19. Hibbert, *Letters and Journals*, p. 17.

20. Woodham-Smith, pp. 118–19. When in 1841 Victoria's half-brother Charles of Leiningen wrote a memorandum recalling the events of 1836, he noted that "from this time onwards the connection between Albert and Victoria was regarded as the one aim to which all energies should be directed." And Albert added, "I was aware at the time of our visit in 1836 of the difficulties attending it."

21. Hibbert, *Letters and Journals*, pp. 17–19. Godfrey and Margaret Scheele, *The Prince Consort: Man of Many Facets* (London, 1977), p. 51.

22. Hibbert, *Letters and Journals*, p. 18.

23. Creston, pp. 186–7.

24. *Dearest Child*, ed. Fulford, p. 302. Writing to her daughter Vicky twenty-four years after the events she described, Victoria recalled the time of her own accession, when she was "a young girl only just eighteen placed in such a position without a single relative to support and sustain her . . . brouillée with my poor mother—so as to be almost at that time at enmity with her—my own brother acting against me."

25. Cited in Creston, p. 199.

26. Hibbert, *Letters and Journals*, p. 21.

Chapter 5

1. *The Girlhood of Queen Victoria*, ed. Esher, II, 296. Melbourne added, on another occasion, "I am always ready to see him, he is such a very clever man, and he don't stay long."

2. *The Letters of Queen Victoria*, ed. Benson and Esher, I, 106.

3. *The Girlhood of Queen Victoria*, ed. Esher, I, 193.

4. Hibbert, *Letters and Journals*, p. 22.

5. *Ibid.*

6. *Ibid.*, 23–4.

7. Cited in Creston, pp. 252–3.

8. Hibbert, *Letters and Journals*, p. 24.

9. *The Letters of Queen Victoria*, ed. Benson and Esher, I, 127; *The Greville Memoirs. Second Part. A Journal of the Reign of Queen Victoria from 1837 to 1852*, ed. Henry Reeve, 2 vols. (New York, 1885), I, 14. The Duchesse de Praslin noted that Victoria "could not hide anger or annoyance," and that "ministers tremble when this young being shows discontent at anything." Cited in Creston, pp. 304–5.

10. *Greville Memoirs, Second Part, Reign of Victoria*, I, 19.

11. Vera Watson, *A Queen At Home* (London, 1952), p. 88.

12. *Ibid.*, 51ff.

13. *Ibid.*, 16–17.

14. *Greville Memoirs, Second Part, Reign of Victoria*, I, 130.

15. *Ibid.*, I, 14.

16. Cited in Creston, p. 261.

17. John Ashton, *Gossip in the First Decade of Victoria's Reign* (London, 1903), p. 18.

Chapter 6

1. Ashton, *Gossip*, pp. 27–9. For London's severe winter of 1838, see *Gentleman's Magazine*, IX, New Series (January–June 1838), 309.

2. Hibbert, *Letters and Journals*, p. 39; *The Girlhood of Queen Victoria*, ed. Esher, II, 58.

3. *The Letters of Queen Victoria*, ed. Benson and Esher, I, 141–2.

4. *Greville Memoirs, Second Part, Reign of Victoria*, I, 94.

5. Hibbert, *Letters and Journals*, pp. 34–5.

6. *Ibid.*, 35.

7. Ashton, *Gossip*, pp. 53–5.

8. *Greville Memoirs, Second Part, Reign of Victoria*, I, 297, 260. Clarendon referred to "the anility of Melbourne." Greville remarked that "any man of resolution and obstinacy does what he will with Melbourne."

9. *The Girlhood of Queen Victoria*, ed. Esher, II, 3.

10. David Cecil, *Melbourne* (New York, 1939; reprint 1966), pp. 192, 181.

11. *Ibid.*, 378.

12. *The Girlhood of Queen Victoria*, ed. Esher, II, 313. Melbourne thought Wellington was overrated; "I do not happen to think he is so great a man," he remarked in 1828. Cecil, *Melbourne*, p. 198.

13. Hibbert, *Letters and Journals*, p. 53.

14. Woodham-Smith, p. 166.

15. Victoria's own penetrating analysis of what disturbed her at this time was simply that it was the natural consequence of too much power being given to one who was too young to wield it maturely. Looking back, at the age of fifty, on this period she wrote that the recollection was "rather painful." "That life of mere amusement, flattery, excitement and mere politics had a bad effect (as it must have on every one) on her naturally simple and serious nature," she wrote to Theodore Martin, Albert's biographer. *The Letters of Queen Victoria, Second Series. A Selection from Her Majesty's Correspondence and Journal Between the Years 1862 and 1878*, ed. George Earle Buckle, 2 vols. (London, 1926–28), I, 584.

16. Hibbert, *Letters and Journals*, p. 42.

17. George Rowell, *Queen Victoria Goes to the Theater* (London, 1978), p. 24.

18. In Victoria's defense it must be pointed out that the specialist Sir Charles Clarke had told Melbourne, who then told Victoria, that even though Flora was a virgin, it was possible for virgins to be pregnant. Hibbert, *Letters and Journals*, p. 42.

19. *The Girlhood of Queen Victoria*, ed. Esher, I, 292–3.

Chapter 7

1. Unfortunately, Albert's diary, which he kept from the age of five, has not been preserved, except for passages copied out after his death. Hermione Hobhouse, *Prince Albert: His Life and Work* (London, 1983), p. 151.

2. Stockmar, who in 1839 was Albert's companion and tutor, told him (and others) that Victoria was showing symptoms of the family disease, of which the chief characteristic was mental instability. Elizabeth Longford, "Queen Victoria's Doctors," in Martin Gilbert, ed., *A Century of Conflict, 1850–1950* (London, 1966), 84 and note, 85.

3. *The Girlhood of Queen Victoria*, ed. Esher, II, 215–16; *Dearest Child*, ed. Fulford, p. 167.

4. Hibbert, *Letters and Journals*, p. 55. "My heart is quite going," she added the following day. *Ibid.*, 56.

5. *The Girlhood of Queen Victoria*, ed. Esher, II, 264–6.

6. *Ibid.*, II, 267–9.

7. Hibbert, *Letters and Journals*, p. 57.

8. *Ibid.*

9. Hector Bolitho, *The Prince Consort and His Brother* (New York, 1934), p. 7.

10. *Ibid.*

11. Hobhouse, p. 21; Scheele, p. 51.

12. *The Girlhood of Queen Victoria*, ed. Esher, II, 316, 311–12.

13. *The Correspondence of Sarah, Lady Lyttelton, 1787–1870*, ed. Mrs. Hugh Wyndham (London, 1912), p. 297.

14. Hibbert, *Letters and Journals*, p. 64.

15. Writing to Vicky in April of 1858, Victoria noted that having a first child was a tremendous shock, a complete outrage to a young woman's feelings of propriety—feelings to which, she added, "the marital act itself was quite shock enough to begin with." In April of 1859 she again alluded, in a letter to Vicky, to "what I suffered, what I felt" when first married—a reference not only to the discomforts of pregnancy but the entire sexual side of marriage.

Early Victorian doctors cautioned that "a first sexual intercourse is, even when sanctioned by marriage and with the most perfect mutual affection, the cause of considerable physical suffering to the female, not infrequently requiring medical attention and the cessation of all sexual activities for some time." Tingsten, pp. 87, 86, 54.

Even in 1859, when she was forty years old, Victoria could still write to her daughter, "I am very much like a girl in all these feelings." *Dearest Child*, ed. Fulford, p. 166.

16. Bolitho, *Prince Consort*, p. 13.

17. So inaccurate was Victorian medical knowledge that doctors informed women that they were least fertile midway between their periods; acting on this belief would have been a sure way to become pregnant. Patricia Knight, "Women and Abortion in Victorian and Edwardian England," *History Workshop Journal*, IV (Autumn 1977), 59. Though officially banned, methods of birth control were known to working-class women. Condoms made of fabric or sheep's intestines had been used for centuries, and in the early nineteenth century, sponges and "gloves" to cover the penis were readily available.

If birth control failed, women often resorted to abortifacients, many of them drastic and sometimes lethal. Victorian newspapers had many advertisements offering to rid women of "temporary inconvenience"—a veiled reference to pregnancy. Duncan Crow, *The Victorian Woman* (London, 1971), p. 102; Françoise Barret-Ducrocq, *Love in the Time of Victoria: Sexuality and Desire Among Working-Class Men and Women in Nineteenth-Century London* (London, 1989), pp. 128–9. It is worth pointing out that in England, until 1884, a woman could be imprisoned for denying her husband his "conjugal rights." Crow, p. 147.

18. H. and A. Gernsheim, *Queen Victoria: A Biography in Word and Picture* (London, 1959), p. 40; Warner, *Sketchbooks*, p. 93.

19. *The Letters of Queen Victoria*, ed. Benson and Esher, I, 283.

20. Contemporary remark by the Duchesse de Praslin, cited in Creston, p. 311. Lehzen's stationery had a picture of a train on it, with the motto "I am coming."

21. Longford, "Queen Victoria's Doctors," in Gilbert, p. 76.

22. Albert's detailed account of the assassination attempt is in Bolitho, *Prince Consort*, pp. 19–20. See also *Greville Memoirs, Second Part, Reign of Queen Victoria*, I, 250. Assassination was in the air; in France in 1840 there were "Death to Kings and Sovereigns" societies, as Leopold informed Victoria. *The Letters of Queen Victoria*, ed. Benson and Esher, I, 286.

23. Longford, "Queen Victoria's Doctors," in Gilbert, p. 76.

24. *Ibid.*

25. *Dearest Child*, ed. Fulford, p. 151.

Chapter 8

1. *Dearest Child*, ed. Fulford, p. 88. "Oh!" she wrote to Vicky nineteen years later, "if those selfish men—who are the cause of all one's misery—only knew what their poor slaves go through! what suffering—what humiliation to the delicate feelings of a poor woman, above all a young one—especially with those nasty doctors." In her letters to Vicky she referred again and again to her illness and unhappiness during her first two pregnancies. *Ibid.*, 94.

2. *Dearest Child*, ed. Fulford, pp. 111–12.

3. *Greville Memoirs, Second Part, Reign of Queen Victoria*, III, 113.

4. Scheele, p. 24; *The Letters of Queen Victoria*, ed. Benson and Esher, I, 381.

5. Woodham-Smith, p. 219, citing Anson's unpublished memorandum in the Royal Archives.

6. *The Letters of Queen Victoria*, ed. Benson and Esher, I, 379, 366. The previous April she wrote that, if Albert were to go on a trip, she would go with him in order to avoid a separation, "even if he was to go to the North Pole." *Ibid.*, I, 329–30.

7. *The Letters of Queen Victoria*, ed. Benson and Esher, I, 457.

8. Hibbert, *Letters and Journals*, pp. 93–4; John Van der Kiste, *Queen Victoria's Children* (Wolfeboro Falls, New Hampshire, 1990), pp. 12–13, gives a broader context for the quarrel. One wonders whether Albert's accusation that Victoria was "starving" Vicky was a veiled reference to the queen's extreme dislike of breast-feeding.

9. Ashton, *Gossip*, p. 181.

10. John W. Dodds, *The Age of Paradox: A Biography of England 1841–51* (London, 1953), p. 89.

11. Details of the royal ball are in Ashton, *Gossip*, pp. 187, 190.

12. *The Girlhood of Queen Victoria*, ed. Esher, II, 316.

13. *Greville Memoirs, Second Part, Reign of Queen Victoria*, II, 58.

14. Victorians believed that because women's brains were smaller than men's, women were far less capable of reasoning and learning—and hence less intelligent. Crow, p. 146.

15. *The Girlhood of Queen Victoria*, ed. Esher, II, 132. Of course, Melbourne had had a searing experience with one particular woman novelist, his wife Caroline Lamb.

16. *Ibid.*, II, 158, 40.

17. Dodds, p. 71.

18. *Ibid.*, 72. Unfortunately, submission often led to harm. A husband could legally "chastise" his wife—and chastisement was broadly defined, to include intimidation, slaps and blows, and whipping. Ronald Pearsall, *Public Purity, Private Shame: Victorian Sexual Hypocrisy Exposed* (London, 1976), p. 9.

Chapter 9

1. Henry Mayhew, *London Labour and the London Poor* (London, 1861–2), II, 402. One workman declared, "I was hardly ever in such a set of stinks as I've been in the sewers and underground parts of the Palace." The odor permeated the grounds, and many areas of the castle were almost uninhabitable because of the horrible smell. Watson, p. 97.

2. Watson, p. 97.

3. Bolitho, *Prince Consort*, p. 77.

4. *The Letters of Queen Victoria*, ed. Benson and Esher, I, 494.

5. Hibbert, *Letters and Journals*, p. 97.

6. Cited in Ferguson, p. 63.

7. Bolitho, *Prince Consort*, p. 59.

8. *The Letters of Queen Victoria*, ed. Benson and Esher, II, 152.

9. *Ibid.*, I, 641.

10. *Greville Memoirs, Second Part, Reign of Queen Victoria*, II, 269.

11. *The Letters of Queen Victoria*, ed. Benson and Esher, II, 197.

Chapter 10

1. Hibbert, *Letters and Journals*, pp. 84–5.

2. In the epidemic of 1848/9, over two thousand people died in a single week; in the last three months of 1849 deaths reached nearly thirteen thousand. In the river districts, where contagion was always worst, inhabitants were described by contemporaries as "more like ghouls and maniacs than human beings."

3. The terrible suffering in Ireland received little mention in Victoria's letters and journal entries; by contrast, the sufferings of the deposed French royal family in 1848 caused her to write reams of sympathetic comment.

4. Hibbert, *Letters and Journals*, p. 89.

5. Michael Tyler-Whittle, *Victoria and Albert at Home* (London, 1980), p. 60.

6. *Greville Memoirs, Second Part, Reign of Victoria*, III, 49. Lady Lyttelton confided to Greville, after her service in the nursery ended, that "the Queen was very fond of her children, but severe in her manner, and a strict disciplinarian in the family."

7. Woodham-Smith, p. 335.

8. *The Letters of Queen Victoria*, ed. Benson and Esher, II, 335.

9. Bolitho, *Prince Consort*, p. 30.

10. On April 4, 1851, Victoria wrote in her journal that Albert went to hear Lyell lecture on antediluvian raindrops while she went to the Haymarket and heard two acts of *Don Cesar de Bazan*. Rowell, p. 44.

11. *The Letters of Queen Victoria*, ed. Benson and Esher, II, 438, 444.

12. Bolitho, *Prince Consort*, p. 131.

13. *Ibid.*, 127–8.

14. *The Letters of Queen Victoria*, ed. Benson and Esher, III, 608.

15. Donald Southgate, *"The Most English Minister"; The Policies and Politics of Palmerston* (New York, 1966), p. 137.

16. *Ibid.*, 279–80.

17. *Ibid.*

Chapter 11

1. Albert wrote to Victoria during her last pregnancy that "that relationship [sex] is sacred, in spite of the pains and trials which women have to suffer." Cited in Woodham-Smith, p. 336.

2. Woodham-Smith, p. 337.

3. Delia Millar, *Queen Victoria's Life in the Scottish Highlands* (New York, 1985), p. 31.

4. One lamentable hunt is described in Bolitho, *Prince Consort*, p. 131. Albert and two companions shot at three stags in a thicket near the Castle, and all missed, time and again. One wonders whether the companions were missing on purpose, reluctant to show up Albert's indifferent marksmanship.

5. Woodham-Smith, p. 264.

6. *Greville Memoirs, Second Part, Reign of Victoria*, III, 109.

7. During the Crimean War, the telegraph operator said, he was kept so busy that he nearly died from overwork. Ferguson, p. 83.

8. Hibbert, *Letters and Journals*, p. 126.

9. *Greville Memoirs, Second Part, Reign of Victoria*, III, 184.

10. Hibbert, *Letters and Journals*, p. 126.

11. Bolitho, *Prince Consort*, p. 147.

Chapter 12

1. *Greville Memoirs, Second Part, Reign of Victoria*, III, 34.

2. *The Letters of Queen Victoria*, ed. Benson and Esher, I, 493.

3. Tisdall, p. 34.

4. George Eliot, writing about Victoria in the early 1850s, thought her looks "deplorable . . . worse and worse the more one looks at her—so utterly mean in contour and expression." Cited in Stanley Weintraub, *Victoria: An Intimate Biography* (New York, 1988), p. 222.

5. Victoria wrote to Vicky shortly after Albert's death that she had "leant on him for all and everything—without whom I did nothing, moved not a finger, arranged not a print or photograph, didn't put on a gown or bonnet if he didn't approve." Hibbert, *Letters and Journals*, p. 157.

6. Woodham-Smith, p. 337.

7. Bolitho, *Prince Consort*, p. 151.

8. *Ibid.*, 166.

9. Van der Kiste, pp. 29–30.

10. *The Letters of Queen Victoria*, ed. Benson and Esher, III, 600; Bolitho, *Prince Consort*, p. 159.

11. *Gentleman's Magazine*, CCI (July 1856), 112.

12. Hibbert, *Letters and Journals*, p. 132.

13. *The Letters of Queen Victoria, Second Series*, ed. Buckle, I, 279. She added, "He was very vindictive, and personal feelings influenced his political acts very much."

14. Millar, p. 66.

15. Woodham-Smith, p. 336.

16. *The Letters of Queen Victoria*, ed. Benson and Esher, III, 231.

17. *Ibid.*, III, 248.

18. Albert's speeches were stupefyingly boring. "The means you have adopted to effect your work of benevolence appear no less deserving of commendation than the object itself," he told the Golden Lane audience. "You have not been content with the bare attempt to force, perhaps upon unwilling recipients, a boon the value of which might not be appreciated, but you have wisely sought to work upon the convictions and natural feelings of the parents and the children you wished to benefit, by extending your assistance to those who, by a small contribution out of their hardly-won earnings, have proved that they are awake to a sense of the vast importance . . . etc. etc." *Gentleman's Magazine*, CCII (January–June, 1857), 485.

An Albertine sentence often had 150 words or more in it, and dozens of hypnotic, sleep-inducing subordinate clauses.

19. Van der Kiste, p. 64.

Chapter 13

1. Letter from Victoria to Vicky, cited in Tingsten, p. 86; Woodham-Smith, p. 338.

2. So recalled Frieda Arnold, one of Victoria's dressers in the 1850s. Ferguson, p. 84.

3. It is significant that, of all the royal relations present at the wedding, only Albert was dry-eyed—and remained so even when Vicky threw herself, weeping, into his arms. The others were bathed in emotion. Albert's composure was a measure of his steely self-control, not his inner feeling. *Gentleman's Magazine*, CCIV (January–June, 1858), 203.

4. *Dearest Child*, ed. Fulford, p. 90; *Dearest Mama: Letters between Queen Victoria and the Crown Princess of Prussia 1861–1864*, ed. Roger Fulford (London, 1968), p. 98; Warner, *Sketchbooks*, p. 118.

5. *Dearest Child*, ed. Fulford, pp. 79, 148; Hibbert, *Letters and Journals*, p. 108.

6. *Gentleman's Magazine*, CCI (November 1856), 629; Tingsten, p. 356.

7. Tingsten, pp. 357–8.

8. Van der Kiste, p. 30; Whittle, p. 92.

9. *Ibid.*, 34.

10. *The Letters of Queen Victoria*, ed. Benson and Esher, II, 438.

11. *Dearest Child*, ed. Fulford, p. 156.

12. In March 1858 Victoria wrote to Vicky that "dear papa, God knows, does everything." Hibbert, *Letters and Journals*, p. 103.

13. *Gentleman's Magazine*, CCII (January-June 1857), 104–5.

14. Richard D. Altick, *The Presence of the Past* (Columbus, Ohio, 1993), p. 272. The term "Fast Girl" was borrowed from the "Fast Men" of the 1840s, foppish characters who affected outlandish dress and speech.

15. Death by fire was a far greater hazard to women in crinolines than is commonly recognized. One French actress was burned to death on the stage when her voluminous skirt went up in flames. A German archduchess, caught smoking, concealed her cigarette in her petticoat and subsequently incinerated herself. Open hearths were an invitation to accidents, as wide skirts swept too near for safety. Peter Quennell, *Victorian Panorama* (London, 1937), p. 96.

16. Altick, p. 508. The baboon lady's manager assured viewers that, although his prize specimen was dead, there was "nothing in the exhibition to offend the taste or disturb the sensibility of even the most fastidious lady."

17. Hibbert, *Letters and Journals*, pp. 136–7.

18. *Dearest Child*, ed. Fulford, p. 118.

19. Hibbert, *Letters and Journals*, p. 105.

20. *Letters of Queen Victoria from the Archives of the House of Brandenburg-Prussia*, ed. Hector Bolitho, trans. Mrs. J. Pudney and Lord Sudley (New Haven, 1938), p. 87. "The way in which luckless women in childbed are usually treated in Germany," Victoria wrote to Vicky's mother-in-law Augusta, Princess of Prussia, "has as its result that they emerge pale, weak and wretched from the treatment, not from the thing itself, and need a long time to recover from the nursing."

21. When Victoria first heard of Vicky's pregnancy, she felt certain that "it will all end in nothing." *Dearest Child*, ed. Fulford, p. 108.

22. Hibbert, *Letters and Journals*, p. 106.

23. *Dearest Child*, ed. Fulford, p. 90.

Chapter 14

1. *Dearest Child*, ed. Fulford, pp. 363, 209.

2. *Ibid.*, 180.

3. *Ibid.*, 91.

4. *The Letters of Queen Victoria*, ed. Benson and Esher, III, 553.

5. *Ibid.*, III, 428.

6. Hibbert, *Letters and Journals*, p. 118.

7. *Letters of Queen Victoria*, ed. Bolitho, p. 115.

8. *The Letters of Queen Victoria*, ed. Benson and Esher, III, 560. "Oh! I am so wretched to think how, for a time, two people most wickedly estranged us!" Victoria wrote early in April. "To miss a mother's friendship—not to be able to have her to confide in—when a girl most needs it, was fearful! . . . I dare not think of it—it drives me wild now."

9. *The Letters of Queen Victoria*, ed. Benson and Esher, III, 572.

10. *The Letters of Queen Victoria, Second Series*, ed. Buckle, I, 241, 297.

11. Bolitho, *Prince Consort*, p. 217.

12. *Dearest Child*, ed. Fulford, pp. 350, 357.

13. Charlot, *Victoria: The Young Queen* (Oxford, 1991), p. 417. Looking back from the vantage point of 1863, Victoria wrote that the news of Bertie's fall from grace in Ireland "broke my Angel's heart." *The Letters of Queen Victoria, Second Series*, ed. Buckle, I, 113.

14. *The Letters of Queen Victoria*, ed. Benson and Esher, III, 599.

15. Hibbert, *Letters and Journals*, p. 154.

16. Whether Albert died of stomach cancer, as some researchers have suggested, or of typhoid, as was believed at the time, can never be known with certainty. It is surprising that Dr. Jenner, an expert on typhoid, and Victoria, herself a typhoid victim, did not recognize the characteristic symptoms earlier in the course of Albert's disease. It must always be remembered, however, that Louis

Pasteur did not develop the germ theory of disease until the year of Albert's illness, 1861, and that the general state of medical knowledge was rudimentary and riddled with inaccuracies. Misdiagnosis was the norm. Lord Clarendon's sarcastic comment was that Albert's doctors "were not fit to nurse a sick cat."

17. *The Letters of Queen Victoria*, ed. Benson and Esher, III, 600–601.

18. *Dearest Mama*, ed. Fulford, p. 30. A few years earlier Albert had told Vicky that he would not care if God took him; he "always felt ready" to die. *Ibid.*, 31–2.

19. *The Letters of Queen Victoria*, ed. Benson and Esher, III, 601–2.

20. Hibbert, *Letters and Journals*, p. 156.

Chapter 15

1. *The Letters of Lady Augusta Stanley*, ed. Hector Bolitho, pp. 239–44.

2. Löhlein, Albert's Coburger servant who was widely believed to be Albert's half brother, an illegitimate son of his father Duke Ernest, was raised by a forester on the estate of Füllbach near Coburg, and Victoria maintained that he was the forester's son. Tyler-Whittle, p. 9 and note.

3. *Letters of Queen Victoria*, ed. Bolitho, p. 189. Feodore had been in England until early November 1861, returning either during Albert's final illness or immediately after his death.

4. *Ibid.*, 119.

5. *Dearest Mama*, ed. Fulford, p. 27.

6. *Ibid.*, 248.

7. Hannah Pakula, *Uncommon Woman*, unpublished manuscript; *Dearest Mama*, ed. Fulford, pp. 23, 193. Victoria's sexual ardor would have surprised many Victorian physicians, one of the most celebrated of whom, Dr. William Acton, wrote in 1862 that "the majority of women (happily for them) are not very much troubled with sexual feeling of any kind." *Victorian Studies*, XXXVI, 83. When Albert died, Victoria was forty-two, only a little past the age at which women experience their strongest sexual desire.

8. *Dearest Mama*, ed. Fulford, pp. 85, 74–5; *The Letters of Queen Victoria, Second Series*, ed. Buckle, I, 62.

9. *Dearest Mama*, ed. Fulford, p. 34.

10. *Letters of Queen Victoria*, ed. Bolitho, p. 135.

11. *Dearest Mama*, ed. Fulford, pp. 107–8.

12. *Ibid.*, 154.

13. *Letters of Queen Victoria*, ed. Bolitho, p. 130; *Dearest Mama*, ed. Fulford, p. 131.

14. *Dearest Mama*, ed. Fulford, pp. 192–3.

15. *Ibid.*, 248–9.

16. Hibbert, *Letters and Journals*, p. 177.

17. *Ibid.*, 178.

Chapter 16

1. Hibbert, *Letters and Journals*, p. 185.

2. *The Letters of Queen Victoria, Second Series*, ed. Buckle, I, 117.

3. *Dearest Mama*, ed. Fulford, p. 197.

4. *Letters of Queen Victoria*, ed. Bolitho, pp. 153, 156.

5. *The Letters of Queen Victoria, Second Series*, ed. Buckle, I, 298–9.

6. *Your Dear Letter: Private Correspondence of Queen Victoria and the Crown Princess of Prussia, 1865–1871*, ed. Roger Fulford (New York, 1971), p. 79.

7. Hibbert, *Letters and Journals*, p. 201.

8. *Dearest Mama*, ed. Fulford, p. 271; *Your Dear Letter*, ed. Fulford, pp. 94, 106.

9. Theo Aronson, *Heart of a Queen: Queen Victoria's Romantic Attachments* (London, 1991), pp. 143–4.

10. *Your Dear Letter*, ed. Fulford, pp. 90–1.

11. Victoria warned Vicky not to change her servants too often and impressed upon her "the inestimable comfort and value of a truly devoted and attached and trustworthy servant." Quoted in Warner, *Sketchbooks*, p. 188.

12. *Dearest Child*, ed. Fulford, p. 365.

13. Tyler-Whittle, p. 122.

14. Hibbert, *Letters and Journals*, p. 202.

Chapter 17

1. *Your Dear Letter*, ed. Fulford, p. 28.

2. Tyler-Whittle, p. 154.

3. *Your Dear Letter*, ed. Fulford, p. 179.

4. *Dearest Mama*, ed. Fulford, p. 281; *Your Dear Letter*, ed. Fulford, p. 161.

5. *More Leaves from the Journal of a Life in the Highlands, from 1862 to 1882* (London, 1884), pp. 228, 231–2.

6. *Your Dear Letter*, ed. Fulford, p. 207. "I saw how dreadfully the wickedness of this world grieved his pure, noble, heavenly spirit," Victoria wrote to Vicky, "how indeed, like our Saviour, he wept over Jerusalem; he mourned over the vice and the strife and the bitterness and unchristian spirit of the world in general." An early edition of Albert's speeches bore the title *The Prince Consort's Golden Precepts. Dearest Mama*, ed. Fulford, p. 64.

7. *The Letters of Queen Victoria, Second Series*, ed. Buckle, I, 378.

8. Robert Blake, *Disraeli* (London, 1966), p. 159.

9. *The Letters of Queen Victoria*, ed. Buckle, I, 397.

10. Blake, p. 78.

11. Hibbert, *Letters and Journals*, p. 220.

12. *Ibid.*, 222–3.

Chapter 18

1. Pearsall, *Purity*, pp. 60–1.

2. Altick, p. 124.

3. Tingsten, p. 106.

4. The sheer boldness of the agnostic stance, taken at a time of overwhelming religious credence, still astounds the researcher. "Let us dream no dreams and tell no lies," wrote the lawyer and agnostic Sir James Fitzjames Stephen [Virginia Woolf's uncle] in 1873, "but go our own way, wherever it may lead, with our eyes open and our heads erect." A very Victorian sentiment; with such heroic words might a Victorian explorer have headed off into the African bush.

5. Hibbert, *Letters and Journals*, p. 211.

6. *Your Dear Letter*, ed. Fulford, p. 186.

7. *The Letters of Queen Victoria, Second Series*, ed. Buckle, II, 173.

8. *Ibid.*, II, 175–6; *The Annual Register . . . for the Year 1871* (London, 1872), pp. 134–5.

9. *Life at the Court of Queen Victoria 1861–1901: illustrated from the collection of Lord Edward Pelham-Clinton*, ed. Barry St. John Nevill (London, 1984), p. 75.

10. Hibbert, *Letters and Journals*, pp. 215–16.

Chapter 19

1. As it proved, the would-be assassin, Arthur O'Connor, had a pistol that was broken and could not have been fired had it been loaded. His assault was very frightening nonetheless, and proved, once again, the alarming vulnerability of the queen. *The Letters of Queen Victoria, Second Series*, ed. Buckle, II, 200.

2. *Life at the Court*, p. 87.

3. *The Letters of Queen Victoria, Second Series*, ed. Buckle, II, 132.

4. Cited in H.L. Beales, *Ideas and Beliefs of the Victorians* (New York, 1948),p. 223.

5. At least eight books were written about the Ashanti campaign. James Morris, *Heaven's Command: An Imperial Progress* (New York and London, 1973), p. 403.

6. Theo Aronson, *Victoria and Disraeli: The Making of a Romantic Partnership* (London, 1977), p. 162.

7. Aronson, *Heart of a Queen*, p. 187.

8. Aronson, *Victoria and Disraeli*, p. 160.

9. Hibbert, *Letters and Journals*, p. 241.

10. *Ibid.*, 244.

11. *Letters of Queen Victoria*, ed. Bolitho, p. 217.

12. Hibbert, *Letters and Journals*, pp. 251–2.

13. *Ibid.*, 243.

14. In his childhood Willy was strapped into a barbarous device intended to stretch his neck muscles, and also treated with "galvanism"—electric shock—for his arm. *Dearest Mama*, ed. Fulford, pp. 203–4, 282, 352; *Your Dear Letter*, ed. Fulford, p. 167. Vicky's daughter Victoria screamed whenever she saw a black gown, and as Victoria was perpetually in mourning, this must have led to a commotion whenever Vicky and her children stayed with the queen. *Your Dear Letter*, ed. Fulford, p. 212.

15. *The Letters of Disraeli to Lady Chesterfield and Lady Bradford*, ed. the Marquis of Zelland, 2 vols. (New York, 1939), II, 259.

16. Until 1896, British law prohibited a man from marrying his deceased wife's sister. It did not, however, prohibit a woman from marrying her deceased husband's brother, as in the famous marriage of Katherine of Aragon and Henry VIII—a marriage much disputed on other grounds.

Chapter 20

1. A private bathroom was, in the early 1880s, not to be taken for granted, even in royal residences. Though Albert's progressive designs for Osborne and Balmoral included water closets, few royal palaces had toilets; Vicky and Fritz and their household still relied on chamber pots, as did most continental sovereigns. In England, upper-class residences in general did not have bathrooms until the 1920s. The Ladies' Lavatory Company built public toilets underground beginning in the 1880s—a great advance in public sanitation—and the British Perforated Paper Company began marketing rolls of toilet paper in 1880. Victoria, however, rejected the modern rolled paper in favor of the traditional squares of paper. *Dearest Child*, ed. Fulford, p. 171; Flora Fraser, *The English Gentlewoman* (London, 1987), p. 171.

2. Frederick Ponsonby, *Recollections of Three Reigns* (London, 1951), p. 15.

3. Aronson, *Heart of a Queen*, p. 171.

4. Hibbert, *Letters and Journals*, p. 280.

5. *The Letters of Queen Victoria, Second Series*, ed. Buckle, III, 413.

6. *Life with Queen Victoria: Marie Mallet's Letters from Court 1887–1901*, ed. Victor Mallet (London, 1968), p. 77.

7. Tingsten, p. 150; *The Letters of Queen Victoria, Second Series*, ed. Buckle, III, 455.

8. Longford, *Queen Victoria*, p. 454.

9. *Letters of Queen Victoria*, ed. Bolitho, p. 251.

10. Hibbert, *Letters and Journals*, p. 290.

11. Ponsonby, p. 43; *The Letters of Queen Victoria, Second Series*, ed. Buckle, III, 637.

12. *The Letters of Queen Victoria, Second Series*, ed. Buckle, III, 607.

13. *Ibid.*, III, 595–6.

Chapter 21

1. Neville, *Life at the Court*, p. 132.

2. This account of the queen's Jubilee is taken from her journal, in Hibbert, *Letters and Journals*, pp. 304–6.

3. *Ibid.*, 307. In the 1880s, during the throes of her struggle with Gladstone, Victoria had often doubted whether the work and energy she applied to her task was appreciated at all. Only a few months earlier, in March of 1887, she had written to her granddaughter Victoria that "I feel very deeply that my opinion and my advice are never listened to and that it is almost useless to give any." Hibbert, *Letters and Journals*, p. 301.

4. *Letters of Queen Victoria*, ed. Bolitho, pp. 259, 261–2.

5. *The Letters of Queen Victoria, Third Series*, ed. George Earle Buckle, 3 vols. (London, 1932), I, 404–5; *Letters of Queen Victoria*, ed. Bolitho, pp. 262–3.

6. Hibbert, *Letters and Journals*, p. 310. Augusta lived two years longer, dying in 1890.

7. Mallet, p. 17.

8. *The Letters of Queen Victoria, Third Series*, ed. Buckle, I, 176–7.

9. *Ibid.*, I, 447.

10. Alan Hardy, *Queen Victoria Was Amused* (London, 1976), p. 147. An American, Mary Waddington, wrote of Victoria: "I watched her while she was talking and I never saw a smile make such a difference to a face. Hers is quite beautiful and lights up her whole face." *Ibid.*

11. *Ibid.*, 142.

12. *Ibid.*, 145, 182, 177.

13. Beatrice, Ponsonby wrote, often neglected government matters "to develop a photograph or . . . paint a flower for a bazaar." *Ibid.*, 189.

14. Hibbert, *Letters and Journals*, p. 321.

15. Eddy followed in his father's footsteps in his pursuit of sexual variety; at least one of his mistresses maintained that he was the father of her child. He had undergone treatment for gonorrhea, and may have had syphilis. Stories circulated to the effect that he frequented at least one well-known homosexual brothel. Weintraub, p. 520.

Chapter 22

1. Hardy, p. 229.

2. Mallet, p. 53.

3. *Ibid.*, 44, 122.

4. Aronson, *Heart of a Queen*, p. 238.

5. Hibbert, *Letters and Journals*, p. 333.

6. This was the future Edward VIII, who after a brief reign was succeeded by his brother George, father of the present Queen Elizabeth.

7. Mallet, p. 72.

8. *Ibid.*, 13–14.

9. *Life at the Court*, p. 141; Mallet, pp. 8–9; Ponsonby, p. 51.

10. Aronson, *Heart of a Queen*, p. 247.

11. *Ibid.*, 251.

12. Hibbert, *Letters and Journals*, p. 334.

Chapter 23

1. Hibbert, *Letters and Journals*, p. 335.

2. Mallet, p. 148.

3. *Ibid.*, 139.

4. Mallet, p. 176; *Life at the Court*, p. 206.

5. Mallet, p. 176.

6. Hibbert, *Letters and Journals*, p. 339.

7. *Ibid.*, 341.

8. Mallet, pp. 183–4.

9. Charles Petrie, *The Victorians* (London, 1960), p. 54.

10. Mallet, pp. 197–8.

11. *Ibid.*, 200–202.

12. Hibbert, *Letters and Journals*, p. 347.

13. Mallet, p. 207.

14. *Ibid.*, 215. "We are abominably served just now," the lady-in-waiting wrote on November 6, 1900. "The footmen smell of whisky and are never prompt to answer the bell and although they do not speak rudely, they stare in such a supercilious way. As for the Queen's dinner it is more like a badly arranged picnic." On November 8, Victoria ordered for dinner a dish of noodles, which never arrived at all.

Chapter 24

1. Jerrold M. Packard, *Farewell in Splendor* (New York, 1995), p. 108.

2. Ponsonby, p. 82.

3. "Grandpapa and the Queen have both been lives of iron," Willy said, "and when it is broken it does not waste away but goes crack!" Packard, p. 139.

4. Packard, p. 154.

List of Works Cited

Author's Note: The printed literature on the life and reign of Queen Victoria is so vast that it can only be suggested in a brief bibliography. The following list includes only books and articles cited in the end notes.

Altick, Richard D. *The Presence of the Past.* Columbus, Ohio: Ohio State University Press, 1993.

The Annual Register: A Review of Public Events at Home and Abroad, for the Year 1871. New Series. London: Rivingtons, 1872.

Aronson, Theo. *Heart of A Queen: Queen Victoria's Romantic Attachments.* London: John Murray, 1991.

———. *Victoria and Disraeli: The Making of a Romantic Partnership.* London: Cassell, 1977.

Ashton, John. *Gossip in the First Decade of Victoria's Reign.* London: Hurst and Blackett, 1903.

Barret-Ducrocq, Françoise. *Love in the Time of Victoria: Sexuality and Desire Among Working-Class Men and Women in Nineteenth-Century London.* London: Penguin, 1989.

Beales, H. L. *Ideas and Beliefs of the Victorians.* Sylvan Press, 1948.

Benson, A.C. and Viscount Esher, eds. *The Letters of Queen Victoria. A Selection of Her Majesty's Correspondence Between the Years 1837 and 1861*. 3 vols. London: John Murray, 1907.

Blake, Robert. *Disraeli*. London: Carroll and Graf, 1966.

Bolitho, Hector, ed. *Letters of Queen Victoria from the Archives of the House of Brandenburg-Prussia*. trans. Mrs. J. Pudney and Lord Sudley. New Haven: Yale University Press, 1938.

———. *The Prince Consort and His Brother*. New York: Appleton-Century, 1934.

Buckle, George Earle, ed. *The Letters of Queen Victoria, Second Series. A Selection from Her Majesty's Correspondence and Journal Between the Years 1862 and 1885*. 3 vols. London, 1926–28.

———, ed. *The Letters of Queen Victoria, Third Series. A Selection from Her Majesty's Correspondence and Journal Between the Years 1886 and 1901*. 3 vols. London: John Murray, 1930–32.

Cecil, Lord David. *Melbourne*. New York: Bobbs-Merrill, 1939.

Charlot. *Victoria: The Young Queen*. Oxford: Basil Blackwell, 1991.

Creston, Dormer. *The Youthful Queen Victoria*. New York: Putnam, 1952.

Crow, Duncan. *The Victorian Woman*. London: Stein and Day, 1971.

Dodds, John W. *The Age of Paradox: A Biography of England 1841–51*. London: Gollancz, 1953.

Esher, Viscount, ed. *The Girlhood of Queen Victoria: A Selection from Her Majesty's Diaries between the Years 1832 and 1840*. 2 vols. London: John Murray, 1912.

Ferguson, Sara. *Victoria and Albert: Life at Osborne House*. London: Weidenfeld and Nicolson, 1991.

Fraser, Flora. *The English Gentlewoman*. London: Barrie and Jenkins, 1987.

Fulford, Roger, ed. *Dearest Child: Letters between Queen Victoria and the Princess Royal 1858–61*. New York: Holt, Rinehart and Winston, 1964.

———, ed. *Dearest Mama: Letters between Queen Victoria and the Crown Princess of Prussia 1861–1864*. London: Evans Brothers, 1968.

———, ed. *Your Dear Letter: Private Correspondence of Queen Victoria and the Crown Princess of Prussia, 1865–1877*. New York: Scribner's, 1971.

Gernsheim, H. and A. *Queen Victoria: A Biography in Word and Picture*. London, 1959.

Hardy, Alan. *Queen Victoria Was Amused*. London: John Murray, 1976.

Hibbert, Christopher, ed. *Queen Victoria in Her Letters and Journals*. New York: Viking, 1985.

Hobhouse, Hermione. *Prince Albert: His Life and Work*. London: Hamish Hamilton, 1983.

Huxley, Gervas. *Lady Elizabeth and the Grosvenors*. London: Oxford University Press, 1965.

Longford, Elizabeth. *Queen Victoria: Born to Succeed.* New York: Harper & Row, 1965.

———. "Queen Victoria's Doctors." In *A Century of Conflict, 1850–1950*, ed. Martin Gilbert. New York: Atheneum, 1967.

Mallet, Victor, ed. *Life With Queen Victoria: Marie Mallet's Letters from Court 1887–1901.* London: John Murray, 1968.

Mason, Philip. *The English Gentleman: The Rise and Fall of An Ideal.* London: André Deutsch, 1982.

Millar, Delia. *Queen Victoria's Life in the Scottish Highlands.* New York and London: Harper and Row, 1985.

Morris, James. *Heaven's Command: An Imperial Progress.* New York and London: Harcourt Brace Jovanovich, 1973.

Nevill, Barry St. John, ed. *Life at the Court of Queen Victoria 1861–1901* Exeter: Webb and Bower, 1984.

Packard, Jerrold M. *Farewell in Splendor: The Passing of Queen Victoria and Her Age.* New York: Dutton, 1995.

Pearsall, Ronald. *Public Purity, Private Shame: Victorian Sexual Hypocrisy Exposed.* London: Weidenfeld and Nicolson, 1976.

Petrie, Charles. *The Victorians.* London: Eyre and Spottiswoode, 1960.

Ponsonby, Sir Frederick. *Recollections of Three Reigns.* London: Eyre and Spottiswoode, 1951.

Quennell, Peter. *Victorian Panorama.* London: B. T. Batsford, 1937.

Reeve, Henry, ed. *The Greville Memoirs. A Journal of the Reigns of King George IV and King William IV.* 2 vols. New York: D. Appleton, 1875.

———, ed. *The Greville Memoirs. Second Part. A Journal of the Reign of Queen Victoria from 1837 to 1852.* 3 vols. New York: D. Appleton, 1885.

Rowell, George. *Queen Victoria Goes to the Theater.* London: P. Elek, 1978.

Scheele, Godfrey and Margaret. *The Prince Consort: Man of Many Facets.* London: Oresko Books, 1977.

Somerset, Anne. *The Life and Times of William IV.* London: Weidenfeld and Nicolson, 1980.

Southgate, Donald. *"The Most English Minister": The Policies and Politics of Palmerston.* New York: St. Martin's Press, 1966.

Tisdall, E. E. P. *Queen Victoria's Private Life.* New York: The John Day Co., 1961.

Tyler-Whittle, Michael Sidney. *Victoria and Albert at Home.* London: Routledge and Kegan Paul, 1980.

Van der Kiste, John. *Queen Victoria's Children.* Wolfeboro Falls, New Hampshire: Alan Sutton, 1990.

Victoria R. I. *More Leaves from the Journal of A Life in the Highlands, from 1862 to 1882.* London: Smith, Elder & Co., 1884.

Warner, Marina. *Queen Victoria's Sketchbooks.* London: Macmillan, 1979.

Watson, Vera. *A Queen At Home: An Intimate Account of the Social and Domestic Life at Queen Victoria's Court*. London: W. H. Allen, 1952.

Weintraub, Stanley. *Victoria: An Intimate Biography*. New York: E. P. Dutton, 1988.

Woodham-Smith, Cecil. *Queen Victoria: From Her Birth to the Death of the Prince Consort*. New York: Knopf, 1972.

Wyndham, Mrs. Hugh, ed. *Correspondence of Sarah Spencer, Lady Lyttelton 1787–1870*. London: John Murray, 1912.

Zelland, Marquis of, ed. *The Letters of Disraeli to Lady Chesterfield and Lady Bradford*. 2 vols. New York: D. Appleton, 1939.

Ziegler, Philip. *King William IV*. Newton Abbot: Readers Union, 1973.

Index